Third Edition

Advocacy and Opposition

An Introduction to Argumentation

Karyn Charles Rybacki
Donald Jay Rybacki

Allyn and Bacon
Boston • London • Toronto • Sydney • Singapore

Vice President, Humanities: Joseph Opiela
Series Editor: Carla F. Daves
Editorial Assistant: Mary Visco
Marketing Manager: Karon Bowers
Production Coordinator: Thomas E. Dorsaneo
Editorial-Production Service: Melanie Field, Strawberry Field Publishing
Text Designer: Paula Goldstein
Cover Designer: Suzanne Harbison
Composition Buyer: Linda Cox
Manufacturing Buyer: Aloka Rathnam

Library of Congress Cataloging-in-Publication Data

Rybacki, Karyn C. (Karyn Charles). 1947–
    Advocacy and opposition : an introduction to argumentation / Karyn Charles
Rybacki, Donald Jay Rybacki. — 3rd. ed.
        p. cm.
    Includes bibliographical references and index.
    ISBN 0-205-19379-X
    1. Persuasion (Rhetoric) 2. Debates and debating. 3. Proposition (Logic)
4. Reasoning. I. Rybacki, Donald J. (Donald Jay), 1945– . II. Title.
P301.5.P47R93   1995
808.53—dc20   95-31346
                                                                          CIP

Printed in the United States of America
10 9 8 7 6 5 4 3 2 1   99 98 97 96 95

iii

Contents

Chapter 3
What Am I Going to Argue About?   30

Chapter 4
How Do I Analyze Propositions?   50

Chapter 5
How Is a Unit of Argument Created?   67

Chapter 6

How Do I Prove My Argument?   83

Chapter 7

How Do I Reason with My Audience?   111

Chapter 8
What Should I Avoid?   132

Chapter 9
How Are Factual Propositions Argued?   155

Chapter 10
How Are Propositions of Value Argued?   171

Chapter 11
How Are Propositions of Policy Argued?   191

Chapter 12
How Do I Present My Arguments to an Audience   212

Appendix   235

References   244

Index   249

Preface

In the first two editions of *Advocacy and Opposition*, our goal was to approach argumentation in a way that preserved the essentials of theory and practice as it existed in competitive debate but to tailor those concepts to fit the needs of the student who is not a member of the debate team. In this, our third edition, we remain committed to offering a practical approach to critical thinking for the beginning student. For instructors who want something more than a traditional approach to policy debating in an argumentation or critical thinking class, *Advocacy and Opposition* offers a theoretical view of the nature of argument in our society; a discussion of ethical principles of arguing as a form of communication; a focus on how arguments are created using the Toulmin model; a complete view of fact and value, as well as policy, as venues of argumentation; and end of chapter exercises for classroom discussion and argumentation assignments that may be completed as either oral or written projects. Those instructors who wish to focus on debating will find an Appendix with rules and formats for debate.

What is new in the third edition?

1. We have made a modest revision overall to better reflect the process of argumentation. We have grouped concepts to show movement from first principles to the production of finished argumentation. The national and international interest in informal logic and using argumentation as a means of seeking knowledge and resolving conflicts is incorporated throughout the book and in the end of chapter suggested readings. We have substantially rewritten most chapters to improve clarity, to define and illustrate concepts in ways more accessible to the beginning arguer, and to reflect new thinking in the field of argumentation.
2. We have provided an expanded definition of contemporary argumentation based on the contributions of rhetoric, dialectic, and logic to the

understanding of argumentation as instrumental communication, clarifying the nature of argument as an instrument for influencing belief and behavior.

3. We have extended the definition of argumentation with new research on the view of argument as a process. We have also expanded the discussion of fields of argument and grouped the basic elements of presumption, burden of proof, and the prima facie case into an early chapter. All of the material on the nature of propositions is grouped into a single chapter instead of spread across several.

4. The discussion of analyzing the proposition has been expanded to better reflect how students should use analysis to build argumentative cases. In particular, we have clarified the relationship between defining terms, interpreting the proposition through those definitions, and making the arguer's own primary inference about the meaning of the proposition that will lead to choosing the actual issues to argue.

5. In recognition of the new thinking in argumentation theory—that arguing to seek knowledge is a goal—we have created a separate chapter for factual argumentation. Our discussion of fact offers two perspectives: factual argumentation done to seek knowledge through testing ideas and factual argumentation done to resolve differences in interpreting facts.

6. We have emphasized the use of electronic data sources and the Internet in analyzing propositions and doing research. The evidence chapter contains additional information on using electronic data bases and suggestions for using the Internet to discover attitudes about a given topic.

7. Dated and contrived examples of evidence, reasoning, and fallacies have been replaced with materials selected from debates on fact, value, and policy during congressional hearings. Materials were chosen with an eye toward the enduring, significant issues that confront our society. We have retained the examples of value advocacy and opposition in action from the hearings on lyrics in rock music, as they have been a great favorite among students. Additional examples of argument in action include factual argumentation on term limits for members of Congress and a policy debate over legislation to attach a royalty fee to digital audio equipment and tapes.

8. We have provided an improved explanation of briefing techniques, including more instruction on how to effectively format briefs, in the chapter on presenting arguments.

We have done substantially more than just update the examples in producing this third edition of *Advocacy and Opposition*. In organizing content to better reflect how students go from learning the first principles of argumentation to producing their own cases of fact, value, and policy, material from the second edition has been divided into twelve chapters rather than the original ten. We have not added new topics but have organized material to make the content more teachable.

Chapter 1 defines argumentation and explains the relationship of contemporary argumentation theory to rhetoric, dialectic, and logic. Chapter 2 extends the definition to view argumentation as a process based on fields of argument; explains the roles of advocate and opponent, the nature of presumption, and the burden of proof; and details the nature of a prima facie case. Chapter 3 discusses the nature of propositions and their classifications as fact, value, and policy. It also explains how to phrase and define the key terms of a proposition. Chapter 4 describes the process of analyzing a proposition in terms of locating the immediate causes of interest in a topic, investigating its historical background, using the definition of key terms to make a primary inference about the topic, and choosing the actual issues to argue through application of the stock issues of fact, value, and policy. Chapter 5 focuses on the Toulmin model as a system for creating individual units of argument that will be logically sound. Chapter 6 explains types of evidence and the rules for testing, searching for, and recording evidence. Chapter 7 teaches the student how to use research in the reasoning process, making the inferential leap from evidence to a conclusion about that evidence. Reasoning patterns of cause, sign, generalization, parallel case, analogy, authority, and dilemma are discussed and illustrated. Chapter 8 examines breakdowns in the reasoning process by reviewing the common fallacies that are committed in creating arguments. Chapter 9 focuses on factual propositions—their use for testing hypotheses and for resolving differing interpretations of fact. Strategies for developing arguments of advocacy and opposition over fact are presented. Chapter 10 discusses value propositions and the role of core values arranged in value hierarchies. The use of criteria for arguing and opposing values is presented. Chapter 11 focuses on policy propositions, the use of problem identification, and the creation of solvent proposals. Emphasis is given to the different systems for approaching policy development and strategies for opposing them. Chapter 12 covers techniques used in presenting arguments for listeners and readers, with an emphasis on oral argumentation. Audience analysis, language use and style, brief preparation, delivery, and managing credibility are discussed. An Appendix summarizes the rules and formats used in competitive debate and discusses the duties of the speakers, cross-examination, and the role of the debate judge.

We would like to thank our reviewers whose suggestions for improving the second edition have shaped this revision: Kathleen German, Miami University–Ohio; Dirk Gibson, Georgia Southern University; Fran Hassenchal, Old Dominion University; and Lee Winet, Suny-Oswego. We also thank Carla Daves, Acquisitions Editor, Melanie Field, and all of the additional editors and production staff at Allyn & Bacon for their assistance. We thank our colleagues who have used the earlier editions and offered their advice on what we might do to improve upon them. Finally, we thank our students who have openly shared their thoughts about what they liked and found frustrating in the second edition. Their input has assisted us in turning this book into what we hope is a better approach to teaching and learning about the process of argumentation.

Chapter One

What Is Argumentation?

The way you feel about "having an argument" may influence your attitude toward this textbook and the course in which it is being used. During the first class meeting, we ask students in our argumentation class to introduce themselves and tell us why they want to learn about argumentation. One student said he and his girlfriend are always arguing, and he wanted to know how to win these arguments. If your definition of *arguing* or *having an argument* is also based on negative, escalating emotions, we hope that this textbook will change your perceptions about the uses and benefits of argumentation.

Arguing or having an argument is essential to our existence as humans. We can speculate that in human prehistory, our distant ancestors argued about how to hunt more productively, how to interpret seasonal signs, and how to regulate their social groupings. Some of this arguing must have involved a certain amount of escalating emotions, but humanity's technological, social, and spiritual growth would probably not have come about if our only definition of argumentation was based on negative emotions. Our advances in every field from communication technology to understanding the Dead Sea Scrolls represent the uses of argumentation by those who are interested in these fields.

Traditionally, argumentation has been thought of as the means we use to justify our opinions and express those opinions to others. As we approach the next century, we see a renewed interest in how everyone can use argumentation. European scholars are exploring how we use argumentation in our day-to-day activities. These scholars see argumentation as "a collaborative, constructive working out of disagreements by verbal interactions in order to resolve a conflict of opinions" (Walton, 1992, p. xi). In addition to the traditional perspective on using argumentation to prove opinions, scholars from many nations are beginning to think of argumentation as the means individuals, citizen's groups, and scientists use to actually discover knowledge (Rowland, 1987).

The Nature of Argumentation

To discover argumentation, all you have to do is observe the daily attempts to influence your beliefs and behavior. Some efforts will be aimed at your emotions, prejudices, and superstitions, but some will use information and reasoning in an attempt to influence you. Most people we encounter—friends, family, teachers, employers, the mass media, advertisers, editorialists, and politicians—offer arguments embedded in persuasive appeals to encourage us to think as they do or behave as they wish us to. From the apparently trivial matter of choosing a breakfast cereal to the more vital decision of what career to pursue, we are constantly exposed to the argumentation of others.

Every day of our lives, each of us authors dozens of written and oral messages intended to influence the beliefs or direct the behavior of others. If you have ever asked a friend to loan you five dollars, begged a teacher to let you turn in a paper a week after it was due, or researched and reported on the advantages and disadvantages of selling sweatshirts to raise money for social activities in your residence hall, you have engaged in argumentation. Some of your appeals may have been aimed at the emotions, prejudices, or superstitions of those you were trying to influence, but some appeals targeted their reasoning abilities. It may not be unreasonable to say that were it not for argumentation, we would not have nearly as much to hear or say, read or write. As a matter of fact, what you have just read is an example of argumentation.

> **Argumentation** is a form of instrumental communication relying on reasoning and proof to influence belief or behavior through the use of spoken or written messages.

By examining this definition we can begin to understand argumentation's purpose, targets, and methods, and its relationship to persuasion. First, think of your definition of *instrument*. You may think of a musical instrument, a surgical instrument, or the instrument panel of an automobile or airplane. In this sense, instruments are tools or implements we use for doing something or understanding how something works. Now, think of an instrument as a set of concepts or ideas that allows you to accomplish something. Language is an instrument for communicating with others. Mathematics is an instrument for counting and measuring. Argumentation is an instrument for influencing others.

Argumentation is a set of concepts or ideas used to understand how we reason and how we convey that reasoning to others for the purpose of influencing them. Like the instrument of language, we use argumentation to communicate with others. Argumentation, however, is a narrower set of concepts and ideas about communicating. We can use communication to vent our feelings, and the form of that venting may seem like argumentation.

BARTHOLOMEW: Can I play ball with you?
    CHADWICK: No!
BARTHOLOMEW: Why?

CHADWICK: Because.
BARTHOLOMEW: Because why?
CHADWICK: Mom! Bartholomew is bugging me. Make him leave me alone!

Even though the form of interaction between Chadwick and Bartholomew seems to be one in which each participant states his reasons, this is not argumentation. Each child is articulating his desire to get his own way, but neither offers reasons to justify such an outcome. Bartholomew and Chadwick each knows in his heart that he is right, and neither considers the legitimacy of the other's belief. Even Chadwick's solicitation of aid from a nominally neutral third party reflects his own interests and discounts the possibility that Bartholomew may have good reasons of his own. The probable result:

MOM: Chadwick, be nice to your little brother. Now you take him along, and let him play. Do you hear me?

Both youngsters learn something from this experience. Chadwick is probably less likely to take such problems to Mom in the future, since her neutrality has become suspect in his eyes. Bartholomew, however, may develop a strategy that renders even this defense useless: Go straight to Mom whenever the prospect of a ball game arises. Chadwick's only defense rests on his ability to use reasoning to make a case that will influence Mom. At that point he discovers argumentation and possibly the winning argument.

CHADWICK: OK Mom, it's just that the guys I play with are all my age, and some of them are bigger than me. I was just worried that Bartholomew might get hurt since we play tackle.

Chadwick's need to be free of Bartholomew is still addressed by this argument, and he has crystallized the issue of his dispute with Bartholomew with such clarity that Mom may well be influenced to see things his way. First, Mom's concern for her younger son's safety is addressed directly. Second, her desire that her older son not be deprived of socializing experiences with his peer group is embedded in the subject of the entire conversation. While she may decide that tackle football is too dangerous for either of them, Chadwick's use of argumentation as instrumental communication gives him a chance to engage her belief in the benefits of his socializing with his peer group and constrain Bartholomew to stay behind.

Most instances of argumentation are more complex than those in the world of sibling disputes mediated by parents. The essence of argumentation, however, is found in the simple pattern of Chadwick's approach to winning Mom's assent in the matter of tag-along Bartholomew: Find the issue that puts the dispute in perspective for the decision maker and provide sufficient proof and reasoning to make a good case for your viewpoint.

Argumentation takes place in situations where people disagree about something, or when they do not know but want to know what something is. Argumentation is always characterized by controversy—either the controversy of opposing views or the controversy of what is the most correct answer. As arguers, we want our views to prevail, so argumentation is always directed to some entity, the *audience*.

The **audience** for argumentation consists of one or more people who have the power or ability to assure the future influence of a belief or pattern of behavior the arguer seeks.

Sometimes we characterize the audience as a nominally disinterested third party, like Mom in Chadwick's dispute with Bartholomew, who will act as a decision maker after hearing both sides of the argument. The self can also be an audience for argument on occasion. In the process of intrapersonal decision making, we frequently engage in internal dialogue, listing the pros and cons of accepting a particular belief or following some course of action. Whether the audience is the self or some other person, argumentation provides a framework for helping that audience determine whether changing or maintaining an existing belief or behavior is more reasonable.

The concept of reasonableness helps us understand the relationship between argumentation and persuasion. Arguers are also persuaders. Persuasion is an attempt to move an audience to accept or identify with a particular point of view. Like argumentation, persuasion is also instrumental communication. Although we will often call your attention to the persuasiveness of arguments in this textbook, our primary purpose is to introduce you to the principles for effective argumentation, the rational subset of persuasion.

What differentiates argumentation from the larger category of instrumental communication—persuasion—is that persuasion operates on both the emotional and the rational levels in communication. Recall our earlier discussion of your role as both consumer and creator of messages intended to influence belief and behavior. We indicated that these appeals might be directed at emotions, prejudices, superstitions, or reason. Some persuasive messages depend more on eliciting an emotional reaction from the receiver than a rational one. Persuasion includes the study of the emotional properties of messages and how the psychological makeup of an audience plays a part in determining to what extent that audience will, or will not, be influenced. The study of argumentation focuses on how proof and reasoning are used to appeal to the rational side of human nature.

A final characteristic of argumentation is that it is rule-governed communication behavior. When you communicate, you engage in rule-governed behavior. One set of rules is the grammar of the language. In addition to the rules we learn in acquiring our native tongue, individual communication contexts have their own particular rules, which may be as broadly applicable as those that pertain to public speaking or as narrow as those that govern communication in a particular family. We learn these communication rules through formal instruction or through informally modeling the behavior of those around us. Because argumentation may occur in a variety of communication contexts, the rules for effective argumentation you will learn from this textbook will be appropriate in several contexts beyond the classroom.

The Historical Development of Argumentation

In this text we emphasize a model of argument developed by the English logician Stephen Toulmin. For centuries, teachers and students of argumentation have struggled to find a way to put into words, to visualize on the page or screen, how human thinking takes place. The value of Toulmin's model of argument is that it gives us a verbal and visual structure for understanding how you think when you put proof and reasoning together to form an argument. A series of these arguments used to develop and clarify an issue constitute a complete argumentative message. To gain a better understanding of contemporary argumentation theory and its evolution, it is worthwhile to review some of the earliest ideas about argumentation and the societal forces that precipitated them.

The formal study of argumentation began in ancient Greece. Citizenship in the democracy of Athens required communication skills. Each male freeborn citizen might be called upon to serve the state in the deliberative processes of the assembly or the judgmental processes of the courts. He might also find himself acting as prosecutor or defense attorney, since the Greek judicial system required each party to the action to represent himself. The Greeks also engaged in public speaking on ceremonial occasions.

The study of *rhetoric*—communication skills necessary to fulfill these requirements—was an important part of formal elementary education. The foundations of argumentation, as studied today, were laid in those ancient schools. Rhetoric was conceived as a humane discipline, grounded in choice, that was primarily designed to persuade or change the listener. The communicator's purpose was to influence choice by developing meaningful probabilities, or arguments, in support of a claim that was being contested. Emphasis was placed on the claims that occurred in the courts, since so much speaking involved arguing one's own case.

One of the greatest of the Greek rhetoricians, Aristotle, viewed the practice of argumentation as central to human nature, "for to a certain extent all men attempt to discuss statements and to maintain them, to defend themselves, and to attack others" (Aristotle, pub. date, 1954, p. 19). Aristotle had defined rhetoric as the ability to find, in a given situation, all the means of persuading an audience to believe a proposition. This involved more than just building workable arguments. The responsibility of the communicator was to investigate everything his audience might be moved by—emotions, political beliefs, and those sources of information that it respected most. The responsible communicator would choose the most ethical, the most probably true, of all of these available means of persuasion.

Efforts to understand how we reason moved in three theoretical directions as a result of Greek teachings about human communication. First, *rhetorical theory* explores how people influence each other through verbal and nonverbal communication. Theories of rhetoric explain "how arguments are made and interpreted by people" (Wenzel, 1990, p. 15). The creation and interpretation of arguments is done in situations where people have to make choices, often when there are good reasons for making different choices. In rhetorical theory, good argumentation occurs in speaking or writing "that effectively helps members of a social group solve problems or make decisions" (Wenzel, p. 12).

Second, *dialectic* explores structures of conversation in which people offer and analyze reasons (Walton, 1992). Dialectic is a formal plan for the give-and-take of an interaction in which you are trying to test opinions or answer philosophical questions, such as, "What is a good life?" Dialectical theory is about "principles and procedures" (Wenzel, 1990, p. 15) for the critical study of a topic. For a dialectician, the formal structure of a forum, discussion, or dialog is the key element of good argumentation. A good system for argumentation produces "the best possible discussions" (Wenzel, p. 12).

Third, *logic*, offers a series of formal rules for distinguishing sound arguments from unsound ones. In logical theory, an argument is thought of as a commodity or product to be tested by applying the rules for making sound arguments. For a logician, "a good argument is one in which a clearly stated claim is supported by acceptable, relevant and sufficient evidence" (Wenzel, 1990, p. 12). Argumentation today derives principles of reasoning from formal logic, but argumentation is described as informal logic. As they are taught today, logical theories of argumentation seem removed from the needs of human communicators. In the twentieth century, "the mathematical logic of propositions and quantifiers [make] the subject even more strict and abstract" (Walton, 1992, p. 1).

The theories of rhetoric, dialectic, and logic each make a contribution to argumentation's function as an instrument to influence belief and behavior.

> [R]hetoric helps us to understand and evaluate arguing as a natural process of persuasive communication; dialectic helps us to understand and evaluate argumentation as a cooperative method for making critical decisions; and logic helps us to understand and evaluate arguments as products people create when they argue. (Wenzel, 1990, p. 9)

From rhetoric, dialectic, and logic, we can identify the characteristics of argumentation as instrumental communication: (1) argumentation involves offering a series of logically related statements or arguments, (2) these arguments involve the use of reasoning in writing and speaking, (3) reasoning is used in arguments to induce belief, (4) arguments constitute a means of persuasion, and (5) for arguments to have social utility, their authors must fulfill certain ethical responsibilities.

The Usefulness of Argumentation

There are good reasons to employ methods of argumentation in many everyday situations because beliefs and behaviors often have serious consequences. In our everyday lives, we use argumentation for practical reasoning. Douglas Walton (1992) describes practical reasoning as "a kind of reasoning that is oriented toward finding a course of action, and deciding whether a course of action is practically reasonable or prudent in a given situation" (p. 33). Practical reasoning helps us make choices about what we should do. We also use argumentation for theoretical reasons. Walton describes this reasoning as "oriented to finding the reasons for and against accepting a proposition as one that is likely to be true or false" (p. 33). Theoretical reasoning helps us decide what we will believe and disbelieve.

Whether our approach is practical or theoretical, we need argumentation to help us in the many instances where differences of opinion, questions, and uncertainties exist. Seldom in human affairs is there a definitive resolution, a 100 percent right or wrong answer to a question or solution to a dispute. Instead, we offer opinions, and information that supports our opinions, about what a plausible or probable answer or solution might be. Finding answers through argumentation is a tentative, give-and-take process that evolves over time. Arguers make cases for a particular set of opinions and modify or revise those opinions as they interact with other arguers. This process offers several pragmatic and philosophical benefits to the participants.

First, argumentation is a reliable method for arriving at the probable truth of something that is in dispute. Beliefs and behaviors arrived at through argumentation result from careful examination of facts and expert opinion, not from responses colored by emotion and prejudice or by habitual predetermined responses caused by triggering stimuli (Ehninger, 1974). Beliefs and behaviors resulting from emotion, prejudice, or triggering stimuli stand the test of time only by serendipity. When you reach a decision through argumentation, you are more likely to feel good about it because it will stand up to your scrutiny and the criticism of others. To test this premise, pretend you are going to buy a new car. Which decision-making process will produce the most satisfaction in the long run, buying a car because the color appeals to you or buying the car with the best track record for safety, mileage, performance, and factory support?

Second, the use of argumentation increases personal flexibility (Ehninger, 1974). When you base belief or behavior on the dictates of an authority figure, tradition, custom, or prejudice, you may be unable to adapt to environmental changes that challenge that belief or behavior. Beliefs and behaviors arrived at through argumentation are less inclined to rigidity. The practitioner of argumentation searches out and develops new patterns of belief and behavior as new situations and new problems arise rather than relying on traditional patterns. Developing argumentation skills is a means of coping with a future in which new knowledge and new ideas may make old truths crumble like the Berlin Wall and the former Soviet Union.

The third pragmatic reason for the use of argumentation is found in the willingness of listeners or readers to change beliefs or behaviors because of the role they play in the process. When you change as a consequence of an argument you have heard or read, you act of your own volition, not because the argument's author has imposed his or her will upon you (Ehninger, 1974). Because argumentation is a two-way process, a dialogue between you and those whose beliefs or behaviors you wish to influence, much of the resistance that would be present if you attempted to force change upon them is defused.

There are also philosophical reasons for the use of argumentation that supplement the pragmatic reasons. First, communication is generally regarded as a liberal art. When we discuss the liberal arts, we typically mean those disciplines that civilize and humanize us. Argumentation is a civilizing, humanizing process since its practitioner must respect both personal rationality and that of the reader or listener. Argumentation treats people as rational beings rather than objects, incapable of thought.

A second philosophical justification for the use of argumentation is apparent when we examine the use of persuasion in our society. Listen to network news or read a national news magazine. It will not take long to find references to "mere rhetoric," "presidential rhetoric," or "a public relations ploy." What the media are really criticizing is not rhetoric or persuasion but how it is practiced. We are suspicious of persuaders who seek knee-jerk responses based on emotions, prejudices, or superstitions. Argumentation overcomes one of the objections to contemporary persuasion by treating its consumer as a rational person. The arguer does not manipulate the receiver but offers the opportunity to participate in the process by respecting the receiver's ability to think.

For the humanizing influences of argumentation to occur, its practitioners must accept substantial personal risk. When people engage in argumentation to sort out practical decisions or theoretical answers, they risk confrontation with their peers. Controversies about what to do or what to think are at the heart of the process of argumentation. Wayne Brockriede (1990) explains the risk of confrontation in terms of how arguing changes the participants: "When two persons engage in mutual confrontation so they can share a rational choice, they share the risks of what the confrontation may do to change their ideas, their selves, and their relationship with one another" (p. 7). The willingness to take these risks can be very beneficial.

One of the ways in which the individual grows is through confronting new ideas and change. As is true of any encounter in which a portion of the self is disclosed, argumentation carries risks that, if confronted, can result in substantial personal growth. Philosopher Henry Johnstone, Jr. (1965) sees argumentation, and its attendant risks, as an essential part of the development of a healthy, fully functioning self. For Johnstone, there is self only when there is risk, and the risk found in argumentation "is a defining feature of the human situation" (p. 17). Thus, accepting the risk of engaging in argumentation is not only a means of making our ideas acceptable to others and thereby achieving interpersonal goals, but it is also a vehicle for intrapersonal growth, testing our ideas so that we may reject those we discover to be unsound or irrelevant.

Limitations in the Use of Argumentation

It is not difficult to find negative examples of people using argumentation. The diatribes of hate groups who argue that one race or religion is superior to all others, the political polemicists who argue that all thinking contrary to their own is wrong, and the seemingly well-meaning researchers who argue that one race is genetically inferior to another are all examples of argumentation that can cause harm. Argumentation does have limitations, since it is practiced by fallible human beings whose motives may not always be above reproach. To achieve its fullest humanizing potential, argumentation depends on the ethics of its practitioners. An unsound argument or one based on shallow or inadequate proof can, through skillful oral and written presentation, be made to appear valid. Thus, as with other means of influencing belief or behavior, argumentation can be subject to abuse.

Ever since the first textbooks on argumentation and persuasion were written, scholars have been concerned with the use of argumentation to promote the selfish ambitions of the individual rather than the good of the group or society. Plato, concerned with the practice of rhetoric in ancient Athens, urged his students to practice dialectic, using a format of questions and answers to arrive at truth. Plato felt that many arguments were mere flattery in the guise of rational thought. Aristotle, influenced by Plato, also warned students that appeals based solely on emotions were unethical. Two thousand years later, the problem remains. Automobiles are sold on the basis of sex appeal, household cleansers are marketed on the basis of social disapproval, and politicians campaign on the basis of form rather than substance.

Since we have listed the virtues of argumentation as a means of influence, you may wonder why the manufacturers of automobiles and household cleansers and the campaign managers of political candidates do not insist on carefully reasoned arguments to gain the public's acceptance. The second limitation of argumentation explains why. The process of argumentation is time consuming. In subsequent chapters, you will learn about the process of phrasing propositions, defining terms, conducting research, and constructing arguments. Influencing belief or behavior through rational processes takes time. Although the ethics of resorting to emotion to transmit the message may be questionable, it can be achieved in a thirty-second spot or in a single picture. After all, would you want your favorite TV program interrupted for half an hour while someone proves why "ring around the collar" will make you a pariah?

Frustration over the second limitation of argumentation can cause its practitioners to engage in ethically questionable behavior. The time necessary to marshal sufficient evidence to support a position and ensure its logical consistency can make the siren song of stimuli that trigger an emotional response all the more alluring. In subsequent chapters dealing with the evidence and reasoning on which argumentation is based, we will provide a set of minimal standards, rules for sufficiency. As a creator of arguments, you should apply these standards rigorously in evaluating your own work. As a consumer of argumentation, you should be equally rigorous in using them. Test what you hear and read to ensure it is not emotive discourse masquerading as argumentation.

The potential abuses of argumentation notwithstanding, we need the ability to argue in order to communicate successfully. We have poked fun at commercials that seem to misuse persuasion and argumentation because these are familiar examples. Realize that these same techniques, which seem creative or merely annoying in the commercials, create serious problems when they are used to sell a point of view on public policy issues, such as a balanced budget, the environment, or education.

Ethical Standards for Argumentation

Because the audience for argumentation often lacks the time or resources to verify every statement made, the creators of arguments bear a heavy ethical burden; what is made to seem most probable or believable is most likely to gain acceptance. Like other forms of communication, argumentation can be used to advance the cause of good or evil. Communication is a social act that implies moral obligations to one's audience (Nilsen, 1974) whether that audience includes the whole of society or a single individual. Our audience often judges our communication as good or bad on the basis of how well we meet those moral obligations. This is the essence of speaker credibility.

Like other forms of communication, argumentation is a matter of choosing what to say. In preparing argumentative cases, you will research a topic, decide which claims and proofs to offer, and choose how to arrange your materials for the most impact. Whether your end product is deemed ethical or unethical will ultimately be determined by your audience. Because we live in a society that holds freedom of thought and speech as a cardinal value, ethical communication protects the rights of free speech while at the same time respecting the rights of audiences.

Stanley G. Rives (1964) suggests that those who engage in argumentation in a democratic society have three ethical obligations: "(1) the responsibility to research the proposition thoroughly to know truth, (2) the responsibility to dedicate his effort to the common good, and (3) the responsibility to be rational" (p. 84). To these we add a fourth obligation: the responsibility to observe the rules of free speech in a democratic society.

The Research Responsibility

An ethical arguer will thoroughly research the proposition to discover, insofar as is possible, what is probably true about the subject. Although no one expects you to learn everything about a given subject, ethical argumentation requires you to be well informed. Your responsibility is to prepare your arguments as thoroughly as you can. This means knowing the subject not only from your viewpoint but from opposing viewpoints as well. It means using the resources available to you to your best advantage.

The research responsibility also requires you to use facts and the opinions of others honestly. Remember that when you think through something you have witnessed, read, or heard, you filter the information through your cognitive maps of experience. You decide how you will interpret reality. In deciding, you have the ability to distort or confuse the facts. Your ethical obligation is to avoid consciously distorting information to mislead your audience.

What is wrong with distortion, especially if it is done in pursuit of a worthy goal? Simply this, you violate the trust of your audience and create the possibility of not being considered a credible source in the future. During the 1960s and 1970s, the arguments used by government officials to justify the Vietnam

War and the Watergate cover-up created a crisis of belief that caused many Americans to question the veracity of any government official on any subject.

Beyond being honest in reporting facts and opinions, you should never fabricate research. Making up information is deceptive and unethical. With information available on almost any subject, a diligent exploration of print and electronic resources will yield what you need to prove your arguments.

Realize that probable truth may exist on both sides of a controversy. Issues in human affairs are seldom one sided. Indeed, we define something as controversial when at least two conflicting points of view exist regarding it. Just because information does not jibe with your point of view does not mean that such information is a lie.

The Common Good Responsibility

An ethical arguer has the welfare of the society as an objective. Many issues argued involve resolving which policy is best, which course of action should be taken. The responsible arguer always creates argumentative positions that stress the benefits of a course of action to society in an attempt to determine the action that best serves the common good. In controversies over values, argumentation focuses on which value or value system ought to prevail for the common good.

The responsibility to seek the common good is a tricky ethical proposition. What appears good to one individual may appear evil to another. The issue of abortion on demand illustrates the problem. For some, the right to an abortion is an essential right of choice, consistent with the societal value of freedom. For others, abortion constitutes murder of the unborn, a violation of the rights of the fetus. Which set of rights is preeminent? The answer is ultimately up to the individual based on his or her values. This issue illustrates the importance of thorough research, for determining the common good is not always an easy task. While research may not provide answers in every instance of conflicting values, it will at least help you to better understand the values or policies in conflict.

Ethical behavior demonstrates character, and the tradition in communication is that a prerequisite of good character is placing the audience's welfare above your own interests. Therefore, ethical argumentation attempts to satisfy acknowledged public wants and needs. You rarely hear a presidential candidate state, "Vote for me because I want to be president." Rather, the candidate asks for votes on the basis that he or she best represents the interests of the electorate.

One aspect of ethical argumentation that promotes the common good is that we live in a society of laws and are obliged to respect these laws. Changing a law is often the motivation for debate and discussion and the responsible arguer advocates changing laws rather than breaking them. Although it is possible to point to exceptional cases, such as the civil rights protests of the 1960s in which "morally repugnant" segregation laws were violated for the purpose of drawing attention to their unjustness, generally the responsible argumentative position is to advocate change. You may, for example, feel that laws against the possession and use of marijuana, laws requiring the wearing of safety equipment, or laws regulating the purchase and consumption of alcoholic beverages are unjust, but to encourage violating them is to advocate anarchy. A responsible arguer makes a case by demonstrating a law's injustice, rather than deprecating the concept of the rule of law in society.

The Reasoning Responsibility

An ethical arguer uses sound reasoning in the form of logically adequate arguments supported by facts and expert opinions. Good or sound reasons are the premier rule of argumentation and rhetoric according to modern theorists (Golden, Berquist, & Coleman, 1992). To engage in communication is to use and respect its rules. When translated into practice, this requires the arguer to assume responsibility regarding the form the message takes. The rules of argumentation will be discussed in subsequent chapters on research practices, constructing arguments, testing their quality, and organizing them into a case. While you do not need to be a slave to rules, ethical argumentation requires that you know and use them to ensure that you properly address your audience's rationality.

The Social Code Responsibility

An ethical advocate respects the rights of other arguers and the audience in order to preserve freedom of speech in a democratic society. Freedom of speech means everyone is entitled to a point of view. Those with opposing viewpoints have an equal right to be heard and deserve the courtesy you expect for yourself. This is a form of the golden rule of communication. Remember, sometime you may be the one who has the unpopular view and your right to be heard will be jeopardized if only majority opinions are allowed free expression.

One social code of argumentation is that while criticism and refutation are important parts of the process, they should be directed toward the arguer's reasoning and proof, not his person. Character assassination is not good argumentation because it diverts attention from the issues and does nothing to further the rationality of your position. Point out the misinterpretations or mistakes in the other person's position, but do not accuse that person of lacking intelligence for having offered them.

Earlier we said that communication was rule-governed behavior. In addition to rules telling us about word order, idea organization, and rational thinking, there are rules of social custom that govern acts of communication. Discover these for the context in which you are arguing and avoid violating them. Because a word is in your vocabulary does not mean it's use is appropriate in every communication context. Social customs include dressing appropriately and avoiding slang expressions and off-color jokes.

A social code that is becoming increasingly important in every communication context is avoiding language that discriminates on the basis of age, sex, race, ethnic origin, or personal characteristics. Because social customs vary greatly, being ethical means being flexible and determining what conduct is appropriate before a given audience. Remember, you will be judged on the basis of how well you operate within the social customs of the group you are addressing.

Ultimately, following ethical standards offers you the best means of arguing well. How will you know when you are arguing well? What is good argumentation? Joseph Wenzel (1990) answers these questions by suggesting that four Cs should guide us.

> [A]rgumentation depends on the arguers being *cooperative* in following appropriate rules and committing themselves to the common purpose of sound decision making. Good argumentation is *comprehensive* in dealing with a subject as thoroughly as possible. Good argumentation is *candid* in making ideas clear and getting them out in the open for examination. Finally, sound argumentation is *critical* in its commitment to basing decisions on the most rigorous testing of positions that circumstances allow. (p. 24)

In defining argumentation as a form of instrumental communication, we view the process as an audience-centered approach to the resolution of controversy. The goal of the practitioner of argumentation is to gain an audience's assent regarding the issue under consideration. Argumentation is not an end in itself but a means to achieving consensus or making a decision.

As we end this chapter, we want you to focus on the idea that argumentation is a *process* or a *means* of communication. In your own argumentation, you may not always succeed in changing the beliefs and behaviors of others. While we all want to be successful in instrumental communication, the most important outcome of studying and practicing argumentation is that it offers a good process, a good means to create arguments. Learning how to use the principles of argumentation will enable you to state without reservation, "This is my argument." Argumentation is a way of growing personally. Even when you do not win an argument, you still grow. As Robert L. Scott (1987) suggests:

> It is less important that we resolve our arguments than that we keep them going for it is in arguing that we realize who we are and what we are. That is, we understand our affiliations and loyalties, our institutions and traditions, and we are to embrace the first person possessive with understanding. (p. 70)

Learning Activities

1. Discuss the advantages and disadvantages of using argumentation as a means of influencing the beliefs and behaviors of others. How will the advantages of argumentation improve your ability to communicate your views in a controversy? How will you overcome the limitations of argumentation?
2. We have used commercials to illustrate the use of emotional responses and to discuss some of the differences between communication that is expressive and communication that is instrumental. To study these differences, find examples of advertisements in magazines or newspapers that seek an emotional response from the reader. For each example, indicate the emotional response sought. Do any of these examples also appeal to the rationality of the audience?

3. Find an example of argumentation that you perceive to be effective and respond to the following questions:
   A. Why is this an example of argumentation? How is it instrumental?
   B. What evidence do you have that the author of the argument is fulfilling the ethical responsibilities of arguing?
4. Think about your most strongly held opinions. Upon what are these based? Examine the sources of these beliefs for evidence of reasoning, emotions, prejudices, tradition, or authority figures.
5. Develop a code of ethical standards for your argumentation class. In particular, the class should determine what social codes will be appropriate. What will you consider to be ethical and unethical behaviors?

Suggested Supplementary Readings

Anderson, J. M., & Dovre, P. J. (Eds.) (1968). *Readings in Argumentation.* Boston: Allyn & Bacon.
   This collection of essays offers views on argumentation ranging from the classical to the contemporary. We recommend the sections on the ethics of controversy and argumentation in society and Sidney Hook's essay on the ground rules for controversy in a democracy, which may be used to formulate a code of ethics for the argumentation class.
Brockriede, W. (1972). Arguers as Lovers. *Philosophy and Rhetoric,* 5, 1–11.
   By characterizing the people who engage in argumentation as rapists, seducers, and lovers, Brockriede explores the ways in which arguers try to force (rape), trick (seduce), or respect (love) their audiences. This article is one of the most well-known discussions of ethical dimensions in argumentation.
Jaksa, J. A., & Pritchard, M. S. (1988). *Communication Ethics: Methods of Analysis.* Belmont, CA: Wadsworth.
   The authors review a variety of contemporary perspectives on ethics, including situational ethics, the truth standard, moral reasoning, and the problem of groupthink. This book contains many case studies of communication ethics on topics such as withholding information, disinformation, and candor.
Nilsen, T. R. (1974). *Ethics of Speech Communication* (2nd Ed.). Indianapolis: Bobbs-Merrill.
   As the title suggests, the nature of ethics and the requirements of ethical communication are examined in depth. Particular emphasis is given to the speaker's obligation to offer the audience the opportunity to make an informed choice. An excellent work on ethics and persuasion.
Rives, S. G. (1964). Ethical Argumentation. *Journal of the American Forensic Association,* 1, 79–85.
   Rives describes the relationship between ethics and argumentation and focuses on the ethical responsibilities of arguers in terms of communication behaviors that regulate argumentation. He takes the perspective that an ideal democratic society would obligate communicators to operationalize three value standards: truth, human welfare, and rationality. These standards are explained in the context of academic argumentation.

Chapter Two

Where Do I Begin in Argumentation?

In Chapter 1, we told you that argumentation is instrumental communication. It is used to influence the beliefs and behaviors of others. Principles of argumentation have evolved over time, and the practice of good argumentation requires that arguers maintain ethical standards appropriate to their society. This information alone, however, is not enough to begin the process of arguing. As with any rule-governed behavior, there are certain first principles, or conventions, you must know as a prerequisite to participating.

We want you to think of arguing as participating in a process that leads to ethical and effective uses of reasoning and proof. To understand how people get involved in the process, it is helpful to extend our characterization of argumentation as instrumental communication. Frans van Eemeren, Rob Grootendorst, and Tjark Kruiger (1987) offer such an extension by explaining common characteristics of the process:

- Argumentation is a social activity.
- Argumentation is an intellectual activity.
- Argumentation is a verbal activity.
- Argumentation is opinion stating, justifying, or refuting.
- Argumentation is directed toward an audience.

To begin the process of argumentation based on this characterization, there are certain conventions about the process that you must know before proceeding. These conventions are: (1) argumentation takes place in a certain social context (a *field*); (2) there are intellectual, verbal, and organizational rules for arguing that are used across all fields (*field invariant*) and there are some rules that are appropriate only in a given field (*field dependent*); (3) there are designated roles (*advocate* and *opponent*) arguers fulfill as they participate in the process of argumentation that obligate them to behave according to certain rule (*presumption* and *burden of proof*); (4) the process of argumentation centers on the audience as decision makers.

Fields of Argumentation

The first convention for beginning the process of argumentation are the concepts that arguments take place within a field and that some elements of the process will not change from one field to the next while other elements will. A *field* of argumentation is a social or professional context in which people argue in order to make decisions or build a body of knowledge. For example, a field is similar to an academic discipline such as history or biology. Theories, examples, and interpretations in each academic discipline have evolved over time as successive historians and biologists contributed to their field's body of knowledge and formed opinions based on research about what something means in the historical or biological context.

Each field has certain elements that are *field dependent.* These elements are particular to that field alone. Definitions and terminology, the jargon that may be incomprehensible to anyone outside of that field, are field-dependent uses of language, the verbal characteristic of argumentation. Standards of proof and reasoning can also be field dependent. Historians and biologists discover information and create knowledge in different ways. We cannot give you a complete list of everything that might be dependent in a particular field. Recall that in Chapter 1 we told you that arguers have an ethical responsibility to thoroughly research a field. Research helps you discover what elements in a field are unique to it. To participate in argumentation, you must be knowledgeable in a field's subject matter and be familiar with the special requirements for arguing that are field dependent.

Think about how the historian and the biologist approach doing research in their respective fields. A rule that exists in many different fields but is conditioned by the subject matter of each is: What constitutes enough cases if one is going to make a generalization? (Lyne, 1990). A historian can develop effective arguments using six cases about the impact of the railroads on the development of the western frontier. A biologist, on the other hand, would be considered irresponsible for drawing a conclusion about cell behavior based on a study of only six cells.

Not all elements of argumentation depend upon the subject matter of a particular field. Some elements, such as the basic mental structures of human reasoning and the tests we apply to determine the quality of information used to prove arguments, do not change as we move from field to field. These elements of argumentation are *field invariant.*

The historian and the biologist both use the same understanding of the reasoning process, that a generalization is made by examining instances of something and forming an opinion about what those instances have in common. Both fields also use the same understanding that good cases, upon which a valid generalization can be based, are those that are representative of all existing cases. The only difference in how history and biology approach generalizing is that each field differs as to how many cases are considered sufficient to support a generalization.

Why is it important, as a beginning step in learning about argumentation, to know the difference between field-dependent and field-invariant elements in argumentation? We all participate in several different fields. If you are taking courses from four different departments, you may be involved in four different fields. If each course requires that you write term papers, analyze case studies, or make comparisons and contrasts on essay tests, you will be a participant in argumentation in four different fields. You must know the field-dependent requirements for using language, the quantity of proof required, and other restrictions particular to each field if you are to be successful as an instrumental communicator in all of them.

It is also important to know the field-invariant elements of argumentation to be a successful participant. There are certain field-invariant rules for language. Whether you are writing for a history professor or a biology professor, both will expect you to know how to spell, use appropriate sentence structure, and organize a term paper according to a standard system for term-paper writing. Equally, there are certain field-invariant rules for arguing that apply across all disciplines, as we suggested in our comparison of history and biology.

In this book, we draw examples from many different fields to illustrate the principles and concepts of argumentation theory. This is possible because argumentation is a set of principles and concepts about how people instrumentally communicate using proof and reasoning and all fields use instrumental communication.

Fields are created by people and, consequently, are not static. A field is always in the process of evolving as new people with new ideas modify it or add to its body of knowledge. You must be on the alert for shifts, as when something that was field invariant in the past becomes field dependent. Equally, because individuals can engage many fields simultaneously, some things that were field dependent in the past may become field invariant in the future.

The third convention for beginning the process of argumentation characterizes the roles of participants and the rules under which they participate. Those who favor change and those who oppose it assume roles that assign certain responsibilities to each of them at the outset of the process. We will use the term *advocate* in argumentation to refer to the person who communicates to encourage a change in the belief or behavior of others. The term *opponent* identifies the person who acts to discourage the change supported by the advocate. This person plays the role of spokesperson for the existing beliefs and behaviors in the field. Using sports as an analogy, the advocate plays offense, the opponent plays defense. The conventions of presumption, burden of proof, and prima facie case development identify the playing field and obligate those who play on it to fulfill certain rule-based responsibilities.

Presumption

Beginning the process of argumentation requires you to identify the beliefs and behaviors that a field presently favors. All argumentation takes place over a piece of figurative ground occupied by existing institutions, ideas, laws, policies, and customs. This figurative ground represents the way things are at present. *Presumption* is the term that specifies who occupies this ground at the beginning of the controversy. Historically, the concept of presumption has reflected one of two viewpoints: artificial or natural.

The concept of *artificial presumption* in the legal system demonstrates how presumption is influenced by a field. In the American legal system, every defendant is presumed innocent until the probability of his or her guilt can be demonstrated by the state, in the case of criminal law, or by the plaintiff, in the case of civil law. This presumption of innocence is termed artificial because it is the result of argumentative ground, having been assigned arbitrarily to one side in the dispute because of a field-accepted belief. The Constitution and the accumulated experience of those in the field of law create a field-dependent presumption in favor of "innocent until proven guilty."

So powerful is this presumption in the American psyche that it often carries over into other fields, as when someone is accused of wrongdoing or malfeasance that is not necessarily a criminal or civil violation of the law. An assumption of innocence here is an artificial kind of presumption; law and custom could just as easily have assigned presumption as the French do: The accused is guilty until he or she proves the probability of innocence.

All fields have their own institutions, ideas, rules, policies, and customs that have been established as the field developed. These elements are often what defines one field as unique from others. We can say that these elements create an order for what is typical, or natural, for that field. Each field has its own natural order and participants in that field usually consider its institutions, ideas, rules, policies, or customs effective and deserving of continuation until someone shows them good and sufficient reasons to change.

Natural presumption derives from the observation of the natural order of whatever field we find ourselves in at a given time. When an advocate challenges a belief or behavior that is the consequence of something in the natural order of a field—an institution, idea, rule, policy, common practice, custom, value, or interpretation of reality—presumption automatically rests with the belief or behavior being challenged. This presumption in favor of the natural order is automatic since a field's natural order is a product of the development over time of things that work for that field. "If it ain't broke, don't fix it" is a bit of folk wisdom that neatly expresses the concept of natural presumption.

Our understanding of natural presumption is drawn from the work of Anglican Archbishop Richard Whately (1828/1963). In discussing presumption, he used the analogy of a company of soldiers inside a fortress. Change would require these troops to march out to meet the enemy; natural presumption would suggest that they remain secure inside their fortress rather than venture out onto an unknown battlefield. Since natural presumption reflects accepted practices in a given field, the natural order of things in the military field suggests that troops do not normally abandon a secure position in favor of an open field. They leave it up to the opposing force to attack their fortified position.

Pragmatically, presumption can serve as a decision rule for determining how the audience will respond to a proposal for change if the advocate for change fails to offer them good and sufficient reasons for making the change. Since presumption tells us what the audience presently views as adequate and deserving of continuation, if good and sufficient reasons are not given, the audience will usually reject a proposal for change. Whately was particularly concerned that those who argue realize what presumption means in preparing an argumentative case. He urged arguers to begin by knowing where presumption lies and to point out who has the burden of proving the change is reasonable and who has the benefit of endorsing the accepted institutions, ideas, rules, policies, and customs in a field. Thus, the convention of presumption helps us understand the responsibilities of the advocate and opponent roles in argumentation.

Presumption is a communication convention with implications for audience analysis. Whately also identified that for which the audience holds deference as a source of presumption. The persons, practices, ideas, or sources of information the audience accepts can be regarded as presumptively occupying the figurative ground. Whether we think of a large field, such as the "American system of democracy," or a narrower field, such as the "genre of horror fiction," those who make up that field tend to favor the existing practices and ideas of the field. They defer to the field's institutions, authorities, opinion leaders, and body of knowledge, which has evolved over time (Bruce, 1993).

The deference those in a field have for that which constitutes it is a natural presumption. People in a field comprise the audience for a proposal to change belief or behavior in it. Knowing those things, especially those sources of information and expert opinion, that the audience has deference for is the best way to discover what will provide a basis for good and sufficient reasons for them to favor or oppose change. J. Michael Sproule (1976) suggests a series of questions to ask in using natural presumption as an audience analysis device.

> The arguer is advised to ask such questions as: (1) to what groups do members of the audience belong? (2) to what sources of information (persons, books, groups) do audience members accord deference? (3) what is the popular and unpopular opinion on a particular subject? (4) what information on a subject might hold the advantage of novelty? Such queries would assist the [arguer] in selecting arguments and evidence best fitted to persuading persons on a given subject. (p. 128)

There is a final perspective from which we may consider the convention of presumption. Usually applied to argumentation as a process for seeking knowledge, presumption can be thought of as a hypothesis to be tested. When people engage in argumentation because their goal is to explore some new idea or reevaluate an old one, to define the boundaries of a concept, or to determine whether something is or is not accurate, they phrase a proposal and test it. The result is argumentation about whether to believe or not believe something (van Eemeren, Grootendorst, Jackson, & Jacobs, 1993 and Walton, 1992).

Argumentation to test hypotheses uses an artificial presumption. "Presumption comes into play where there is an issue or question that is open in the sense that the relevant, available evidence does not resolve the issue one way or another with sufficient weight to close discussion of the issue" (Walton, 1992, p. 42). The issue or question is phrased as a hypothesis although we will use the label *proposition* in Chapter 3. The hypothesis is given provisional, artificial acceptance and then argumentation takes place to determine if that acceptance should continue or should be rejected after thorough reasoning. Those who participate in hypothesis-testing argumentation may take the traditional roles of advocate and opponent, in which one side supports the accuracy of the proposition and the other denies it. A hypothesis may also be tested by using a format for argumentation in which all participants play the roles of both advocate and opponent.

You may recognize this form of argumentation from your experience in science or social science courses. The scientific method is a logical system for testing a hypothesis, often through a study or an experiment. A social scientist proposes that the lyrics in Country-Western music are more likely to contain negative characterizations of marriage and fidelity than the lyrics of any other form of popular music. She states the hypothesis: Country-Western lyrics suggest negative images of marriage and fidelity to listeners. She then assembles evidence by studying the content of lyrics in Country-Western and non-Country-Western songs and publishes her research in a social-science journal.

Our first social scientist has initiated an argument about the content, and likely impact on listeners, of the lyrics of Country-Western songs. Another social scientist reads the article and believes it misrepresents the meaning of these lyrics. He analyzes them and finds that the lyrics are more likely to suggest positive characterizations, and he publishes his findings. Both researchers may continue their debate over the hypothesis, analyzing more songs and publishing their findings. They may also choose to work together to determine whether the hypothesis is accurate by conducting a laboratory or field experiment to determine how Country-Western fans characterize these lyrics.

The debate tournaments that high school and college students participate in provide another venue for hypothesis testing. A debate topic is selected for the school year and students participate in contests to advocate or oppose the hypothetical statement or proposition. The testing of the hypothesis occurs as affirmative (advocate) and negative (opponent) teams argue back and forth, with a judge (audience) evaluating who best tests the hypothesis on the basis of the strength of arguments, quality of evidence, and soundness of reasoning. In tournament debate, testing the hypothesis of the debate topic relies on artificial presumption. Presumption is automatically granted to the negative team at the beginning of each debate, and the affirmative team has the burden of proving the presumption should be overturned. Whichever team is most successful in convincing the judge that its test of the hypothesis is accurate "wins" the debate. We may, then, view presumption from three different perspectives:

1. Presumption identifies existing institutions, ideas, laws or rules, policies, practices, or customs.
2. Presumption identifies what sources of information and expert opinion constitute good and sufficient reasons for accepting or rejecting a proposed change in belief or behavior.
3. Presumption is a decision rule that determines what the advocate must prove in testing the proposition as a hypothesis.

Whether artificial or natural, presumption grants initial possession of the figurative ground to the person fulfilling the role of opponent. The opponent represents an existing institution, idea, law or rule, policy, practice, or custom and is responsible for denying that good and sufficient reasons exist to change it. We assume that what exists should be maintained unless good reasons surface to change it. Presumption simply describes what exists without making any kind of judgment about its worth or effectiveness. Consider the following description:

> The existing curriculum at Northern State University involves courses which are mostly worth four credit hours, although a few one, two, and three-credit courses exist. Student schedules and faculty teaching loads are designed around the four-credit-hours-per-course system. Some faculty and students would like to have the system converted to a three-credit standard.

In this case, presumption states that a system of four-credit courses exists and functions at Northern State University. Presumption does not suggest this is necessarily good for learning or teaching, just that it is present and that in the field of Northern State University, no one presently sees any reason to change it. Controversy over the credit-hour system would revolve around the efforts of advocates to present a series of good reasons for changing the system and the efforts of opponents who, using the benefit of presumption that the four-credit standard has worked, defend the policy on the basis of its successful functioning.

In argumentation the importance of the convention of presumption lies in the responsibility it places upon the advocate. Since advocates do not have the benefit of presumption, which favors no change, they must show good and sufficient reasons why we can no longer rely on those beliefs or behaviors that are afforded presumption because they presently exist. We may summarize presumption in the following principles:

1. The term *presumption* describes a situation that currently exists and points out a prevailing order.
2. The opponent initially occupies the figurative ground over which the argument will be contested.
3. Presumption only describes; it does not judge the value or lack of value of the existing beliefs, institutions, ideas, laws or rules, policies, or customs presently occupying the ground.

Burden of Proof

Once presumption has been determined, an advocate must discover and provide good and sufficient reasons to support a change in belief or behavior. It is the responsibility of the person performing the role of advocate to provide these reasons in order to fulfill the burden of proof.

Presumption describes the preoccupation of ground in argumentation by the opponent; the *burden of proof* is the obligation of the advocate to contest the ground by offering arguments that are logically sufficient to challenge presumption. The process of argumentation is much like a balancing scale. Arguing is a shifting or transferring of the weight of evidence and reasoning from one side to the other (Walton, 1988). The audience for argumentation is part of the balancing mechanism as it may shift its support from advocate to opponent, or opponent to advocate as each side's arguments are presented. The scale is finally tipped when the audience decides to accept or reject the proposed change based on which side's evidence and reasoning ultimately has more weight.

To fully understand what the burden of proof involves, recall that presumption describes what exists without passing judgment on it. The advocate, in fulfilling the burden of proof, both passes judgment on and criticizes present belief or behavior and recommends a new belief or behavior. He or she begins by specifying or naming what it is that should not continue—the existing belief or behavior awarded preoccupation of the ground by presumption. To fulfill the obligation of burden of proof, the advocate must demonstrate why whatever presently occupies the disputed figurative ground should not continue to do so. The content and scope of the burden of proof is specified by the statement of the proposition argued.

The burden of proof may be thought of as the obligation of the complaining party in a dispute. In civil law, this obligation would be identified with the responsibility of the plaintiff to proceed first and make a case against the defendant, proving the complaint by a preponderance of evidence. If you were dissatisfied with an automobile you had purchased and decided to sue the dealership, as the plaintiff you would have to demonstrate through the introduction of evidence and testimony that you had been harmed or damaged in some way as a result of the dealer's actions. In criminal law, the state acts as advocate and must prove beyond reasonable doubt that the accused is guilty of the crime. This constitutes the state's burden of proof.

In a controversy, the burden of proof always falls upon the party who would lose if the complaint were rejected or if a settlement did not occur. In the case of your suing the auto dealer, as the person bringing the complaint, you would lose if you could not demonstrate that you had been harmed or if you could not prove the harm was a consequence of the dealer's actions. In the example of criminal law, the presumption of innocence means that if the prosecution was unable to demonstrate the guilt of the accused at a sufficiently high level of probability, the state's case would be lost.

In some fields, the requirements for the burden of proof may not always be as clear as they appear in legal argumentation. This is why audience analysis to determine presumption can be useful. It will help you discover exactly what your audience expects you to prove. If you were a student advocate addressing a Northern State University policy-making body made up of faculty and administrators, you might determine that their attitudes favored maintaining the four-credit-hour standard because faculty would be expected to undertake additional course preparation and demand a salary increase for the extra work load. You would have to show that the greater good to students, obtained from changing to a three-credit-hour standard, would justify the salary increase or the increased faculty work load.

Sometimes you have to make an educated guess regarding how much proof is sufficient to fulfill your burden to support change. Those who already support the change will require a simple affirmation of their beliefs; they require proof that confirms change is good and shows them how to change. An uncommitted audience may be open to the change but may require substantial reasoning and information to see that change is a good idea. An unbelieving audience may resist the change no matter what proof is presented but may sometimes be reached by your demonstrating that there are areas upon which agreement can be achieved. The latter is a common practice in labor-management negotiations and diplomatic relations. How many arguments are necessary and how much proof must support them depends upon an audience's expectations and degree of commitment.

The burden of proof is the logical opposite of presumption. The advocate has the responsibility of proving that the change being proposed is supported by good reasons. The opponent has the advantage of relying on existing belief or practice that will continue if the advocate fails to make a good case for change. We may summarize the burden of proof in the following principles:

1. The advocate has the responsibility to make a case of good and sufficient reasons for change. This is the burden of proof.
2. In fulfilling the burden of proof, present beliefs and behaviors described by presumption are judged and evaluated based on the available evidence, and an alternative pattern of thought or action is proposed.

How do you know when you have fulfilled your burden of proof? The advocate's responsibility to fulfill the burden of proof is discharged when a prima facie case is presented.

The Prima Facie Case

To overcome the presumption that a belief or behavior is adequate and deserving of continuation, the advocate must present a fully developed case strong enough to justify a change unless successfully challenged by countering arguments. Literally, a *prima facie case* is one that "at first sight" or "on the face of it" is sufficient to justify changing belief or behavior. A prima facie case causes us to suspend our reliance on presumption as a guide for belief or behavior. This suspension of presumption will either be temporary, if valid countering arguments are provided, or permanent, if the opponent is unable to establish a reason to continue to rely on the original presumption.

Because he or she would lose the dispute if a prima facie case were not presented to fulfill the burden of proof and suspend presumption, the advocate normally initiates the argument by speaking or writing first. This initial presentation must be prima facie and sufficient to support the proposal for a change in belief or behavior. The legal system once again provides an example to clarify the concept. In order to establish the guilt of a person accused of a felony, the prosecution must present an indictment of this individual that suspends the artificial presumption of innocence. This presentation must constitute a prima facie case.

Suppose Ralph is accused of auto theft. A prima facie case would, at the very least, consist of evidence and testimony supporting the following arguments:

An automobile was reported missing from the dealer's lot.

Subsequent to receiving this report, the city police apprehended Ralph with the vehicle in question in his possession.

Ralph's possession of the automobile was unlawful. He had not purchased it, nor had he received consent of any dealer representative to take it for a test drive.

Proving these three arguments would constitute a prima facie indictment of Ralph for grand-theft auto. The presumption of Ralph's innocence would be suspended until his attorney had mounted a successful defense. The defense attorney would have the responsibility of attempting to reestablish the presumption of Ralph's innocence by attacking the truth of one or more of these arguments or by introducing argumentation demonstrating extenuating circumstances mitigating Ralph's guilt.

The advocate is responsible for developing a *topical* prima facie case. In the field of an argumentation class or tournament debate, the advocate and her or his opponent agree to a proposition that identifies the broad, general topic to be argued. In ordinary conversations, and in the argumentation that takes place in some fields, it is easy to drift from topic to topic. When you want to make a specific case for or against some proposed change, that is not a desirable quality. Sticking to the topic you agreed to argue, the proposition, prevents the audience from becoming confused about the issues.

If you had agreed to argue about changing Northern State University's credit-hour system, the proposition might be stated as: Northern State University should adopt the three-credit-hour course as the university standard. In providing a prima facie case, the advocate would not contest the amount a student pays per credit hour or the manner in which fees are collected, since these issues are clearly outside the bounds of the proposition. Tuition constitutes a different topic requiring a different proposition and has as much relevance to a discussion of the credit-hour system at Northern as unpaid parking tickets would have to Ralph's guilt or innocence on the auto-theft charge.

In addition to being topical, a prima facie case for a proposition of value or policy must demonstrate *inherency*. Argumentation is used to decide whether or not change is justified. To justify change, the advocate must examine both the deficiencies in existing beliefs or behaviors and the reason for their existence. Inherency is concerned with the nature of cause. Advocates propose changes in belief or behavior to remedy problems or to fulfill the need for knowledge. They must identify what causes the problem or the need knowledge and demonstrate that the nature of the cause is such that it can only be overcome by a change in belief or behavior.

Inherency addresses questions such as: What is the cause of the problem? Is change necessary to overcome this cause? If we do not change, will the cause disappear and the problem correct itself? Why do we need new or reevaluated knowledge? Cause establishes that the problem exists as a direct result of existing belief or behavior. If the cause is found in behaviors that operationalize these beliefs, inherency is termed *structural*. If the cause is found in the beliefs of a field, inherency is said to be *attitudinal*.

We generally assume that if a problem's cause cannot be found, we cannot determine how best to remedy it, and if there is nothing to stimulate a quest for more knowledge, we will not pursue it. If an advocate cannot identify cause, he or she cannot develop a logically complete argument. Thus, inherency is a crucial part of an advocate's prima facie case. If the advocate fails to identify a cause for a problem or cause as a reason to seek knowledge, it will be impossible to determine if there is a good reason to change our belief or behavior.

Finding the cause establishes that a problem or need exists as a direct result of existing belief or behavior. If the cause is found in the institutions, laws or rules, policies, and sometimes the customs of a field, inherency is structural. This is the easier type of inherency to find through research because structures are typically recorded or codified in constitutions, handbooks, court cases, legislation, and rules of conduct. But not all structures are recorded. Unwritten customs and standard practices may evolve in a field over time, and new members of the field must learn them through experience. For example, rituals and superstitions that are believed to bring good luck in the athletic field are seldom recorded or talked about, but they exist with a very potent force for those in athletics.

Structural inherency results when fields adopt formal or informal systems that operationalize a strong or widely held belief. Institutions, laws or rules, policies, practices, and customs are the fabric that allow members of a field to engage in the activities that typify it. Structural inherency argues that a problem's cause is found in the behavior these formal and informal systems require of people. In searching for inherent causes, the advocate examines institutions, laws or rules, policies, practices, and customs to see if their presence or absence is what has caused a problem or need.

Inherency is attitudinal when the cause of a problem or need results from beliefs, ideas, or values that are central to a field. Attitudinal inherency is usually found in the articulated opinions, feelings, or emotional reactions of the people who comprise a field. Attitudinal inherency may be more difficult to find through research because we do not always verbalize beliefs, ideas, or values. More difficult does not mean impossible to find. In meeting your ethical obligation to do research, you can find many of these beliefs, ideas, or values by examining published mission statements, ethical codes, or survey research results and by interviewing, or reading essays by, opinion leaders in a given field.

Attitudinal inherency can be a powerful barrier to changing belief or behavior, even when many in a field deem such a change necessary. To illustrate the power of attitudes, consider the following examples. The opinion that women are less capable of studying mathematics than men can keep women from pursuing careers in many scientific fields. The feeling that college athletes are dumb jocks who receive preferential treatment can make them exiles in the classroom. Emotional reactions to the seeming unfairness of the tax system has led some to cheat on their taxes. Attitudes are often difficult to identify, but they play a powerful role in causing us to accept something as true or false, to value one thing over another, or to act or refuse to act in a certain way.

In our example of argumentation concerning Northern State University, if the principal reason we have for wanting to change Northern's credit-hour system is that the present system is (1) too restrictive of a student's options in choosing courses or (2) does not get maximum productivity from staff and facilities, we would be citing problems that are built-in features of the existing four-credit-hour system. Inherency in this case is structural; the problem is caused by the four-credit-hour policy. This policy has been in effect for a number of years and is considered deserving of continuation by Northern's policy makers.

Faculty members' belief that a three-credit-hour system would increase their work load also serves as an inherent barrier to change. If faculty members prefer the four-credit-hour system, they have little or no inclination to change it. The problems with the system perceived by student advocates could only be solved by implementing a change that the existing power structure is ambivalent toward putting in place.

The role of faculty attitude in preventing change illustrates that it is possible for structural and attitudinal inherency to be present at the same time. It is a characteristic of controversy that there may be several causes for a problem's existence. To solve a problem, however, it is necessary to remove its prime cause. The advocate and opponent, in examining existing beliefs and behaviors, frequently disagree over whose explanation most clearly represents the probable truth about what causes a problem or need to exist. Conceptually, inherency is important in determining whether a prima facie case has been presented because it forces arguers to examine the reasons why things exist and to explore whether they will correct themselves by the natural processes of change.

We may summarize the concept of prima facie argument with the following principles:

1. The advocate has the responsibility of presenting a prima facie case, which at face value justifies a change in belief or behavior.
2. The form and content of the arguments offered determines the face value of an advocate's case.

3. A prima facie case must be both topical and inherent.
4. Presentation of a prima facie case causes the suspension of presumption unless it is successfully challenged.

The question may still remain: How do you know when you have discharged your responsibilities as an advocate regarding the burden of proof? How will you know what to oppose if you are the opponent? The content and scope of the burden of proof is determined by the wording of the proposition that expresses the change in belief or behavior the advocate proposes.

Further, what constitutes a prima facie case can be determined by the use of certain field-invariant, stock questions that can be applied to propositions in any field. Early theories of rhetoric developed a series of questions that were crucial in legal proceedings. These questions established the content and scope of the burden of proof for legal propositions. They are similar to the questions the prosecutor considered in preparing the case against Ralph. For fields of argument other than law, similar sets of questions exist. They are commonly referred to as *stock issues*, the questions that listeners or readers want answered before they will accept the advocate's arguments as sufficient to warrant a change in belief or behavior. These questions focus the controversy and are naturally derived from the proposition being argued.

This chapter has covered conventions, roles, rules, and responsibilities, that shape participation in the process of argumentation. These conventions establish the figurative ground over which argumentation takes place and some of the rules arguers must follow for argumentation to be logically complete. An advocate, as the person seeking a change in belief or behavior, must prove the case in order to overcome presumption, which artificially or naturally favors no change. The playing field of argumentation is regulated by the rule that advocates and opponents must not deviate too far from the topic. In making a prima facie case for change, the advocate must prove that an inherent cause exists that serves as a good reason to make a change in belief or behavior. The opponent has the benefit of the presumption that existing elements in a field are considered adequate by the field and deserve continuation in the absence of a prima facie case for changing them. The next chapter expands on what you must do to enter the process of argumentation as we examine the function and wording of argumentative propositions.

Learning Activities

1. Discuss what the three different views of presumption mean to the roles of advocate and opponent in argumentation. Should we always assign the roles before determining presumption? In which communication contexts might you use the view that presumption rests with existing institutions? In which would it be appropriate to discover the beliefs of an audience? Which fields make extensive use of hypothesis testing as a form of argumentation?

2. Choose an ongoing controversy such as smokers' versus nonsmokers' rights, abortion versus right to life, environmental protection versus the need for employment. Which side in the controversy has presumption? Which has the burden of proving that change should occur?

3. Scholars often argue over whether a proposed theory has accuracy or legitimacy in their field. Two theories of communication—fantasy theme analysis and the narrative paradigm—are examples of such argumentation. Choose one of the following debates for examination:

   A. *Advocate:* Bormann, E. G. (1972, December). Fantasy and Rhetorical Vision: The Rhetorical Criticism of Social Reality. *Quarterly Journal of Speech,* 58, 396–407.
   Opponent: Mohrman, G. P. (1982, May). An Essay on Fantasy Theme Criticism. *Quarterly Journal of Speech,* 68, 109–132.

   B. *Advocate:* Fisher, W. R. (1985, December). The Narrative Paradigm: An Elaboration. *Communication Monographs,* 52, 347–367.
   Opponent: Rowland, R. C. (1987, September). Narrative: Mode of Discourse or Paradigm? *Communication Monographs,* 56, 264–275.

   How does the advocate identify presumption in the field of speech communication? Does he present good and sufficient reasons for accepting the proposed theory of communication? How does the opponent deny the theory is accurate? Are his reasons effective enough to cause you as the reader to reject the accuracy of the proposed theory?

4. Find an editorial from a current newspaper or magazine that you believe is intended to alter behavior. Analyze it in terms of the following:

   A. What is the locus of presumption?
   B. How does the arguer fulfill the burden of proof?
   C. In your opinion, has the arguer succeeded in creating a prima facie case?
   D. Assume that you will be the opponent for this case and indicate what you might argue in response.

Suggested Supplementary Readings

Golden, J. L., Berquist, G. F., & Coleman, W. E. (1992). *The Rhetoric of Western Thought* (5th Ed.). Dubuque, IA: Kendall/Hunt.
   This book surveys rhetorical theory from the Greeks to the present. We recommend you examine the portion of Chapter 8 relating to Richard Whately and his development of the concepts of presumption and burden of proof. Also examine Chapter 13, "Stephen Toulmin on the Nature of Argument," which describes the philosophy behind the model and discusses the superiority of the Toulmin model as a means of generating understanding.

Sproule, J. M. (1976). The Psychological Burden of Proof: On the Evolutionary Development of Richard Whately's Theory of Presumption. *Communication Monographs,* 43, 115–29.
   A review of the development of the concept of presumption in Whately's several revisions of his *Elements of Rhetoric.* Sproule concludes that Whately felt

presumption should be determined on the basis of audience beliefs and attitudes. He suggests how arguers might use the theory of presumption as a guide to audience analysis and argues that the psychological makeup of the audience should determine the responsibilities of advocate and opponent.

Vasilius, J. (1980). Presumption, Presumption, Wherefore Art Thou Presumption? In D. Brownlee (Ed.), *Perspectives on Non-Policy Argument*, (pp. 33–42). ERIC Document ED 192 382.

Originally presented at the 1980 Desert Argumentation Symposium at the University of Arizona, this paper offers ten justifications for using presumption to test hypotheses in value argumentation. Vasilius examines the problems faced by Cross Examination Debate Association (CEDA) debaters in determining the responsibilities of advocates and opponents. She explains how employing hypothesis testing as the philosophical basis for argument resolves this problem.

Walton, D. N. (1992). *Plausible Argument in Everyday Conversation.* Albany, NY: State University of New York Press.

Douglas Walton is one of the scholars on the cutting edge of new applications of argumentation and the extension of theories of argument. Chapter 2 is an extensive discussion of presumption in various contexts. We particularly recommend Walton's discussion of presumption as an advanced explanation of the concept "I presume something" as the basis for argumentative theories of natural presumption.

Chapter Three

What Am I Going to Argue About?

In Chapter 2 we said argumentation always takes place over a figurative piece of ground, and its limits are defined by a proposition stating a change in belief or behavior. A clearly stated proposition is crucial to establishing the responsibilities of advocate and opponent in the process of argumentation. In this chapter, propositions are defined, three classifications of propositions are presented, and guidelines for phrasing propositions and defining their terms are offered.

The Nature of Propositions

Stating the proposition identifies the limits of the topic of argument, places the burden of proof with the advocate, and gives presumption to the opponent. Propositions are formed about controversies in a field. A controversy is a dispute or difference of opinion about something. Physicists wonder why so few students readily catch on to scientific thinking. Physics professor Alan Cromer (Begley, 1993) suggests that science and objective thinking are unnatural activities. Others in the field disagree. NASA argues that an American space station is a better investment of national resources than more social programs (Cramer, 1991). Social service agencies disagree with this view. Students and administrators at Harvard, Tufts, and the University of Iowa propose regulations that prohibit faculty from dating students in their classes (Begley, 1993). Some in the campus community respond that this infringes on the Declaration of Independence's espousal of the pursuit of happiness as a fundamental American right.

Since controversies commonly arise over questions of "what happened," "what is," "what judgment shall I make in this situation," or "what is the best course of action to follow," the limits of controversy must be identified so both advocate and opponent know the boundaries of the argumentative ground. The proposition serves as the starting line for the process of argumentation.

> The **proposition** is a statement that identifies the argumentative ground and points to a change in belief or behavior.

The proposition defines the locus of disagreement and whether that disagreement is over some proposed change in belief or behavior. To argue effectively in ways that will offer sound reasons to your audience, you must state the controversy in a way that readily identifies what the argument is about. By identifying the locus of disagreement in the form of a proposition, you will be able to fulfill three objectives in successfully participating in argumentation.

Selecting Terms for Definition

The first objective is that arguers define the terms that describe the argumentative ground. By phrasing the locus of disagreement in the form of a proposition, important words or phrases that may need definition are made more obvious to both the arguers and their audience. One question frequently arises: What do the advocate and opponent mean when they use particular words or phrases? The proposition provides a semantic framework for argument and allows the advocate and opponent to offer interpretations of the important words and phrases contained in it.

Let us examine a possible proposition for argumentation: *The federal government should significantly strengthen the regulation of mass media in the United States.* This is a proposition for policy argumentation, but the same objective also applies to propositions for factual and value argumentation. In order for the advocate to fulfill the burden of proof, she must identify and define the terms in the proposition that the rational reader or listener must understand in order to realize what sort of change the advocate seeks. In the example, three key phrases establish the figurative ground of the argument: (1) federal government, (2) significantly strengthen the regulation of, and (3) mass media. Only by determining the meaning of these terms can the advocate convey what the proposition means and what her burden of proof includes.

Although the opponent does not begin the process of definition, he is not obligated, in all instances, to accept the definitions provided by the advocate in her initial presentation. In some instances, an early step in the argumentative process for the opponent involves arguing about the definition of specific terms in the proposition. Hence, the proposition is an important first step in clarifying the boundaries of argumentative ground.

The advocate for our proposition concerning federal regulation of mass media, for example, might choose to define one key phrase in this way: Mass media means films and video cassettes that depict explicit sexual acts between children under the age of twelve and adults of the opposite or same sex. The opponent may have the same uneasy feeling you just had since he has now been cast in the role of defender of the right of pedophiles to obtain child pornography. Any presumption deriving from his role as opponent is stripped away or even reversed by this definition of mass media, since it is difficult to conceive of many people accepting the notion that if child pornography exists, it deserves to continue until good reasons are provided to show otherwise.

Our sample proposition is one for academic argumentation, about which more will be said shortly. In this instance, we see why an opponent might contest a definition since failure to do so would place him at an extreme disadvantage. The opponent might suggest child pornography is not included in the argumentative ground since it does not meet commonly accepted standards of what we define as mass media. Such an argument over the way a term has been defined would ask the audience to make a decision based on determining who has the most reasonable definition of key terms in the proposition. There is no universal list of rules for making such a decision, but the practices for defining terms given at the end of this chapter offer many usable ideas for determining which terms to define and how to define them.

Specifying Direction of Change

The second argumentative objective fulfilled by having a proposition is that it identifies the alteration of belief or behavior sought by the advocate and resisted by the opponent. A proposition must specify the action to be taken or the belief to be altered. By identifying the change sought, the proposition identifies both the advocate's burden of proof and the benefit of presumption the opponent may draw upon to deny that the change is good or necessary.

Taking our sample proposition once again, let us assume that the advocate has offered the following definitions:

federal government: the Federal Communications Commission

significantly strengthen the regulation of: impose a specific code of standards to govern the depiction of acts of violence

mass media: all television programming broadcast by the three major networks, independent stations, and cable or pay television systems

The change sought involves increased regulation of the depiction of violence in television programming. If you are reading carefully, you probably recognize that the way the proposition is defined directs change at both entertainment and news programming. The advocate has the burden to prove that such a change is necessary, desirable, and achievable. The opponent has the benefit of presumption that the present system of regulation by the Federal Communications Commission and the code of standards and practices of the various broadcast companies have been considered adequate and are deserving of continuation.

Even without definitions, the proposition pointed to the kind of change the advocate is expected to support. To state that the federal government should significantly strengthen the regulation of mass media in the United States is to point the advocate in the direction of supporting greater control. The proposition identifies the agency for change the advocate must employ—the federal government. It identifies the type of change—significantly strengthened regulation. It points to the target of change—mass media in the United States.

Change is also specified when the proposition is one of value or fact. Readers or listeners are asked to alter their beliefs regarding how something is valued or understood. In a value proposition, such as, "Preventing the sale and use of controlled substances on school property is more important than an individual student's right to privacy," the agency for change is the audience. They are asked to make a mental commitment to value safety over privacy. The advocate's burden to prove that change is necessary, desirable, and achievable involves arguing one value's supremacy over the other. In a proposition of fact, such as, "The use of controlled substances on school property is increasing," the audience is asked to believe the trend indicated in the proposition and the advocate's burden is to prove it is occurring. Even before definitions were supplied, these propositions set general boundaries for argument that were flexible enough to afford both advocate and opponent the opportunity for interpretation.

This characteristic—flexibility—is usually found in propositions from the academic classroom-tournament debate field. Propositions in other academic and nonacademic fields are formed when there is a feeling that actions, available knowledge, or value judgments might require change. These propositions are often very specific about the objective the advocate seeks.

A proposition in the legal field is usually found in the statement of criminal charges or a plaintiff's complaint in a civil case. Defendant X has violated law or statute Y. If X is the owner of an adult bookstore, and if Y is designed to prevent the production, distribution, sale, or exhibition of child pornography, then argumentation between prosecutor and defense attorney is joined over whether X is guilty of violating Y. The proposition being argued is specific and leaves fewer opportunities for interpretation than the academic proposition introduced earlier.

Fewer opportunities does not mean none. While we indicated that the opponent in an academic controversy might object to the definition of mass media as child pornography, his legal counterpart, the defense attorney, might employ a similar strategy. The presumption for child pornography is as weak in the legal field as it is in the academic. Recognizing this, the defense attorney may attempt to redefine the proposition and put the law, rather than his client, on trial. Where presumption is found can be broadly interpreted. Rather than focusing on the specific act of selling pornographic materials, the defense attorney might turn to the law as a source of presumption. The First Amendment to the Constitution states, "Congress shall make no law" regarding a number of institutions, one of which is the press. Since there is strong presumption for this document, the defense attorney might argue that the law under which his client is charged represents a greater threat to society than do the materials he is accused of producing, distributing, selling, or exhibiting because it violates the Constitution.

The clash of values in this example, and the feelings they evoke, are typical of argumentation in many fields because real consequences result from how controversies are resolved. Disputes over pornography usually take place over the figurative ground of which value is more important: freedom of the individual or public morality. Such examples of value conflict are common and may create paradoxes such as the American Civil Liberties Union defending the right of American Nazis to march in Skokie, Illinois, where a number of Holocaust survivors live. The point of considering this value conflict is that the direction of change specified in the proposition should be as clear as possible. Identification of presumption may also require a definitional process to determine exactly what argumentative ground is at stake.

In your personal experiences with argumentation, the proposition may have been a declarative statement as simple as, "I think we should go to a movie tonight" or as vexing as, "If you really loved me, you'd prove it." This is not always the case. In naturally occurring argumentation, propositions are not always clearly stated at the outset of the controversy. The failure to state exactly what we are arguing about probably accounts for most of the instances of misunderstanding that occur in interpersonal controversy. Propositions in many fields may not be clearly stated in advance, but when they are, they are narrow and open to fewer interpretations than propositions for academic argument.

Propositions for academic argumentation often seem easier to cope with than those in other fields because they are always clearly stated in advance. Since academic argumentation exists solely for the purpose of developing skills and testing ideas, the disagreements are usually artificial or induced. To maintain interest in an academic exercise, it becomes necessary to have a proposition that is broad enough to allow interpretation and to provide sufficient intellectual challenge to the student who may have to work with it over a period of time. The seemingly unitary nature of many propositions in other fields is neither characteristic of, nor desirable for, propositions in academic argumentation.

In our example on regulation of mass media, controversy over what to regulate need not involve a discussion of television violence, since mass media include movies, music, newspapers, books, and magazines as well as television; neither is violence the only critical issue that might be considered. This is an example of a proposition that could be argued over an extended period of time, by a number of people, without becoming boring or repetitive. It shares one important characteristic with propositions in other fields: It points toward some alteration of belief or behavior. If it did not, there would be nothing to argue, and the misunderstanding and bypassing, which occurs in some argumentation, might result. When the opponent in our earlier example of academic argumentation challenges the validity of the advocate's definition of mass media as child pornography, he is saying that the change in belief and behavior she supports points in a direction not reasonably suggested by the proposition they agreed to argue.

What are academic argumentative propositions about? Issues of social equality, the process of government, international relations, and economics are often topics for classroom argumentation. As a result, you may find yourself learning about past, present, and future events while you are developing and refining your skills.

Identifying Key Issues

The third objective fulfilled by a specifically worded proposition is the aid it provides in the identification of key issues. In Chapter 4 we devote more specific attention to the identification of intrinsic or stock issues; at this point, it is sufficient to state that issues are central questions suggested by the specific wording of a proposition and its definition by the advocate. "An issue is an inherent and vital question within a proposition: inherent because it exists inseparably and inevitably within the proposition, and vital because it is crucial or essential to the meaning of the proposition" (Mills, 1968, p. 96). Issues become the contested points in argumentation, the areas of disagreement between advocate and opponent. If the proposition can be said to define the potential boundaries of argument, the issues suggested by it provide the internal structure or framework for argumentation.

Issues grow directly from the definition of the proposition that the advocate provides since this definition narrows and clarifies its meaning in academic argumentation. Earlier, we offered the following definitions:

federal government: the Federal Communications Commission

significantly strengthen the regulation of: impose a specific code of standards to govern the depiction of acts of violence

mass media: all television programming broadcast by the three major networks, independent stations, and cable or pay television systems

Our broad proposition has now come to mean something very specific: The Federal Communications Commission should crack down on television violence. If the opponent accepts these definitions as reasonable, argumentation can proceed on the issues associated with the narrowed proposition. These become the advocate's burden of proof.

What might these issues be? They are questions that a reasonable person, such as our advocate or opponent, might ask before accepting the change in the Federal Communications Commission's regulative behavior required by the narrowed proposition.

Is violence depicted on television?

Does something harmful occur because of the depiction of violence in television programming?

Would there be any advantage or benefit in controlling the depiction of violence in television programming?

Is the way in which the Federal Communications Commission deals with the depiction of violence in television programming insufficient at present?

Is the Federal Communications Commission the best government agency to regulate the depiction of violence in television programming?

What might the consequences be of having the Federal Communications Commission regulate the depiction of violence in television programming?

These questions represent issues that give shape and structure to the process of argumentation over the figurative ground. By locating areas of disagreement, potential and real, the arguers specify for each other, and for the listener or reader, the aspects of belief or behavior over which controversy exists. Issues, which sharpen the locus of disagreement, constitute the basis for determining whether to alter or maintain current interpretations of reality.

Those who were reading carefully enough earlier to notice that the definition of mass media includes both entertainment and news programming probably have a few questions right now. What does the advocate mean by violence? Does the use of the term *depiction* mean that while television could not show the act on the screen, it could show its consequences? Good questions! In your role as opponent, listener, or reader you would probably get a sense of the answers from the arguments the advocate provided in upholding her burden of proof. That might not always be the case. This points to a problem that can occur when we define a proposition. If we are not careful, all our definition accomplishes is shifting confusion from the meaning of terms in the proposition to the words and phrases we used in attempting to narrow and clarify its meaning.

You might also ask what happened to First Amendment freedoms. If the lawyer defending the pornography merchant could try to get his client off the hook by claiming the law under which he was charged was unconstitutional, couldn't the opponent in this academic controversy invoke the same defense? After all, doesn't freedom of speech give CNN the right to bring us pictures of the latest acts of violence in Eastern Europe or ABC the right to bring the sexual exploits of the characters on "NYPD Blue" into our living rooms? These questions point to a particular feature of the academic proposition that is important in issue identification. We call your attention to a six-letter word in our sample proposition, *should*, a word that is common to many academic propositions.

One of the artifices of academic argumentation is that it frequently concerns itself with what ought to be rather than what will be. In a sense, we proceed from the assumption that if something should change, it can change, be it belief or behavior. We ignore the fact that in reality it might not, no matter how strong the proof or compelling the reasons. Before dismissing academic argumentation as a frivolous twentieth-century equivalent of the thirteenth-century disputation over how many angels can dance on the head of a pin and dropping your argumentation course, consider the following: The suspension of disbelief involved in academic argumentation is no different than that which operates in other fields.

The government agency that passed the antismut law our hypothetical prosecutor used in attempting to bring our purveyor of child pornography to justice probably did exactly the same thing. The government representatives asked themselves whether something should be done, answered affirmatively, and passed the law. They may never have considered whether it violated the First Amendment. If they did, they decided either that it probably did not or, more probably, that it was a question for the courts. As a practitioner of academic argumentation, you will find yourself often concerned with what ought to be, keeping in mind that your purpose is to develop skills and test ideas.

Since academic argumentation often involves arguing both sides of a proposition or listening to the argumentation of classmates, you may find yourself arguing or listening to arguments about something you do not really believe. We have referred to this mysterious field of "academic argumentation," which is not really a field. Academic argumentation as a field consists of textbooks and scholarly journals on the theory and practice of argumentation, your argumentation class and others like it, and the competitive contests high school and college students participate in. The subjects we use for propositions in academic argumentation come from the great variety of fields that exist in society.

Because the goal of academic argumentation is to teach how to advocate and oppose propositions, and because the subject matter is selected from the panoply of human activities, you may hear or read cases other arguers make for ideas or actions that you believe so distasteful, so wrong, that they would never happen in our world. The courts, Congress, or the public would not allow them to happen. Distasteful or wrong proposals put forth to resolve problems or satisfy needs are often made with the best of intentions. Some group or agency concludes that "something ought to be done," finds a course of action, and undertakes it. This sometimes produces decisions that are distasteful or harmful, as was the case when officials of the Reagan Administration oversaw the sale of arms to Iran to generate funds to support the Contras' guerrilla war against the Sandinista government in Nicaragua in circumvention of the Boland Amendment.

The perception that something should be done, that one value is more important than another, or that we must alter our understanding of something, carries no guarantee that when a change is made, it will turn out to be desirable or it will not have some unforeseen, long-term consequence. Good argumentation in any field explores the extent of desirability and searches for potential drawbacks. As you examine propositions for argumentation in your class or in other fields, you must practice the suspension of belief or disbelief in order to consider all aspects of the implied change. In sum, when you set out to discover what belief is best or what should be done, taking care in defining terms and examining all possible issues growing out of the proposition are important, albeit time-consuming, steps.

Summary of the Nature of Propositions

1. The proposition specifies the scope of the controversy, providing boundaries for argument. Defining selected terms of the proposition helps to clarify these boundaries.
2. The proposition expresses the advocate's goal, asserting the alteration in belief or behavior for which assent is sought.
3. The proposition delineates the advocate's responsibilities regarding the burden of proof and the opponent's opportunities that may result from identifying presumption, and it suggests potential issues that constitute the argumentative ground.

The Classification of Propositions

We classify propositions according to the ends sought by their advocates, a change in either belief or behavior, and have already referred to the three types of propositions commonly argued—*fact, value,* and *policy.* These correspond to the most common sources of controversy: (1) disputes over what happened, what is happening, or what will happen; (2) disputes asserting something to be good or bad, right or wrong, effective or ineffective; and (3) disputes over what should or should not be done.

Propositions of Fact

Propositions of fact seek to alter our beliefs. They do so by asserting an appropriate way to view reality or seek knowledge. *Illegal immigration deprives U. S. citizens of jobs,* asserts a relationship between the presence of illegal aliens and some qualitative or quantitative harm. *The lyrics of Country-Western music convey negative images of marriage and fidelity,* asserts a relationship between the word-symbols in lyrics of this music genre and potential attitudes its listeners may develop as a result. We may not accept the probable truth of these propositions without further explanation. Proof of their asserted relationships would require identification of those areas in which the presence of illegal aliens in the United States causes the consequence specified and analysis of the lyrics of Country-Western music to determine if such negative images exist in them.

Propositions of fact are further classified in terms of the change in belief that is sought—whether it is about the past, the present, or the future.

Past Fact
  Life evolved naturally from existing conditions on earth.
  Few American presidents have enjoyed favorable press coverage while in office.

Present Fact
  The American mass media is relatively free from government regulation.
  Trade sanctions against China are necessary for the protection of some American industries.

Future Fact
  The Internet will change how we interact with each other.
  Most wildlife species will cease to exist outside of zoos in the next century.

In each of these factual propositions, the controversy concerns the relationship between something and what we are asked to believe about it. To determine the truth of the relationship in the case of past or present fact propositions, the process is similar: Discover what is required to establish the probable truth of the statement and proceed to verify it. Propositions of future fact depend on discovering the probability that something will occur in the future. In Chapter 9 we explore proving propositions of fact in more detail.

Propositions of Value

Like the proposition of fact, the proposition of value attempts to alter belief by dealing with our subjective reactions to things and our opinions of them. The proposition of value establishes a judgmental standard or set of standards and applies them. Any attempt to demonstrate something as good, right, or effective ultimately depends upon the criteria for what constitutes goodness, rightness, or effectiveness. The advocate of a proposition of value normally applies her own criteria, especially if she believes them to be understood and accepted by her opponent, her listener, or both. Notice the values involved in the following academic value propositions:

The rights of endangered animal species are more important than the rights of indigenous human populations.

American commercial broadcasters have sacrificed quality for entertainment.

Protecting the environment is a more important goal than satisfying America's demands for full employment.

"This season's new television shows are the worst ever!" "Brand X popcorn is the best." These are assertions of judgment based on subjective standards of "worstness" and "bestness" that the person making them has applied. Both are propositions of value.

If the advocate's burden of proof relative to propositions of fact may be discharged through data, then how may propositions of value be determined as true? Once again, the concept of what is probable is important to keep in mind. Because they reflect the subjective judgments and tastes of the individuals who advance them, propositions of value can only approach the level of probable truth, but they cannot even approach this level unless we know the criteria on which they are based. Take the statement, "Brand X popcorn is best," for example. What makes something best? In the case of popcorn, is it price, nutritional value, flavor, the amount each kernel expands during popping, or the percentage of popped kernels?

Some of these criteria could be objectively verified, such as the percentage of popped kernels. We could test this standard of "bestness" as if we were trying to prove a proposition of fact about the percentage of popped kernels in a batch of popcorn. Other standards, such as flavor, are judgmental. Knowing the criteria used to evaluate the subject of the proposition allows the listener to assess both their reasonableness as criteria and the extent to which they are probably effective criteria for making an evaluation of the subject. In Chapter 10, we will discuss the development of cases for value argumentation in more detail.

Propositions of Policy

Unlike fact and value propositions, which are aimed at altering our beliefs, policy propositions seek a change in behavior. They suggest that something should be done. *The Food and Drug Administration should impose tougher labeling standards on over-the-counter drugs* is an example of a policy proposition as was our earlier example of federal regulation of mass media. They do more than attempt to alter our beliefs about their subjects. If we give our assent to these propositions, we are agreeing to changes in behaviors, ours or someone else's. The policy proposition calls for action to be taken.

The policy proposition is common in most fields. It is characterized by the word *should*, which only suggests something ought to be done not that it necessarily will be done. The word *should* requires the advocate to indicate the specific change she supports and to prove it is *necessary*, *desirable*, and *viable* in upholding her burden of proof. It may have occurred to you that these latter words, *necessary*, *desirable*, and *viable*, are suggestive of a set of value propositions. That is one of the secrets to successfully advocating or opposing policy propositions—subpropositions of fact and value that function as main points are used to develop cases. Advocates use factual main points to establish a rationale for believing problems exist. Existing policies are evaluated to determine what causes the problems. Opponents use factual main points to encourage the audience to believe these problems do not exist. They use evaluative main points to characterize the strengths of existing policies. Both advocates and opponents make value judgments about the advocates' proposed policy.

Let us examine some typical policy propositions used in academic argumentation to discover their complexity. What aspects of fact and value do you find? What actions are implied?

> The federal government should significantly strengthen the guarantee of consumer product safety required of manufacturers.
>
> The federal government should control the supply and utilization of energy in the United States.
>
> The United States should restore normal diplomatic relations with the government of Cuba.

These topics all deal with significant and highly complex political, economic, and social issues. How might you go about demonstrating that any of the changes suggested are necessary, desirable, and viable? Through examination of supporting factual and judgmental points—these policy propositions would be accepted only if arguments concerning certain subpropositions of fact and value were accepted.

To demonstrate why the alteration in behavior suggested by a policy proposition should be accepted, the advocate's burden of proof might require her to begin by demonstrating that:

> a problem exists (fact subproposition)
>
> because of this, people are harmed (fact and value subpropositions)
>
> despite people being harmed, the means of dealing with this problem are presently either inadequate or nonexistent (value and fact subpropositions)

Because acceptance of the alteration of behavior suggested by policy propositions rest on a foundation of fact and value, the concept of proving them probable is once again pertinent. In marshaling proof and good reasons for a prima facie case, the advocate supports what she believes to be the best course of action. Chapter 11 provides a complete discussion of argumentation involving policy propositions.

Summary of the Classification of Propositions

1. Propositions of fact assert a relationship between things or between persons and things; with the exception of propositions of future fact, the advocate's burden is to prove them to be probable by direct verification.
2. Propositions of value assert the worth or lack of worth of something; the advocate's burden is to prove them to be probable through the application of criteria developed by the individual or discovered from the field.
3. Propositions of policy assert that a course of action or behavior should be taken; the advocate's burden is to prove the policy change is reasonable by using subpropositions of fact and value in creating a prima facie case for the policy.

With the nature and classification of types of propositions firmly in mind, we turn to phrasing argumentative propositions so that they properly assign presumption and the burden of proof.

Phrasing the Proposition

Phrasing propositions concerns choosing language that will properly establish the argumentative ground. The importance of wording a proposition for academic argumentation cannot be overemphasized. Clear phrasing is needed to provide a meaningful basis for the process that follows. A failure in proposition wording is an invitation to misunderstanding and poor analysis of its component issues (Zeigelmueller, Kay, & Dause, 1990).

First, the proposition should be phrased as a clear statement of the change in belief or behavior the advocate will seek. To do otherwise confuses the assignment of presumption and the scope of the burden of proof. Consider the proposition: *Something should be done about strikes by professional athletes.* This proposition fails to meet the first rule for phrasing a good proposition. "Something" is vague, and determining burden of proof and presumption is very difficult. "Something" could involve nationalizing all professional sports leagues, imposing a federal ban on strikes by professional athletes, having the federal government or some other institution set the terms of contract settlements between professional athletes and team owners, and so on. If the idea of arguing this subject is to consider the viability of a policy of arbitration that does not disrupt the professional sports season, a more appropriate wording of this proposition might be: *An independent labor relations board for professional sports contract negotiations should be created to arbitrate all labor-management disputes.*

The advocate knows she will have the burden of proving that a special arbitration board will accomplish something positive—uninterrupted sports seasons. Presumption is also more clearly specified in the revised proposition. The opponent may expect to defend labor's right to strike granted by successive pieces of federal legislation and the accepted practice of withholding services when a union perceives management to be intractable. Both advocate and opponent have a better understanding of the argumentative ground in this proposition. As a result, the analysis each will undertake in preparing to argue will benefit.

A second rule to observe in phrasing a proposition is that the proposition should contain one central idea. Having improved our sample proposition by clarifying the change it seeks, let's see what happens when more than one central idea is introduced. *An independent board should be created to arbitrate all labor-management disputes in professional sports and to mandate the use of video replay of contested plays in professional sports.* This is no longer a single proposition. It now contains two separate and unrelated topics. They are related only to the extent that both deal with professional sports. Further, the advocate is committed to affirm a policy about labor-management relations and a different one about officiating.

A proposition with more than one central idea saddles the advocate with separate burdens of proof for each idea—mandatory arbitration and mandatory use of video for contested plays—and the opponent now finds himself with two separate areas of presumption to defend. This introduces unnecessary complication into the argumentative process. Phrasing a proposition around only one central idea facilitates and improves the process of analysis. As an arguer breaks down a proposition into its component issues, he or she looks for the questions that are central to it. If the proposition contains multiple ideas, the process of issue identification becomes more difficult. Both advocate and opponent may find it impossible to establish an internally consistent argumentative position for our poorly worded proposition because it calls for changes in two distinct areas.

A final rule for phrasing propositions is that they should be couched in neutral terms. The wording should favor neither side in the controversy. The advocate who falls prey to temptation might word a proposition with emotive language: *An independent labor relations board should set the terms of contract settlements between greedy owners of professional sports teams and overpaid players.* Such value judgments should be saved for the development of arguments about the proposition. In the field of academic argumentation, we strive to phrase propositions neutrally so that both advocates and opponents have an equal opportunity for making factual interpretations and value judgments based on their diligent research and careful reasoning. Emotionally loaded words rob them of that opportunity.

Summary of Rules for Phrasing Propositions
1. Propositions should be phrased to indicate the direction of change in present belief or behavior that the advocate is responsible for supporting.
2. Propositions should be phrased as a single, declarative statement containing one central idea.
3. Propositions should be phrased in neutral language so that the cause of neither advocate nor opponent is favored at the outset.

Defining the Key Terms

Recall that it is the advocate who initiates argumentation and has the responsibility of providing the initial definition of terms. Since each arguer must locate the issues in the proposition, definitions can be used to identify and clarify key concepts for advocate and opponent. Select the terms in your proposition that you believe need clarification and formulate definitions.

The definition of terms in the proposition may become a contested part of an advocate's argumentation, thus it is advisable for both advocate and opponent to be well versed in the process of definition. Note that disputes over definitions may also arise regarding terms in a given issue. The following discussion of terms that may need defining, and ways to define them, is intended to help you create rules of definition in arguing fact, value, and policy. Arguers are obligated to make clear exactly what they mean when they use a particular word or phrase. To that end, we provide some general rules for defining terms, categories of terms that require definition, and suggestions for how to go about the process of definition.

Rules of Definition

The Inclusionary Rule.   Phrase definitions in such a way that they include everything that appropriately falls under the term. Recall the policy proposition: *The federal government should significantly strengthen the regulation of mass media in the United States.* We indicated the term mass media has the potential for including more than just television. If the advocate defined mass media as television, the definition would automatically rule out argumentation over books, newspapers, radio, or magazines. You must take care not to narrow the proposition so sharply that an important issue is ruled out by your definitions. If both advocate and opponent agree that television is a suitable definition of mass media, there is no problem. The advocate, however, should be prepared to defend this definition of mass media if it is questioned.

The Exclusionary Rule.   Phrase definitions to exclude those things not appropriate to the terms (just the opposite of the inclusionary rule). Your definition should not be so broad as to include things that do not properly fall into the category of the term. For instance, defining *mass media* as "all communication" would include interpersonal and intrapersonal communication, types of communication not aimed at a mass audience. Notice the problem in the following example. To define *human* as "a tool-using and tool-making animal" results in the inclusion of all members of the species primates in the category human. Chimpanzees use objects as projectiles or clubs and have been observed making tools to facilitate the harvesting of termites. Zoologists suggest that other animal species use, and even may create, tools.

The Adaptation Rule.   Phrase definitions so that the meanings are appropriate to the proposition's figurative ground. While it may be perfectly legitimate to define the *Federal Communications Commission* using the names of its members, it may not be appropriate to use such a definition if you are arguing about things it ought to regulate. Likewise, mass media might be defined in terms of technical specifications for the transmission of television and radio signals, but such a definition may not be appropriate to an argument whose figurative ground involves significantly strengthening federal regulation.

The Neutrality Rule. Phrase definitions to avoid unnecessary emotionality. Just as it is inappropriate to use emotionally laden language in phrasing a proposition, it is inappropriate to use loaded language in defining terms. It would be inappropriate to define the *Federal Communications Commission* as "a group of nearsighted reactionaries more concerned with protecting network profits than promoting the public good" or to define a *teachers' union* as "an organization of socialist radicals undermining the quality of education." Definitions should be descriptive of the term defined, not of your feelings about it. In arguing the actual issues of your case, you will have ample opportunity to make those feelings understood and appreciated by your listeners or readers.

The Specificity Rule. Phrase definitions so that the terms themselves are not a part of the definitions. It may be true that "a rose is a rose is a rose," but to define a term using the term itself does not give the audience a clearer picture of its meaning. For example, what do you learn from the following definition? "The Federal Communications Commission is that commission in Washington, D.C., concerned with communications." Included in the need to be specific is the need to provide noncircular definitions. While it may be true that having money means not being poor, it scarcely improves our understanding to define *wealth* as "the absence of poverty" and *poverty* as "the absence of wealth."

The Clarity Rule. Phrase definitions so that they will be understood more readily than the terms they define. To define *federal government* as "that central government, commonly known as the United States government, to which the fifty states have agreed to subordinate certain powers as specified in the U. S. Constitution," is unnecessary and fails to improve our understanding of the argumentative ground. Although the preceding is an extreme example, the problem of cloudy definitions is common, particularly on technical topics. Try to avoid using too much jargon in defining terms whenever possible. Not every participant in a field is comfortable with its jargon. You may be arguing in the field of Washington politics, but do you and your audience recognize these terms used by lobbyists?

> **Horse:** A member of Congress who introduces or endorses a bill created by a lobbyist.
>
> **Tiger:** A member of Congress who is wildly enthusiastic about a lobbyist's bill.
>
> **Dog:** A member of Congress who responds negatively to a lobbyist's bill. (Zeman, 1989)

Terms Needing Definition

Five categories of terms usually require definition: those that are equivocal, vague, technical, new, or coined. As an advocate, you are defining terms for both your opponent and for your audience. Either may not understand your definitions and may object to them out of confusion. As an opponent, you may choose to challenge the advocate's definition by providing your own.

Equivocal terms have two or more equally correct meanings. Many common words in the English language have more than one standard meaning. Consider the word *bridge*. Arguments in the fields of music, engineering, and dentistry may be about bridges, but each field has a distinctly different meaning for the term. Also, consider the word *enemy*. We normally think of an enemy as a foe, someone who is hostile, an unfriendly agent. Can *enemy* be defined as something more positive? It has recently become common to adopt the maxim "the enemy of my enemy is my friend" as a definition of a person or agent who may be considered supportive. You cannot always rely on context to help establish the intended boundary for an equivocal term. Care must be exercised in making clear the meaning you intend.

Vague terms have shades of meaning; they lack clear-cut definitions, so that each listener or reader is free to supply his or her own meaning. Consider *freedom of speech*, which can have as many meanings as there are political views. Some terms, such as *democracy* can be both equivocal and vague. There are different versions of democracy, such as a "democratic people's republic" and a "Jeffersonian democracy." At the same time, what constitutes the American version of democracy is subject to a great deal of interpretation. What does the term *good* or *inferior* mean to you? Value terms, terms of ideology and attitudes, are often vague. Because the term's meaning is open to so many interpretations, it must be defined clearly if the proposition's figurative ground is to make collective sense to the advocate, the opponent, and the audience.

Technical terms are jargon or specialized words belonging to a particular field or profession. Since many controversies involve the use of scientific or technical terminology, exact definition of terms such as *bioeugenics* is necessary if meaningful argumentation is to occur. Terms with a limited or specialized meaning should not be left undefined, since the reader or listener may not know their meaning but may supply one anyway. This is especially important when concepts are discussed in terms of their acronyms. An HMO is a health maintenance organization, a form of PPGP, prepaid group practice, not to be confused with HBO, a premium cable television service, or PPG, the Pittsburgh Plate Glass Company.

New terms are additions to the language, words or phrases that do not exist in the common vocabulary. These words often begin as jargon in a particular field and are incorporated into the lexicon of other fields as their use spreads. Because computers are common equipment in so many fields, the language of computer technology and use offers a variety of new terms. A *cyberpunk* is a young, computer-literate person who may seem to live through his or her computer experience. *Cyberspace* is the world one can enter by electronically connecting with

other computer users, a favorite hangout for cyberpunks. *Virtual reality* is the sim-
ulation of sensory experiences that touch-sensitive gloves and special glasses
attached to a computer with special software can provide. *Surfing the Internet*
refers to the practice of scanning or browsing through the data bases and electronic communities of such services as America Online, Prodigy, and Compu-
Serve.

Coined terms are those invented when a convenient term does not already
exist. Many coined terms are shorthand expressions for complex ideas. *Techno-
phobia* is a "fear of technology." Coined terms sometimes alter existing terms,
including proper nouns, to describe ideas or practices. *Fedexing* is verbal shorthand for "sending something by private carrier" (so-termed because Federal
Express is the best-known private carrier for mail and packages). Coined terms
are also created to describe current developments in an evocative manner. *Oprahtization* was coined to describe the use many Americans make of talk shows, such
as "The Oprah Winfrey Show," as a source of information and opinions. Oprahtization is used in such contexts as "the Oprahtization of American politics" to
describe the extensive use of radio and television talk shows by political candidates. A person influenced by Oprahtization is characterized as part of the *tel-
electorate* (half television viewer and half voter). Coined terms can become
standard English; consider that *television* was a coined term at one time.

How to Define Terms

Terms may be defined by using a *synonym*—a more familiar word similar in both
denotative and connotative meaning. This is how standard dictionaries typically
define terms. For example, to be *nugatory* means to be "worthless or ineffectual."
To provide a more specific definition for *reproduction* in an argument about video-
tape recorders you might use its synonyms: *copies, prints,* or *representations.*

Terms may be defined by the *function* an object, instrument, or organization performs. Some terms make more sense when described in terms of what
they do. Charles R. Schuster of the National Institute on Drug Abuse functionally defines what members of the One Hundred and First Congress's Judiciary
Committee should understand *drug abuse* and *drug addiction* to mean:

> Drug abuse is a unique problem in which the individual seeks to alter, or
> indeed to "experiment" with the functioning of the nervous system in an
> attempt to change how they feel and how they see the world. . . . Drug abuse
> is a voluntary behavior; the casual user makes a free and conscious decision to
> break the law and use mind altering substances. Drug addiction is a disease of
> the brain, resulting from repeated self-administration of these substances.
> (Drugs in the 1990's: New Perils, New Promise, 1991, p. 159)

If you choose to define functionally, be sure that the explanation clarifies
rather than obfuscates. To define *radial valve gear* as "a gear employing a combination of two right-angle motions for the purpose of cutting off the steam supply to the cylinder at an early stage in the piston's stroke" is to define both
functionally and unclearly. People unfamiliar with steam locomotives will associ-

ate the word *gear* with the things in a car's transmission or a grandfather clock, but there are no gears as such in the valve gear of a steam locomotive.

Terms may be defined through *examples*. A common technique, employed in this and other textbooks, is to explain something by providing examples of it. When you define by example, you attempt to clarify meaning by naming concrete, representative instances of the term. Suppose we were arguing the proposition: *Social science is the most important general requirement for graduation.* If we do not know to what extent our audience shares our definition of *social science* we might define by example: "By social science, I mean the study of history, sociology, anthropology, political science, or economics."

Terms may be defined by referring to *authoritative definitions*. In a sense, a standard dictionary serves as an authority for the definition of words, but caution must be exercised in using standard dictionaries. The dictionary merely provides you with a list of all the ways in which users of words commonly define them. To discover just how equivocal many English words can be, consult an unabridged dictionary.

Because specificity is a goal in defining, it is best to refer to a specialized dictionary, an encyclopedia particular to a field, or a recognized expert in the field, for example, medical dictionaries, legal dictionaries such as *Black's Law Dictionary*, encyclopedias such as *The Encyclopedia of Social Science*. These can be good sources for definitions when the precise meaning of a term in the clinical, jurisprudential, or sociological sense is required. Popular periodicals and newspapers can be sources of authoritative definitions when an expert's concept or definition is provided in an article. *TV Guide* can be a good source of definitions of terms pertaining to the mass media, since it regularly reports on university research about media. In one study, *violence* was defined as:

> Any deliberate act involving physical force or the use of a weapon in an attempt to achieve a goal, further a cause, stop the action of another, act on an angry impulse, defend oneself from attack, secure a material reward, or intimidate others. (Hickey, 1994, p. 38).

Terms may be defined *operationally*. When we seek to clarify the meaning of a term by explaining it as the consequence of a single step or series of steps we employ an operational definition. A stockbroker tells you that "net income on this investment should be fifteen cents per share." You look puzzled and say, "I was sure that stock would pay more." Realizing you do not understand *net income*, the stockbroker defines it operationally: "If you take the total amount of income paid as dividends on the stock and deduct the amount paid in taxes and brokerage fees, the resulting figure will be the net income on the investment." In arguing policy propositions, operational definitions are often used when the new policy the reader or listener is asked to support is specified.

Terms may also be defined *behaviorally*. To define something that cannot be experienced directly, we may sometimes clarify the term by describing the behaviors commonly associated with it. It may be difficult to define *staff burnout* but relatively easy to describe the kinds of behavior associated with burnout cases: apathy toward change, absenteeism, and mistakes on the job. Behavioral definitions can be particularly useful in describing a theory or phenomenon, such as how we think. *Ontology* is a theory about how we acquire knowledge. It is easier to understand if we define it in terms of people learning through narratives about experiences or as the behavior of humans telling each other personal stories of their experiences.

Finally, terms may be defined by *negation*. This type of definition indicates what the term does not mean. There are some terms we can more easily define by negation. For example, someone who is *single* is "not married," someone who is *insolvent* is "not able to meet financial obligations." Sometimes definition by negation is the clearest way to define a term: "A *full-time undergraduate student* is any individual enrolled for not less than twelve semester hours who has not previously received a baccalaureate degree from an accredited college or university."

This chapter has equipped you with the principles of propositions; their function in argumentation; their classification as fact, value, and policy; phrasing them appropriately; and defining their key terms. Propositions are accepted or rejected by the audience on the basis of whether the advocate makes a prima facie case to develop them, or the opponent offers effective counterarguments and a defense of existing beliefs or behaviors as worthy of continuation. The next step in the process of arguing is learning how to analyze the proposition to determine which specific issues you will argue.

Learning Activities

1. Examine the following propositions. Identify the kinds of propositions—fact, value, and policy—represented. Be prepared to discuss how each example does or does not meet the rules for wording propositions suggested in this chapter.

Energy
A. Renewable energy sources are preferable to fossil fuels.
B. By 1999 the United States will run short of fossil fuels.
C. The federal government should implement an accelerated program of conversion to renewable energy sources.

Ecology
A. The present system of environmental protection creates toxic waste dumps.
B. The United States should significantly improve its environmental protection policy.
C. The protection of the national environment ought to take precedence over the expansion of industrial production.

Law Enforcement
A. The judicial system should reform the system of juvenile and family courts.

B   Crimes by juveniles are the most serious crimes against persons. *value*

C. The American judicial system unfairly favors the juvenile offender over the victim. *value*

Foreign Policy

A. U.S. foreign policy commitments <u>overextend</u> the federal budget.

B. U.S. foreign policy commitments ought to reflect the <u>American belief</u> in the principle of democratic government. *policy*

C. The United States should substantially reduce foreign aid to nations that fail to protect the rights of their citizens. *policy*

Education

A. The <u>quality of education</u> in American public schools ought to be the nation's first priority. *policy*

B. The education of college professors does not place sufficient emphasis on teaching techniques. *value*

C. The Department of Education should create and maintain a core curriculum for all public schools. *policy*

2. Taking the propositions in activity 1, imagine you are listening to an advocate's speech on each topic. As a member of the listening audience, identify what words or phrases in each proposition you feel would need to be defined.

3. Select three topic areas that you might like to investigate in greater depth in completing future assignments. Formulate specific fact, value, and policy propositions that these topic areas suggest to you. Search the reference section of your library for possible sources within the field of each topic to serve as a source of definitions of key terms in your propositions.

Suggested Supplementary Readings

Cronkhite, G. (1966). Propositions of Past and Future Fact and Value: A Proposed Classification. *Journal of the American Forensics Association*, 3, 11–16.
Discusses how value propositions should be analyzed to determine the arguments that will focus attention on the value, the choice of criteria, and the facts that match the value object to the criteria. This article emphasizes that the choice of arguments will be based, in part, on how much time the arguer has to develop a position and what the audience is likely to accept without much argumentation.

Mills, G. E. (1968). *Reason in Controversy* (2nd Ed.). Boston: Allyn & Bacon.
Although many of the examples are dated, this book offers one of the most thorough discussions of propositions, analysis to determine issues, and discussion of traditional policy argumentation.

Chapter Four

How Do I Analyze Propositions?

Advocates and opponents need to know what specific arguments to use as they prepare to capture the proposition's argumentative ground. In this chapter we begin consideration of the process you should follow in putting together an argumentative package in advocacy of, or opposition to, a proposition. This process is called *case development*, and it begins with analysis of the proposition.

The process of analysis is field invariant for propositions of fact, value, and policy. Choosing specific arguments that you will use in constructing your case of advocacy or opposition is usually field dependent although certain ideas, such as the cost of something and its benefit, may be used across several different fields. The ultimate goal of the process is to discover the actual issues you will argue. *Actual issues* are the questions central to the specific need for knowledge or difference of opinion identified by the wording of the proposition you are preparing to argue. Actual issues are found through a four-step process of analysis: (1) locating the immediate cause of concern about the topic, (2) investigating the history of the topic, (3) defining key terms and creating the primary inference of the topic, and (4) determining the actual issues in the controversy.

Locating the Immediate Cause

Locating immediate causes of interest or concern about a topic is a matter of monitoring media and paying attention to what people in a field and across many fields are talking about. In our society, mass media and the use of personal computers to link up with others are some of the best sources for finding out what is on people's minds, what most concerns them at a given point in time. The mass media focus our attention on topics by airing or printing stories about them. The Internet, which we will discuss in Chapter 6, has tremendous potential for researching immediate cause. With more than 5,000 discussion groups and 2,500 electronic newsletters available (Elmer-Dewitt, 1993), you can discover what people fear, suspect, applaud, or simply want to know more about, almost instantaneously.

What the news-mass media chooses to talk about can have a significant impact on what people are concerned about. Recently, "CBS This Morning" did a week-long "heart-smart" series about warning signs of a heart attack and prevention measures. Our family physician said that the following week, visits by patients claiming to be suffering from heart-attack warning signs were up 30 percent. While, happily, none of these patients had real problems, our physician said this is a common phenomenon following a news series on heart attacks or other illnesses that people greatly fear. Thus, we can say that viewing a series of news stories about heart attacks is the immediate cause of people's concern that they might be having one.

Immediate Cause in Factual Propositions

The causes of a desire for knowledge or a difference of opinion are usually significant events, occurrences, or circumstances in the present or near past. To find them, arguers must ask themselves why people are focusing on this topic at this time. A significant, sometimes harmful, event will often be the immediate cause for argumentation about the need for factual knowledge or the interpretation of existing facts.

The publication of a controversial study, such as *The Bell Curve* by Charles Murray and Richard Herrenstein or a field study of an inner-city school where 70 percent of African American and Latino students graduate on time and many go on to college, stimulate argumentation over a hypothesis that race influences intelligence (Hancock, 1994, and Morganthau, 1994). A growing demand by the children of biracial couples to drop all classification of people into racial groups and scientific studies that claim race is no more than a mixture of social prejudice, myth, and superstition create arguments about the factual basis for classifying people into racial groups (Morganthau, 1995).

Analyzing the immediate cause helps you discover why a proposition of fact is sufficiently important to justify argumentation. You will find indications of your proposition's importance by studying recent history: Is it viewed as a controversy in the news? What are opinion leaders saying about it? Are people doing research, holding seminars and symposiums, issuing position statements about the topic? When you discover what is being said about the proposition, examine the consequences that are attached to a given interpretation of fact.

Immediate Cause in Value Propositions

In value propositions, controversy exists over opposing evaluations of a person, object, event, or idea. The purpose of argumentation is to decide how we should judge something—a political candidate, a product, a federal program, an artistic performance, or a moral standard.

In value argumentation, analysis of the immediate cause of the controversy seeks to discover why making a judgment about something is salient at this time. When we argue value propositions, we are arguing about both the criteria used to judge something and the extent to which whatever is being judged measures up to the criteria. In order to achieve this, we have to discover as much as possible about the judgmental criteria and what it is we are judging. Thorough analysis of the field specified by the proposition will help you discover this information.

Locating the immediate cause is necessary to help you discover whether values are presently in conflict. If the question is one of privacy versus public safety, do societal attitudes seem to favor safety at the expense of privacy or vice versa? What are our nation's lawmakers and opinion leaders saying about how we should value the subject of the proposition? Do these authorities and agenda setters offer criteria that will serve as standards of judgment?

Search the field of your proposition. Has there been an important discovery that has led to a value controversy? Has a significant event taken place that has focused national or international attention on the topic? For example, the more popular the Internet becomes as a medium of communication, the more people have begun to make value judgments about it. An immediate cause for concern was the posting of a "fantasy murder" on one bulletin board. Setting up crime-solving challenges, and even suggesting creative ways you might fantasize about doing away with an enemy, is not uncommon for some groups of Internet users. This incident, however, was an immediate cause of concern because the victim, a real person, was named, and the murder involved torture and sexual abuse. This incident served as the immediate cause for argumentation about the value of much Internet use and the moral standards of many users (Levy, 1995).

Immediate Cause in Policy Propositions

We become concerned about a change in policy when some person or group of persons believes a problem exists. Immediate cause stems from events that suggest the nature of the problem. You should look for significant, harmful events and explanations of why these events occurred. The analysis of immediate cause is important for proving inherency in policy propositions. Inherency arguments identify the cause of a problem. The cause of a problem must be identified if you, as advocate, are to proceed any further in developing a prima facie policy case. If you cannot locate the cause, both immediate and possibly in the past, you will have little success in solving the problem. Locating immediate cause helps discover inherency arguments. Finding the immediate cause will usually lead you to ask if the cause has some historical basis.

Investigating the History

Investigating the contemporary and historical background provides you with pertinent information. Even in instances where the immediate cause of a controversy

over fact is obvious, discovery of historical episodes of dissatisfaction or conflicting interpretations of similar episodes, provide important insight, especially if the
investigation includes a thorough examination of past efforts to understand a
body of factual information relevant to the controversy.

If you were involved in arguing the proposition, "Violence portrayed on
television causes violence in the schools, the community, and the home," your
background investigation might include examining social science research on the
causes of violent behavior in children. You would discover that efforts to understand the impact of seeing violent entertainment on the receiver did not begin
with the advent of television. Earlier in this century, educators, parents, and min-
isters were concerned about the effects of movies and comic books on children.
You may find other historical connections to the present controversy since the
issue of violence and television is not a new one. Considering the proposition of
fact in its historical context is important; such propositions are often argued on
the basis of trends growing out of past experience and extending into the future.
An understanding of past beliefs about fact can be used to argue their propensity
to continue in the future.

Because values are for the most part slow to change, you must examine the
background of a proposition of value extensively to identify shifts. Advocates and
opponents must study the artifacts that reflect the society's structure and values
(Warnick, 1981). Artifacts include such documents as the Constitution, Supreme
Court and other decisions interpreting the Constitution, the Declaration of Independence, legislation, mission statements, and codes of ethics. If, for example,
you are engaged in an argument about abortion, artifacts might include the
Supreme Court decision in *Roe v. Wade* and the Bible. The relevant artifacts ger-
mane to the value object and judgment may vary considerably with the topic, but
some, such as the Constitution, are basic to many controversies.

You will also find relevant artifacts in a particular field of argument. Does
the proposition suggest a field, such as science, politics, economics, or law? Does
the proposition suggest a particular ethical system or code of conduct such as an
economic system, the Judeo-Christian moral code, a political system, or a professional code of conduct? The importance of placing the proposition in its
appropriate field is that the field may suggest criteria appropriate to making your
value judgment about something.

If you discover that values have changed over time, the ability to understand
how change occurred may be essential. Is the immediate cause you have located
significant enough to motivate a person or group to commit to a value change?
Nicholas Rescher's (1969) widely cited discussion of the process by which values
change suggests that values are seldom accepted or abandoned absolutely, except
in the rare circumstances of religious or ideological conversions. Instead, values
are changed through processes of redistribution, emphasis or deemphasis, restandardization, and retargeting.

When *value redistribution* occurs, society adopts the value of a minority
group that has successfully promoted a different way of attributing importance
to that value. In the past two decades, some insurance companies have promoted
"women's work," or "housework," as being equally valuable as the work of wage

earners and, therefore, worthy of insurance coverage against the possibility that the homemaker might die or become incapacitated. This places a new connotation on the value of housework by putting it in an insurable category of labor.

Environmental change can cause *value emphasis* or *deemphasis*. Some deeply entrenched value, perhaps one that is not even openly stated, is suddenly threatened by a change in the physiological or psychological environment and takes on a different level of importance relative to other values. In the analysis of a value topic, emphasis or deemphasis may be part of what has produced the immediate controversy. A nearby toxic waste accident can suddenly make the protection of the community or the right to feel secure in your own home seem extremely important, while 500 miles away people in an area of high unemployment may be excited about the jobs that will be created by the opening of a toxic waste disposal site outside their city limits.

You may be familiar with the phrases "standard of living" and "quality of life"; both refer to a system of defining that which is attained. One way in which values change is through a *value restandardization*. Societal goals in particular are subject to social, economic, and technological change. John L. Peterson's book *The Road to 2015* (1994) suggests a matrix of trends that will shape the next century. Among these trends are science and technology, space, the environment, health, social values, population, economics, transportation, energy, and politics. Presently, Americans consider air travel and the automobile to be the fastest, easiest means of getting from point A to B and back again. In the future, Peterson states that good transportation for business and leisure purposes will be a network of "maglevs" (high-speed trains that run on magnetic technology). Technology, along with trends in other fields, will change what we perceive as a good quality of life.

All of us have goals that operationalize enduring values. Since a goal does not always help us to maximize attainment of a particular value, we find ourselves engaging in *value implementation retargeting*. In this case, the value itself has not undergone a change; what has changed is the manner in which we pursue the value. Most people in our society place good health high in their personal hierarchy of values. Government and private medical plans reflect the value we place on good health. This value has not changed substantially, but the manner in which society pursues it has. Instead of focusing on the treatment of disease, medical care has shifted toward the prevention of disease—the "wellness" concept.

Above all, in examining the historical background of your topic, search for previously predominating societal and field dependent values and identify conflicts among them. Such conflicts may be current or long-standing. Sproule (1980) identifies certain values that frequently appear in juxtaposition with each other—freedom, equality, morality, safety, and privacy.

We can determine criteria for making evaluations by investigating historical background. The examination of common sources of value is a good starting point, followed by careful consideration of the field in which the value proposition resides. Some useful questions that can help you to find value criteria include the following: What are cultural values or norms that pertain to the thing you are evaluating? What are the particular standards of value that have been historically established for making this or similar value judgments? Why do individuals or members of a field presently value something as they do?

Learning the history of your policy proposition can also be useful in developing arguments. The notion of the history of a proposed change should be given a very liberal definition. History may be the last two years or the last two hundred years, depending upon the specific proposition. Your research may be restricted solely to the field of your proposition, or it may require you to look at other fields as well. For example, if you are arguing a policy proposition on controlling military spending, examining past efforts to solve the problems of the high cost of equipment maintenance might include an examination of the system by which military contracts for replacement parts are let to vendors and the history of those companies that win these contracts. The investigation might also include research on how the private sector deals with the same problem. How do civilian airlines cope with the high cost of replacement parts? Your investigation of the topic's historical background could even stretch beyond the field of aviation to include an evaluation of how other government agencies that use technologically sophisticated equipment obtain replacement parts. What you learn might suggest possible solutions to the immediate problem, their workability, and disadvantages.

In particular, you should examine earlier attempts to institute a policy of this sort—attempts that seem identical to or that embody the same principles as your policy proposition. Examine the field of your proposition to discover whether they succeeded or failed and whether legislation is presently pending in regard to the policy. For example, if your policy proposition concerns a balanced federal budget, investigate U.S. history for instances when the budget was in balance. How was balance achieved, and what caused the budget to go out of balance? What attempts were subsequently made to balance the budget? Why did they fail? What was said about them?

You must learn the history of your topic. You need to know if the presence or absence of a policy has created dissatisfaction in the past. Because policy making is usually consistent with the traditions of our society in general and with the specific field that is considering a policy change, you must examine relevant value systems and predispositions toward the topic. Policies are typically consistent with past action, so if an action has been deemed inappropriate in the past, it may still be regarded this way. If you know a policy has not been regarded as appropriate, but it is the course of action you wish to advocate, you will have just succeeded in discovering an inherent barrier to change—attitudes.

Finding the immediate causes and exploring the historical background of the controversy provides you with a frame of reference from which to argue a proposition of fact, value, or policy. These two steps in the process of analysis also give you some clues to your audience's understanding of your proposition. To focus your own interpretation of the proposition, the third step in the process of analysis requires that you use your definitions of terms to make a primary inference about the meaning of your proposition.

Defining Key Terms and Creating the Primary Inference

Almost all propositions need some interpretation to clarify the exact change in belief or behavior you seek from your audience. Although this can be done as you develop individual arguments, effective arguers introduce their cases by focusing the proposition in such a way that the individual arguments will collectively make sense to the audience. The reason we define key terms in a proposition is to clarify what we mean and how we intend the audience to understand the proposition. How you define terms also narrows the range of possible issues you should argue.

Advocates must develop a case that on first hearing or reading seems logically complete and that the audience will feel comfortable in accepting as probable. This is the concept of the prima facie case. Opponents may choose to defend what the benefit of presumption has identified as deserving of continuation because it works effectively: an existing idea, law or rule, policy, practice, or custom. Opponents may also choose to attack each and every part of the advocate's prima facie case.

Each side in the process of argumentation needs to use the definition of terms. The interpretation of a proposition made on the basis of your definition of terms is called the *primary inference*. An inference is a conclusion you have reached on the basis of information you have examined. We make inferences by drawing a conclusion from available information.

> The **primary inference** is the conclusion you draw about what you believe the proposition means based on the information contained in your definitions of key terms.

Consider this proposition: *Government support of the arts is necessary to their survival.* Suppose you have defined the the key terms as follows:

government support: stipends to college professors who teach art history

the arts: paintings, sculpture, and folk handicraft from human prehistory to the present

necessary to their survival: the continuation of instruction in art history

Notice what this does to focus the proposition. As an advocate, you now must develop a prima facie case on the proposition: *The government must pay college professors to teach the history of painting, sculpture, and folk handicrafts to guarantee that such courses are taught.* This is a much different inference than if you had defined government support as the National Endowment for the Arts and the arts as the work of living artists in the fields of photography, painting, sculpture, and performance art.

Both advocates and opponents must identify the primary inference they see as existing in a proposition although they are not obligated to identify the same one. If the opponent chooses to accept the advocate's definition of terms, he has tacitly agreed to her primary inference. He should develop his arguments in direct response to arguments she creates from the primary inference dictated by her definition of terms. Opponents are not obligated to accept the advocate's definition of terms or agree to her primary inference as the best interpretation of the proposition. An important strategy of opposition is determined at this point in issues analysis: Should an opponent provide his own definition of terms and argue that the advocate's primary inference is flawed?

Suppose the advocate defined *government support* as federal funding for day care centers; *the arts* as activities that day care centers use to occupy children's time; and *necessary to their survival* as not limiting their services only to the children of families who can afford to pay for day care. As the opponent, you should ask yourself if this is really in the spirit of what people in the fields of art, politics, and education mean by government support for the arts. You will probably answer no and choose to define terms more appropriately, making your own critical inference that you believe is a more reasonable interpretation of the proposition. This is the essence of arguing the issue of *topicality* introduced in Chapter 2. Contesting the advocate's definition of terms and possibly providing your own definitions is important when you believe the advocate has unfairly or mistakenly interpreted the proposition through her definitions.

How is a primary inference made from the definition of key terms? Recall that arguing is part of rule-governed communication behavior, and the nature of the English language supplies some of those rules. In English grammar there are three forms of sentence structure: simple, compound, and complex. A simple sentence has a subject, a verb, and a single independent clause (called the *predicate*).

Government support of the arts (the subject) is (the verb) necessary to their survival (the independent clause that is the predicate of this sentence).

In Chapter 3 we told you that propositions should be phrased as a single, declarative statement that has one central idea. A declarative sentence is a statement asserting the relationship between the subject of the sentence and the independent clause. In the case of our example, there is an asserted relationship between government funding of the arts (subject) and the survival of the arts (independent clause). To avoid multiple central ideas or confusing qualifications of the central idea, propositions should not be phrased as compound or complex sentences. Compound and complex sentences do have uses in argumentation that we will address in the next chapter. In this chapter, we want to focus on the simple, declarative sentence and how to use definitions of key terms for issues analysis.

Key Terms in Factual Propositions

A proposition of fact is much like an item on a true-false test. When you try to figure out if you should mark such an item true or false, you do the same thing an arguer does in making a primary inference. You look for the key terms in the item, define for yourself what the subject and predicate mean in terms of the material you studied, and decide if your definitions suggest the statement is a true or false one. In factual propositions, you focus on key terms, whose definitions will help the audience understand what must be shown to make the statement probably true or probably false.

Consider this factual proposition: *John Wilkes Booth was not responsible for Abraham Lincoln's death.* We have always been taught that the truth is Booth killed Lincoln. Americans do not usually question the truthfulness of this statement of fact. Neurosurgeon Richard A. R. Fraser (1995) makes a prima facie case for considering our factual proposition a probably true statement. How can that be? After all, several witnesses saw a man they knew to be Booth shoot the gun that lodged a bullet in Lincoln's brain. Fraser selected one key term in the proposition to make his primary inference. He operationally defined *responsible* in terms of recognized medical practice in the treatment of low-kinetic-energy bullet wounds caused by 1860s firearms, such as Booth's derringer. Fraser's primary inference is: Substandard medical treatment caused Lincoln's death.

Key Terms in Value Propositions

In the case of value propositions, words or phrases in both the subject and predicate of the sentence may require definition. Making a value judgment often has connotative implications. Value-laden terms such as *desirable, effective, beneficial, injurious, disadvantageous,* or *harmful,* for example, must be defined. The definitions of value-laden terms are the source of criteria you will use to make value judgments as you develop individual arguments for your case. Consider what must occur for us to deem an effect serious or adverse. What renders a policy beneficial? Criteria specify the attributes that something must possess to be evaluated in a certain way, and they serve to clarify the nature of the figurative ground over which value argumentation takes place.

Value-laden terms should be defined in such a way that they suggest a series of statements capable of being supported with proof and reasoning. If you are arguing about the effectiveness of U.S. foreign policy, ideally your criteria would set observable standards by which effectiveness could be determined. Some possible criteria might be: (1) an effective foreign policy keeps us out of wars, (2) an effective foreign policy makes us more friends than enemies, (3) an effective foreign policy encourages the development of democratic institutions in other nations, and (4) an effective foreign policy treats all nations equally.

Key Terms in Policy Propositions

The advocate in policy argumentation must also decide what portions of the proposition require definition. Since the most identifiable characteristic of a policy proposition is that it points toward a change in behavior, some new course of action, defining that course of action is one of the advocate's responsibilities in case construction. If the advocate fails to define what is meant by this specified course of action, asking listeners or readers to adopt the action as their own will not be very convincing. They may not understand what they are being asked to do. We do not usually change our behaviors when we are unsure about what the change involves. Equally, decision-implementing bodies are unlikely to change if the details of the decision are unclear.

There are many legitimate methods for defining the terms of a policy proposition, and the advocate has choices to make regarding which other terms require definition. Whether to define more than the proposed action is one of those choices. In some propositions, the subject—the agency that will undertake change or that will undergo change—may be clearly stated: *The International Olympic Committee should hold all future Summer Olympics in Greece*. In other examples the subject is not as clearly identified: *The federal government should expand support for the arts*. The agency to expand support in this proposition could mean the National Endowment for the Arts, federal block grants to the fifty states, or some new agency created to sponsor the arts and cultural activities.

Remember, the definitions you choose for key terms are most important in deciding what you want the proposition to mean as you plan your argumentative strategy. Whether you are advocate or opponent, using your definitions of key terms to make a primary inference helps you focus the topic and make decisions about case development. Once you have made your primary inference, you are ready for the final stage of issues analysis—determining the actual issues you will use in arguing your case.

Determining the Issues

Thus far in the process of analysis you will have discovered the immediate cause that brings your topic to the audience's attention, examined the topic's historical background, and used your definitions of key terms to make a primary inference about the proposition. This will give you enough information to determine which main points you should argue, as well as some subpoints you should use to develop those main points. You may not use every potential issue that you discover, but you should consider all potential issues that are relevant to your interpretation of the proposition.

In Chapter 1 we told you that argumentation theory has evolved over a long time, dating back to the days of ancient Greece and Rome. In their refinement of Greek rhetoric, Roman authors identified four kinds of questions crucial to legal disputes: (1) questions of fact—did the accused commit a crime; (2) questions of definition—if the accusation is theft, might the act have been borrowing; (3) questions of justification—if the act was theft, did the accused steal out of dire need; and (4) questions of procedure—was the charge properly made (Fisher & Sayles, 1966). The nature of these legal controversies, and the need for judges to determine which party to the dispute more nearly represented the "truth," was a driving force behind the development of rhetoric in Greece and Rome. While rhetoric was developed in the legal context, its study produced workable theories of argumentation and persuasion applicable to controversies in other contexts as well.

In Chapter 2 we said there are field-invariant stock issues that can be used to analyze propositions. Like the Roman series of stock questions to ask in any legal case, propositions of fact, value, and policy each have a set of stock questions that can be applied to determine what the potential issues might be for any topic.

Stock Issues for Factual Propositions

The advocate's selection of actual issues in a proposition of fact will be determined by two factors: What constitutes her burden of proof in establishing a prima facie case for the proposition of fact, and what can be demonstrated to be most probably true with the resources of proof and reasoning available to her? Propositions of fact are argued to decide whether the primary inference is probably true or probably false.

There are two stock issues to use in finding the actual issues for building your factual case:

1. What information confirms (or denies) the alleged relationship between the subject and the predicate of the primary inference?
2. What techniques of reasoning (covered in Chapter 7) should be used to demonstrate this relationship?

The first stock issue asks you to meet your research responsibility by finding out if there is enough available evidence to prove arguments about probable truth. The second pertains to your responsibility to reason with your listeners or readers. Arguing facts is at the very heart of the process of argumentation. Notice the connection between the stock issues of fact and the definition of argumentation we gave you in Chapter 1. We said argumentation is instrumental communication that relies on proof (stock issue one) and reasoning (stock issue two).

At first glance, the stock issues of fact seem very simple—find information and use reasons. This does not mean that factual argumentation is superficial or that substantial cases cannot be created for propositions of fact. To develop his case that John Wilkes Booth was not responsible for Abraham Lincoln's death, Richard Fraser had to build an intricate chain of reasons and do extensive research. Fraser researched known and commonly used medical practices in the treatment of gunshot wounds during the Civil War. From that information, he developed a series of reasons why Lincoln's on-the-scene physicians were probably guilty of malpractice, leading to the conclusion that inept medical treatment, not the head wound itself, was most probably the reason Lincoln died.

Whether you are arguing about differing interpretations of fact, testing a hypothesis about what something should mean, or seeking to establish a new interpretation of recently collected facts, use the stock issues of fact to help you identify the actual issues to include in your case development. Ask, What research do I have that proves the probable truth of my primary inference? and What reasoning techniques should I use in making my inference?

Stock Issues for Value Propositions

Propositions of fact attempt to determine what is most probably true of a past, present, or future relationship inferred by the proposition. Value propositions differ in that they attempt to establish what is the most acceptable application of judgment to a particular person, place, event, policy, or idea. In value argumentation, the controversy centers around which of two or more opposing evalua-tions is most credible.

Values are deeply rooted mental states and are formed early in life. They predispose us to categorize something as existing somewhere along a continuum ranging from highly positive to highly negative. A value held by an individual or a group may not be verbalized until it comes into conflict with some other value about which judgment is going to be made. Because no two people possess exactly the same life experiences, the potential for value conflict is present when people begin to make judgments. Values are not independent of each other. They exist in a hierarchy, with some values deemed more important than others in a given set of circumstances.

The advocate's role in arguing a proposition of value is to provide good and sufficient reasons, a prima facie case, for her audience to evaluate the subject of the proposition in the same way she does. The opponent's role in value argu-mentation is to examine the soundness of her arguments and to examine the pre-sent value attributed to the proposition's subject. Value propositions take a particular form that aids both arguers. The subject of the value proposition sen-tence is termed a *value object*. The value object names some idea, person, action, agency, tradition, practice, or custom that exists or is proposed. The *value judg-ment*, the predicate of the value proposition sentence, identifies broad criteria by which the value object can be measured. A value judgment or a general evalua-tion—good-bad, fair-unfair, safe-harmful, effective-ineffective—is what is in-ferred as appropriately assigned to the value object.

In Chapter 3 we said the proposition should always be phrased in such a way that change is implied and so the advocate supports a change in the judgment normally assigned to the value object. This is important because in some instances, the value proposition reflects two equally prized objects and the advo-cate's task is to argue the primacy of one over the other:

> The freedom to publish or read anything is more important than the moral objections that its content may raise.
> The preservation of the professional sports season for the fan is more important than the economic interests of the players and owners.

Notice that both propositions could be reversed and argued from the opposite perspective. They are worded in such a way as to specify the argumentative ground to be disputed by the advocate and opponent.

In other propositions, the value object and the value judgment are unitary in nature:

> Modern art is aesthetically deficient.
> Ronald Reagan will be remembered as the greatest president of the twen-tieth century.

Even though only one value object and judgment is supplied in these proposi-tions, there are still ample opportunities for disagreement.

You identify issues that will develop a prima facie case for a value proposition in the same way as for a proposition of fact. Stock issues once again take the form of vital questions that must be answered if the arguer's case is to be accepted. The three stock issues that shape value advocacy and opposition are:

1. By what value hierarchy is the object of the proposition best evaluated?
2. By what criteria is the value object to be located within this hierarchy?
3. Do indicators of the effect, extent, and inherency of the value object show that it conforms to the criteria?

These questions help determine the nature of the dispute, the judgmental criteria used to resolve it, and the kinds of arguments used to measure the value object by these criteria.

Advocates and opponents of value propositions will discover appropriate value hierarchies and criteria for judging values by examining present causes of concern about a value judgment and the relevant historical background of the value topic. We will have more to say about using value hierarchies and criteria for case development in Chapter 10, but for now, we need to consider what a value hierarchy is and how it influences making value judgments.

To understand the nature of value hierarchies, consider your life as a college student. Each week, those who teach you have certain expectations about what you should do as a student in their classes. Most college professors enjoy their subjects and consider that subject to be one of the most important in producing an educated person. Each professor places his or her subject near the top of a personal hierarchy of valuable knowledge. Equally, these professors expect you to place the course they teach, and your work in it, high on your own personal hierarchy of valuable courses.

Where you place a given course is conditioned by several variables, such as: Is this a course in your major? Is this a professor who stimulates you to learn? Do you perceive the class as easy or difficult? How much work is required of you each week? If you are required to take a course in geography but dislike having to study maps, think the professor's lectures are boring, and resent the number of pop quizzes, you may not place this course very high on your personal hierarchy of valuable courses. On the other hand, if you must get an A in this required course to receive a scholarship, even though your other dissatisfactions with the course remain, you may place the geography course near the top of this semester's hierarchy of valuable courses. Why? Because you have an important criterion to measure what makes something a valuable course: A valuable course is one that will allow you to get a scholarship.

The value hierarchy for a given value proposition and the criteria you will use to make the evaluation result from how you define key terms and make your primary inference. The central issue of value argumentation is: Does the value object meet the criteria for evaluation? If only a single criterion has been advanced, it is obviously deemed sufficient to allow a proper evaluation to be made. If multiple criteria are advanced, is it necessary for the value object to meet them all in order to be judged in the manner described by the proposition of value? If this is not the case, the criteria can be applied independently. Demonstrating that the value object meets any one of them would be sufficient to warrant the judgment specified by the proposition. The exchange of arguments in value controversies is sometimes devoted to whether these criteria are independently sufficient or necessary in toto.

Stock Issues for Policy Propositions

Policy propositions concern changes in behavior ranging from the passage of new legislation or the creation of new institutions to the course of action an individual should follow. Policy propositions imply that a critical decision to do something be considered.

The stock issues policy propositions use to develop a prima facie case are:

1. Is there a reason for change in a manner generally suggested by the policy proposition?
2. Does the policy proposed resolve the reason for change?
3. What are the consequences of the proposed change?

These stock issues not only help you discover the kinds of arguments that must be advanced for an advocate's case to be prima facie but also demonstrate the relationship between fact, value, and policy. Notice that one possible response to the question posed in the first stock issue, "things are bad now," takes the form of a value judgment, as does the response to the third stock issue, "things will be better in the future." Notice that the second stock issue forces consideration of a statement of fact, "the proposed policy resolves the problem."

Determining the actual issues to be argued for and against a proposition of policy proceeds in much the same way as it does for fact and value propositions: matching what can be proven from an investigation of the immediate cause for concern and its historical development against the imperative of using the stock issues of policy for ensuring that the advocate's case is prima facie. If the advocate has defined the proposition operationally, she will have satisfied the requirements of the second stock issue and only needs to justify a reason for this change and to explain its consequences.

If it appears that movement from fact, through value, to policy exponentially increases the complexity of argumentation and the options available to advocates and opponents of change, that is because appearances in this case are not deceiving. Not only are the issues more numerous and the strategies more intricate, but you will also recall that, insofar as academic argumentation is concerned, policy propositions are worded in such a way that they afford the advocates of change a wide latitude in interpretation. Thus, the constraints on issue selection by the opponents of change and the uncertainty of what actual issues the advocate will argue appear to be compounded by policy propositions. While this is true, the opponent's plight is not hopeless. He still has presumption on his side, and since the advocate's burden of proof is more complex, she has more opportunities to make a mistake.

The opponent has two other things to keep in mind as he analyzes the proposition. First, he only needs to defeat the advocate on one of the stock issues in order to prevail. This means that he can develop a series of generic arguments that would apply to a number of different interpretations of the proposition. If the proposition is one that is likely to require the advocate to urge adoption of an expensive program, the opponent could develop a generic argument about the undesirability of either raising funds or diverting funds from existing programs. While the opponent would still be required to apply this and other arguments he advances to the advocate's specific case, he has something to argue regardless of the advocate's interpretation of the proposition. If it is too farfetched, the opponent will engage his second alternative for coping with the uncertainty of his position.

In academic argumentation, defining the proposed action so that it conforms to the wording of the proposition is known as *being topical*, one of the advocate's responsibilities. For those of you learning the techniques of policy argumentation, this is a matter of some concern as well as a question of ethics and good faith between you and your audience. By agreeing to argue a certain proposition, your audience trusts that you will indeed argue it. If you have consented to argue the advocate's side of the question, "Should the federal government be required to operate on a balanced budget?" you break faith with your audience when you twist the proposition by arguing in support of a freeze on the production of weapon's grade nuclear material on the basis that this freeze would keep such material out of the hands of terrorists, and "Oh, by the way," balance the budget by reducing defense spending. The opponent analyzing the proposition of policy can at least expect the advocate's case to be topical and know that he has the winning position if he can prove that it is not.

The process of analysis is the same for propositions of fact, value, or policy although the breadth and depth of analysis changes. Advocates and opponents of change should examine the immediate cause and historical background of the controversy that brought the proposition into a position of prominence. After defining those terms that require definition and deciding how the terms form a primary inference, advocates and opponents should then decide which actual issues they will argue in presenting their case for or against change.

Issues are established both by the demands imposed by the stock issues of fact, value, and policy and by the resources of proof and reasoning that you decide are most appropriate to building your case. The next step you should take in preparing to advocate or oppose change is a step in the direction of the library. Chapter 6, which discusses the types and tests of evidence and how to locate it, will help you make this trip a profitable one. Before you head off to the library, however, it is helpful to have a sense not only of the issues that will become the main points of your case but also of the framework to use in creating the individual arguments that develop each issue. In the next chapter, we will demonstrate the use of the Toulmin model as a system for creating a unit of argument.

Learning Activities

1. Examine the propositions listed below. Select one for issue analysis. What is the immediate cause of the controversy in the proposition? What are some important elements in the history of the topic? What key terms should be defined, and what primary inference can be formed from those definitions? What are the actual issues that might be argued by the advocate? By the opponent?
   A The federal government should provide a program of comprehensive health care for all U.S. citizens.
   B. All military intervention into the affairs of other nations in the Western Hemisphere should be prohibited.
   C. Political action committees undermine the democratic process.
   D. The further exploration of space should be a priority in the 1990s.
   E. A national program for recycling would save substantial amounts of our national resources.
2. Read the essay "How Did Lincoln Die?" by Richard A. R. Fraser in *American Heritage*, February/March, 1995, pp. 63–64 & 66–70. What led Fraser to argue about this subject in 1995? What historical background does Fraser use to build his argument? What actual issues did Fraser choose to argue? Does he create a prima facie case of factual argumentation?
3. Phrase your own proposition of fact, value, or policy. What terms require definition? What type of definitions should you provide? What is the primary inference that your definitions lead to? What is the immediate controversy in your proposition's topic area? What issues may be argued by advocates? By opponents?
4. Patricia Aburdene and John Naisbett's *Megatrends for Women* (1992) hypothesizes a number of trends that will affect women in the future, including their roles in politics, sports, religion, and "the menopause megatrend." Choose one of these trends, or the trend assigned by your instructor, and make a presentation to the class. Explain the trend in terms of a value hierarchy it suggests and what values it implies. What degree of importance does society presently attach to these values? How will the future affect the present hierarchy of these values?

Suggested Supplementary Readings

Brown, L. R., Kane, H., & Roodman, D. M. (1994). *Vital Signs 1994*. New York: Norton.
    Similar to John Peterson's *The Road to 2015*, these authors discuss the trends that are shaping our future. They focus on worldwide trends in food, agricultural practices, air quality, economics, energy, transportation, the military, and global societies. This view of future trends anticipates restructuring of

value hierarchies resulting from shifts in population patterns, food productivity, disease, and a host of other factors.

Davis, K. C. (1990). *Don't Know Much About History.* New York: Crown. Investigating the historical background of a topic can be difficult if it has been a while since you studied history. Crown has done a series of *Don't Know Much About . . .* books for readers who want a review of such subjects as history, science, and literature. Davis offers a review of key dates, people, events, causes, and the concepts behind them in American history. He provides comparisons and contrasts between events in the past and present to help make connections between issues from the past and how we interpret those issues today. An added value of this book and others in the series is the extensive bibliography of where to go for detailed accounts of each subject.

Greenhaven Press. (1988). *The Mass Media: Opposing Viewpoints.* San Diego: Author. We have used a number of examples about the mass media and we thought you might like to examine the pros and cons of media content and use in America. This anthology of articles offers advocacy and opposition argumentation on media bias, government regulation of the media, the media-politics connection, and harms of advertising. Greenhaven's *Opposing Viewpoints* series offers a wide variety of anthologies on controversies we presently consider important. The series is a great source for preparing issues analysis and getting a sense of how figurative ground is contested.

Chapter Five

How Is a Unit
of Argument Created?

In argumentation, controversy over a proposition is disputed in terms of issues. The stock issues for fact, value, and policy help you find the important points for developing a prima facie case or arguing against one. Using the stock issues to discover actual issues gives you *main points* for the overall organization of your ideas. Each of those main points must be developed through one or more specific arguments that help the audience understand how and why that main point is probably true. Each individual argument that develops a main point can be thought of as a *unit of argument*, a building block in case construction.

For example, earlier in your life you may have been involved in a controversy over the policy proposition: *You should eat your vegetables.* A prima facie argument advocating this proposition probably included the main point: "Vegetables are necessary for your good health." This main point might have been developed through units of argument, headlined by two subpoints about the connection between veggies and health: "Vegetables have vitamins and minerals," and "Vitamins and minerals are vital to proper growth."

The Toulmin Model of Argument

Whatever topic you choose to argue, your position as advocate or opponent emerges through a series of claims supported by grounds and warrant, terminology developed by British logician Stephen Toulmin (1958; and Toulmin, Rieke, & Janik, 1984) to classify the parts of an argument. There are many interpretations of how to use Toulmin's thinking on the structure of an argument. In this chapter, our interpretation is that the model should be used as a blueprint for creating your individual units of argument. We recommend that you develop your cases of advocacy and opposition by labeling the issues to be argued as *contentions* (argumentation jargon for a main point) and by using the Toulmin model to create one or more units of argument that will prove each contention's probable truth.

Claims

Argumentation begins when an advocate makes one or more claims. A *claim* is your own opinion, the conclusion you form from information on the topic. You want the audience to understand and accept your conclusions as believable. A claim is a conclusion that does not stand alone and something the listener or reader can ultimately agree or disagree with. In this sense, claims both begin and end the process of argumentation. Claims begin the process by showing where an arguer has taken a stand. Claims also end the process, showing what the listener or reader is expected to accept as true or probable. Disputes concerning claims center on whether they are capable of being supported by proof and reasoning and shown to be true-probable, untrue-improbable.

There are four categories of claims, each of which performs a different function:

factual claims: argue what was, is, or will be

definitional claims: argue how something is to be defined or categorized

value claims: argue evaluation or pass judgment on something

policy claims: argue that something should be done

Factual claims resemble propositions of fact in that they are concerned with things that can be verified. They are concerned with past, present, or future fact. The arguer asserts that something did exist, now exists, or will exist in the future and then proceeds to offer whatever proof can be discovered to demonstrate it. Theoretically, the best proof of factual claims derives from direct observation and experimentation (Ehninger, 1974). Practically, most of us have to rely on print and electronic sources of information for material to prove our factual claims. What might you use to prove each of the following factual claims?

Failure to resolve the hostage crisis led to President Carter's defeat in 1980.
The United States is winning its war on drugs.
A cure for cancer will be discovered by the year 2000. *I don't know.*

The second type of claim common to argumentation is the *definitional claim.* Such claims are used when the precise definition of a term becomes a contested issue. Definitional claims are concerned with how something is defined, as a particular type or category of act, individual, object, or idea. The following are examples of definitional claims:

Mass media are commonly considered to be (are recognized as) television, radio, film, recordings, magazines, newspapers, and books.

Computer literacy is (defined as) the basic knowledge needed to use computers.

The U.S. invasion of Panama in 1989 was (should be categorized as) a case of international aggression.

Like the value propositions they resemble, *value claims* show the arguer's evaluation or judgment. Value claims express an attitude toward something and they are identified by the use of evaluative language. The following are examples of value claims:

Return of the Jedi has the best special effects of the three films in the Star Wars trilogy.

The social security system is a poor substitute for effective retirement planning.

Television advertising is more effective than newspaper advertising.

The *policy claim* is like the policy proposition. It states that an action should be taken or a behavior should be altered. Because policy claims advocate change, they always concern the future. The following are examples of policy claims:

You should floss your teeth once a day.

You should purchase U.S. savings bonds.

You should register to vote.

Claims, regardless of type, are what arguments are about. Because they have a sentence structure similar to that of propositions, it is not surprising to discover that claims assert relationships between people, things, and ideas or actions. For example, in advancing the claim, "The social security system is a poor substitute for retirement planning," the arguer seeks to relate an institution (the social security system) to a judgment about it (is a poor substitute). Standing alone, this claim represents the arguer's opinion of the social security system. Opinion statements of this sort are usually insufficient to alter an audience's belief or behavior. More is required.

A final point about claims concerns how they are worded. Since claims express complete thoughts, they have the properties of formal sentences. Claims may be phrased as simple statements, with one relationship asserted, or as compound statements, with multiple relationships asserted. A compound sentence has two or more independent clauses in its predicate. Compare the following simple claim statements with their corresponding compound statements.

Personal income tax fraud is increasing. (factual claim)

Personal income tax fraud is the willful evasion of one's obligation to pay assessed taxes on salaries and remunerations. (definitional claim)

Personal income tax fraud is harmful to the well-being of society. (value claim)

Tax law enforcement should be strengthened to prevent personal income tax evasion. (policy claim)

A compound claim statement differs in that it argues more than one relationship in its assertion. Compare the following examples of compound claim statements with their simple counterparts:

> Personal income tax fraud is increasing and becoming more difficult to prosecute.
>
> Personal income tax fraud is the willful evasion of one's obligation to pay assessed taxes and a violation of federal and state laws.
>
> Personal income tax fraud is harmful both to U.S. citizens and to institutions.
>
> Tax laws should be revised to more equitably distribute the tax burden and more stringently punish the tax evader.

Recall that in discussing propositions, we indicated it was unwise to have multiple ideas stated in a single proposition. In wording claim statements that serve as subarguments, compound statements often make argumentation more economical. By offering a single claim to argue that tax fraud harms two entities, individuals and institutions, the arguer saves time and keeps related ideas together in her listener's or reader's mind. In addition, compound statements allow the arguer to set up patterns of reasoning through comparisons. "The seriousness of income tax evasion is demonstrated by the fact that tax fraud is increasing more rapidly than crimes against persons and property." The types of crime are unrelated, but the compound statement gives the audience a basis for comparison and a measure of the extent of tax fraud.

Thus, the arguer's task in making a claim is to present a well-defined and supported position for the listener or reader to consider. In doing this, the arguer offers not only a claim but also the grounds and warrant that support it. The relationship between them is such that an argument is the movement from grounds, accepted by the listener or reader, through warrant to claim (Brockriede & Ehninger, 1960). These three elements make up the primary triad of a unit of argument in the Toulmin model. A unit of argument is the structure for forming opinions from information you have collected on the topic. This unit of argument corresponds to the rational processes people use in making decisions (Golden et al., 1992).

Although the arguments you hear or read may not have all three elements clearly identified, the elements of the primary triad are basic to the structure of all argument. They represent the reasoning process invoked when someone makes a statement that requires support before someone else is willing to accept it as true or probable. If we say, "X is the cause of Y" (a claim) and, to support this opinion, we add, "Y happens every time we find an X present" (information about the co-occurrence of X and Y), we have created a unit of thought about X and Y. If we were uncertain that the audience saw the connection between X and Y in the same way we did, we might state more of our thinking, "X has certain properties that result in the creation of a Y" (a statement about how one thing causes another thing).

If the audience accepted our opinion that X causes Y because it shared our opinion, there would be no argumentation over the relationship between X and Y. Since argumentation takes place when people have differences of opinion or want to test all the ways in which the relationship between X and Y might not hold up, stating a claim is usually not enough for a unit of argument to make sense. In Toulmin model form, we would write up this unit of argument as:

CLAIM: X causes Y.
GROUNDS: X is present in this instance, and we also have evidence that Y is present.
WARRANT: An X has certain properties that give it the ability to produce a Y.

The following example demonstrates how the the concept of the prima facie case comes together with the conventions *presumption* and *burden of proof* discussed in Chapter 2 as a case is developed through a series of units of argument. This example addresses the first stock issue of a policy proposition, the reason for change. It also demonstrates why claims alone are inadequate and require the support of grounds and warrant to make the message worthy of agreement.

PROPOSITION: All students at this university should take course work sufficient to develop competency in a second language as a requirement for graduation.
PRESUMPTION: The existing state of affairs is that only some students choose to study a second language sufficiently to develop competency in its use. Presumption indicates that it is not necessary for all students to develop second-language competency and that the present system of graduation requirements should continue.
FIGURATIVE GROUND CONTESTED: Graduation requirements for students seeking undergraduate degrees.
BURDEN OF PROOF: The advocate of the proposition to change the present graduation requirements at this university has the burden of demonstrating a reasonable case for changing those requirements.
PRIMA FACIE CASE: The advocate seeks the suspension of presumption by presenting arguments that are within the bounds of the topic and are inherent and that a reasonable person would accept at face value. For example:
CLAIM 1: All students need second-language competency.
CLAIM 2: Students with second-language competency have more employment options upon graduation.
CLAIM 3: At present, it is extremely unlikely that the curriculum will be changed to make second-language competency a university-wide requirement for graduation.

You are probably unmoved by this message unless the proposition states something you already believe. In that case, your attitude would override the presumption established by the wording of the proposition because you already think having competency in a second language is a good thing. Not everyone agrees with you! As advocates for the proposition, we would fail to be certain that we had established a prima facie case if all we presented were a series of claims since claims are generally not accepted at face value. However, if we also provide the grounds and warrant that support our claims, they become good reasons for a reader's assent, a prima facie case.

CLAIM 1: All students need second-language competency.

SUPPORT: The United States is part of a global economy, trading with people from many different cultures. The United States is a multicultural nation whose people speak many languages; in particular, Spanish is commonly spoken as the language of choice by almost 30 percent of our population. This information suggests college graduates need competency in a second language.

CLAIM 2: Students with second-language competency have more employment options upon graduation.

SUPPORT: Research shows that many U.S. companies, private philanthropic and religious organizations, and the U.S. government give preference to job applicants with second-language competency. Some states with large Latino populations require competency in Spanish for state government positions.

CLAIM 3: At present, it is extremely unlikely that the curriculum will be changed to make second-language competency a university-wide requirement for graduation.

SUPPORT: The university has experienced a decline in enrollment and is reducing the size of the faculty. The administration is not predisposed to add new requirements for graduation that would necessitate increasing the size of the faculty by requiring an extensive number of new sections of foreign language classes.

Grounds

Since a claim alone is insufficient to alter belief or behavior, you must consider the second major element of the Toulmin model: grounds. Grounding the claim provides the foundation of information on which an argument rests, the proof required for a rational person to accept the claim as true or probable. The relationship of claims to grounds is such that "the claim under discussion can be no stronger than the grounds that provide its foundation" (Toulmin et al., 1984, p. 26). *Grounding* is that element in the argument given to the listeners or readers that enables them to answer such questions as What information supported this claim? or Upon what foundation is this claim based? Common ground, which the audience already knows and accepts, may exist, and you may draw on it to support claims. You may also add information to it to increase the probability of the audience's accepting your claim as true.

Suppose the audience for our proposal on second-language competency as a graduation requirement already knows that some states with large Latino populations require competency in Spanish as well as English as a condition of employment. A simple statement of this fact can be used to ground Claim 2.

CLAIM 2: Students with second-language competency have more employment
    options upon graduation.
GROUNDS 1: Our state requires competency in Spanish, as well as English, to
    be employed by the state.

This bit of information the audience already possesses may not be sufficient
to ground the claim because it refers only to competency in Spanish and only to
jobs with the state. We should add a second source of information to ground the
claim's conclusion that second-language competency in general, will offer students more employment opportunities. Our revised unit of argument might look
like this:

CLAIM 2: Students with second-language competency have more employment
    options upon graduation.
GROUNDS 1: Our state requires competency in Spanish, as well as English, to be
    employed by the state.
GROUNDS 2: Research done by the Department of Labor shows that compe-
    tency in French, Spanish, German, Arabic, Japanese, or Chinese is the sin-
    gle most important factor in being hired by a multinational corporation.
GROUNDS 3: The office of the U.S. Secretary of Foreign Affairs reports that
    college graduates with competency in a second language are more fre-
    quently hired for government posts than graduates who speak only English.

We sometimes use the generic term *evidence* to classify all proof in the form
of facts and opinions discovered through research and used to ground claims.
Since other parts of the Toulmin model may also use evidence, this element in
the primary triad is labeled *grounds* to avoid confusion. Experimental observations, statistics, expert opinion, personal testimony, matters of common knowledge, or previously established claims make up the pool of material used as
grounds in an argument. More specific information on the nature and application of evidence is provided in Chapter 6.

The field in which argumentation takes place often influences the form and
substance of individual arguments that make up a particular instance of argumentation. We have discussed law as one field that possesses features that make
it unique, such as the artificial presumption of innocence. Knowing the field of
argument gives you some insights into the kinds of evidence that appropriately
grounds claims and the expectations that surround the kinds of reasoning that
warrant accepting claims based on such evidence.

Some aspects of argument, however, are independent of the particulars of
a given field. Although a geologist and a criminal lawyer use different strategies
in preparing and presenting their arguments, both need a structure to follow in
building those arguments. The same is true when you begin to create your own
arguments. This system for constructing arguments is transportable to any field
since argumentation is based on a series of common elements.

Claims must always be supported by grounds; claims alone are only tentative hypotheses until something supports their veracity. If we make the claim, "All
students need second-language competency," you might reasonably ask, "Why

do they need it?" Grounds used to support a claim are selected to provide specific information pertinent to that claim as distinct from all other possible claims. Grounds should always point toward the claim, leading the audience directly toward the conclusion specified by it. It would be foolish to attempt to prove our claim by citing statistics that indicate that at present only about one student in three completes existing graduation requirements. The grounds do not logically fit the claim. Sometimes, the logical fit between a claim and the information that grounds it is clear in our own minds but may be a mystery to the reader or listener without further explanation. The third element of the primary triad in the Toulmin model provides such explanations.

Warrant

The third element in the primary triad is called the warrant. It shows why if one accepts the validity of the grounds, one can also safely accept the validity of the claim. *Warrants* indicate how, given the available grounds, it is reasonable for the listener or reader to make the inferential leap from them to the claim. "The assertor's task is normally to convince us not just that it was legitimate for him to adopt the initial claim for himself, but also that we should share it and so rely on it ourselves" (Toulmin et al., 1984, p. 46).

Warrants provide us with specific information about how the arguer reasons. By showing the relationship between grounds and claim, warrants demonstrate that making the mental leap from one to the other is rational. The easiest way to show this relationship is to verbalize how you reasoned from the grounds to the claim in forming an opinion. Chapter 7 will explain more about the reasoning process, but we can return to our "X causes Y" example for a simple demonstration of how to explain your reasoning process as the warrant step in a unit of argument.

CLAIM: X causes Y.
GROUNDS: X is present in this instance, and we also have evidence that Y is present.
WARRANT: An X has certain properties that give it the ability to produce a Y.

Look very carefully at the wording of the warrant. The warrant describes how reasoning from cause is done. For one thing to be the cause of another, it must have the ability or properties to make the second thing occur. We can explain why we believe that X causes Y with the information that the two always occur together (the temporal property of causal reasoning). The mental leap that takes us from this property—X and Y being connected in time— to the claim that X causes Y is the cue to the reader or listener on the nature of causal reasoning. This provides additional support for our mental leap: X has certain properties above and beyond the temporal connection to Y, making it capable of bringing about Y.

A warrant does not always have to describe how you reasoned in forming a claim statement based on the grounds. You may draw on what the audience knows as material for the warrant. Warrants are found in things already accepted as true as a part of common knowledge, values, customs, and societal norms. In addition, natural laws, legal principles, statutes, rules of thumb, or mathematical formulas may establish warrants. Warrants take the form of information that shows a relationship between a claim and the grounds used to support it.

Consider how we might warrant our claim about the connection between having competency in a second language and getting a job upon graduation.

CLAIM: Students with second-language competency have more employment options upon graduation.

GROUNDS 1: Our state requires competency in Spanish, as well as English, to be employed by the state.

GROUNDS 2: Research done by the Department of Labor shows that competency in French, Spanish, German, Arabic, Japanese, or Chinese is the single most important factor in being hired by a multinational corporation.

GROUNDS 3: The office of the U.S. Secretary of Foreign Affairs reports that college graduates with competency in a second language are more frequently hired for government posts than graduates who speak only English.

WARRANT: What is true of our state, the research on multinational corporations, and the U.S. Department of Foreign Affairs is probably true of most prospective employers of college graduates. (This is a warrant that explains the reasoning process of generalizing: What is true of some is true of most or all.)

If we wanted to use a warrant drawn from things that are already accepted as true by the listener or reader, our unit of argument might look like this:

CLAIM: Students with second-language competency have more employment options upon graduation.

GROUNDS 1: Our state requires competency in Spanish, as well as English, to be employed by the state.

GROUNDS 2: Research done by the Department of Labor shows that competency in French, Spanish, German, Arabic, Japanese, or Chinese is the single most important factor in being hired by a multinational corporation.

GROUNDS 3: The office of the U.S. Secretary of Foreign Affairs reports that college graduates with competency in a second language are more frequently hired for government posts than graduates who speak only English.

WARRANT: It is common knowledge that the more useful skills a graduate possesses, the more likely he or she is to find employment upon graduation.

The warrant justifies movement from the grounds to the claim by describing how you reasoned to connect grounds to claim or by calling upon commonly accepted belief to demonstrate the connection. In the ebb and flow of everyday argument, warrants are often unstated. The audience must discover them for itself. Very often, it is the warrant that defines the locus of controversy between advocate and opponent. We reason from claim to grounds or grounds to claim, and it is the warrant that specifies the reasoning. Thus, a claim stands or falls on the validity of the warrant. If you have ever confronted a claim and the grounds that purported to support it and felt that it just didn't make sense, it may have been because you were unable to find a warrant reasonably linking one to the other.

JEANNE: Phil really isn't a very good student.
KATHY: Why?
JEANNE: Because he's on the football team.

Kathy probably wonders, "Why does being a football player automatically make Phil a poor student?" Her question arises from the lack of a sensible warrant.

From this facetious example we can learn two things about the nature and use of warrants. First, warrants are a vital part of argumentation. If a clear link between grounds and claim is not provided, the audience's rationality may prevent it from accepting the claim. Second, the arguer should always select a warrant that the audience is likely to understand and accept as rational. It "makes sense" that students might have more employment opportunities upon graduation if they have competency in a second language. It "makes no sense" that being on the football team equates to poor academic achievement. The warrant is essential in argument, but it is helpful only to the extent that it is understood by the intended audience.

Summary of the Elements of the Primary Triad
1. A *claim* is a conclusion that does not stand alone but requires further proof before the audience is willing to accept it as verified.
2. *Grounds* are information of fact or opinion used to provide verification for the claim, commonly labeled *evidence*.
3. *Warrant* is the reasoning that justifies the mental leap from grounds to claim, certifying that given the grounds, the claim is true or probable.

Claim, grounds, and warrant do not always provide sufficient proof and reasoning to establish the argument. Because arguers face the need to be clear, accurate, and specific, it is sometimes necessary to build in additional support and qualification for the claim using the elements of the secondary triad of the Toulmin model: backing, qualifiers, and rebuttals. These constitute the things that show an argument's strength or force. Backing is not always required to build an effective argument, but we recommend that you use backing while learning argumentation skills. Qualifiers and rebuttals are necessary when you must show your audience the limitations on the probable truth of your claims.

Backing

The audience may require more information before they agree that given the grounds, and in light of the warrant, the claim should be accepted. Warrants sometimes require clarification and additional information. Since "warrants are not self-validating" (Toulmin et al., 1984, p. 62), the effective arguer demonstrates that the warrant supplied should be believed. *Backing* offers explicit information to establish the reliability of the warrant used in arguing the claim. "An argument will carry real weight and give its conclusions solid support only if the warrants relied on in the course of it are both sound and also to the point" (Toulmin et al., 1984, p. 63). Backing your warrant offers support that your point can be made using a particular kind of reasoning or by drawing on what the audience already knows to help them make the mental leap from ground to claim.

The type of information the arguer must use to provide backing may be either general or specific, depending on the requirements of the situation. As the warrant serves as justification for making the leap from grounds to claim, backing justifies belief in the warrant itself. Like the warrant, backing may be unstated, left to the imagination of the listener or reader. If the audience is knowledgeable on the subject being argued or familiar with the grounds used, backing, and even the warrant, may be unnecessary. However, in circumstances where the audience may not have much prior knowledge, the arguer is well advised to supply both warrant and backing to increase the believability of the position.

CLAIM: Students with second-language competency have more employment options upon graduation.

GROUNDS 1: Our state requires competency in Spanish, as well as English, to be employed by the state.

GROUNDS 2: Research done by the Department of Labor shows that competency in French, Spanish, German, Arabic, Japanese, or Chinese is the single most important factor in being hired by a multinational corporation.

GROUNDS 3: The office of the U.S. Secretary of Foreign Affairs reports that college graduates with competency in a second language are more frequently hired for government posts than graduates who speak only English.

WARRANT: What is true of our state, the research on multinational corporations, and the U.S. Department of Foreign Affairs is probably true of most prospective employers of college graduates.

BACKING: A ten-year study of the employment rates for new college graduates done by Eastern State University's School of Business confirms that, in general, graduates with competency in a second language found employment faster and at higher salaries than graduates with a competency in only the English language.

In this example, providing both warrant and backing is not argumentative overkill. They help the listener or reader understand the impact of second-language competency on securing employment, and the backing adds the further bit of significant information that these students probably make more money. If after analyzing your audience, you are undecided about whether to include warrant and backing, it is usually wisest to go ahead and include both. Claims seek to alter belief or behavior, and people are predisposed to resist change. Including grounds, warrant, and backing in each unit of argument makes that unit of argument clearer for the audience. Clear arguments, offering specific information, are more likely to lead to success in advocating or opposing propositions. Warrants and backing help an audience to interpret and understand the factual basis upon which your claim rests.

Qualifiers

The second element of the secondary triad in the Toulmin model helps the arguer indicate the force or strength of the claim. Not all arguments have the same strength. *Qualifiers* show the degree of force the arguer believes the claim possesses. Not all claims must be qualified; in some instances the arguer is certain of the correctness and strength of the claim. If in investigating a topic you discover exceptions or instances that disconfirm your claim, you will have to account for those exceptions in your argument. Consider the following examples of qualified and unqualified claims:

> Qualified: Except for those students who can pass a competency exam in a language other than English on admission to the university, students need a minimum of two years of study in a second language to develop competency.
> Unqualified: Students need a minimum of two years of study in a second language to develop competency.

The limitation of the first claim is suggested by the modal qualifier "except for those. . . ." Modal qualifiers are "phrases that show what kind and degree of reliance is to be placed on the conclusions, given the arguments available to support them" (Toulmin et al., 1984, p. 85). Modal qualifiers typically take the form of adverbs, adverbial phrases, or prepositional phrases that modify the action suggested by the claim's verb. The following are examples of frequently used qualifiers:

sometimes
presumably
necessarily
certainly
perhaps
maybe
in certain cases
at this point in time
with the exception of
in all probability

The use of such qualifying terms indicates the strength or limitation of your claim. Qualified claims provide the arguer with a means of advancing an argument in circumstances where the reliability or applicability of the claim is not absolute or universal. The arguer using qualified claims is communicating honestly, alerting the listener or reader to the fact that the claim is not valid in all instances or is not absolutely true. The use of a qualified claim does not necessarily signal that the opinion it states is unsound, merely that it is not absolutely verified or verifiable.

Rebuttals

The final element of the secondary triad in the Toulmin model also provides a means of accommodating the limitations of claims. *Rebuttals* are added to claim statements that need to be limited to indicate the circumstances under which they may not be valid. Strategically, the use of a rebuttal anticipates objections to the claim. Rebuttals help us avoid errors in reasoning and reflect that we are dealing with what is generally true, not absolutely true.

In our example, attachment of a rebuttal would alter the unqualified claim as follows:

> Students need a minimum of two years of study in a second language to develop competency.
>
> Students need a minimum of two years of study in a second language to develop competency, unless they fail one or more courses and require tutoring and remedial course work.

You may feel using qualifiers and rebuttals is not a very good idea, since they seem to diminish the strength of arguments. The use of qualifiers and rebuttals acknowledges that argumentation is not an exact science and that human affairs are seldom discussible in absolute terms. There are two circumstances in which the use of rebuttals is particularly important if you are truly committed to being honest with your audience.

The first circumstance exists when grounds, warrant, and backing support the claim only under certain conditions. This occurs in our example, calling for the qualifying statement we provided. The second circumstance occurs when grounds, warrant, and backing provide only partial support for the claim. What if second-language competencies desired by U.S. employers were restricted to Spanish and Native American languages? The claim would have to be restricted, stating a need in terms of a limited number of languages for graduates who plan on working in the United States.

Summary of the Elements of the Secondary Triad
1. *Backing* provides the credentials that help establish the legitimacy of the inferential leap from grounds to claim.
2. *Qualifiers* show the amount, or degree, of force that a claim possesses.
3. *Rebuttals* limit claims, showing circumstances under which they may not be true and anticipating objections to the claim.

The Toulmin model provides a useful system for creating individual units of argument. Individual arguments, however, are seldom sufficient to advocate or oppose each issue adequately in your development of a fact, value, or policy case. Since an issue serves as a main point in your case, and main points must be developed with substructure, a series of units of argument form that substructure.

Simple, Chain, and Cluster Arguments

A *simple* pattern of argument exists whenever a single claim supports an arguer's contention. Assume for a moment you are married and have two children. While out running some errands, you see a sports car on a dealer's lot and decide you must have it. When you get home, you and your spouse argue the policy proposition: *We should trade the station wagon in for a sports car.* Your spouse claims owning a sports car is impractical: It has two seats (grounds 1), there are four family members (grounds 2), family income restricts you to one car (grounds 3), going anywhere as a family would require twice as many trips and make long family trips impossible (warrant). You didn't get your sports car, but hopefully you do get the idea behind simple patterns of argument. A simple pattern of argument is useful when a single telling point needs to be made to win the argument. However, the simple pattern also makes the job of the person you are arguing against simpler, and, if the point is not a telling one, your use of a simple pattern may give your opponent an edge.

A *chain* of argument exists whenever a series of claims are linked together in such a way that each becomes an integral part of the next, providing grounds, warrant, or backing. Assume that when you go to work next Monday you learn that you have been promoted and given a big raise. You can now afford a second car, and the dealer still has the one you want. The policy debate resumes, and your spouse changes tactics by arguing that sports cars are dangerous. This argument relies on a chain of interconnected claims rather than a single one.

First, sports cars are smaller than most other cars on the road. Second, because they are smaller, drivers of larger cars are less likely to see them. Third, because they are less likely to be seen, sports cars are more likely to be involved in accidents. Fourth, because they are more likely to be involved in accidents, and those accidents will involve larger cars, the occupants of sports cars face greater risk of injury or death, therefore making sports cars dangerous.

While it is organizationally more complex, a chain of argument is not necessarily any stronger than a simple argument. Since a chain is no stronger than its weakest link, it is not necessary to refute every argument your spouse offered to get your dream car. Arguing that a sports car's superior handling and braking increases its ability to avoid potential accidents calls the third claim in the chain into question and possibly keeps you from having to drive to work the next day in the family station wagon.

Cluster arguments are those in which a number of claims independently point to the same conclusion. Suppose the dealer gets the car you want in a shade of red so visually arresting that even your spouse admits that no one could miss seeing it as you drive down the street. The argument now shifts to the main point that sports cars are too expensive, supported by the following claims. First, the price of sports cars is higher than the price of cars in general. Second, the cost of insuring a sports car is higher than the cost of insuring a car in general because of the surcharge that most insurance companies add. Third, the cost of driving a sports car is higher than the cost of driving most other cars because its high performance engine requires the use of more expensive, premium fuel. Fourth, the cost of repairing a sports car is higher than the cost of repairing other cars because the parts are more expensive.

While the main point in the cluster argument is supported by four claims, as was the main point in the chain example, the cluster argument is not only organizationally complex but also stronger than the simple argument. Like claims in a chain, claims in a cluster add up to support the main point. Unlike claims in a chain, claims in a cluster do so independently. As a result, calling the validity of any claim in a cluster into question does nothing to diminish the validity of the remaining claims. Responding to your spouse's third claim with an argument that better fuel mileage offsets the higher price of premium gas may call it into question. This victory, however, does nothing to diminish the probative force of the claims about higher purchase price, insurance premiums, or repair costs or get you out from behind the wheel of the family station wagon.

Advocates and opponents frequently use all three patterns of argument—simple, chain, and cluster—in presenting their cases. Contesting a definition of terms or the classification of something may easily be developed with a single unit of argument. Some contentions may best be developed by relying on chain linkage and others by cluster independency. Whether a simple, chain, or cluster grouping of units of arguments is best depends upon the topic and field of argument.

In a given field, on a given topic, a chain of units of argument can be very persuasive. You will remember that in the last chapter we referred to Richard Fraser's factual argument about who was really responsible for the death of Abraham Lincoln. Fraser used a chain of units of argument to lead the reader from his first claim that the on-the-scene physicians were deficient in their knowledge of accepted medical practice through a series of interconnected claims to the final claim that the doctors, not Booth, were responsible for Lincoln's death.

In this chapter we have given you a system for building units of argument. Argument units are used to make a complete case for or against your proposition based on the issues you discovered in doing the analysis of the proposition. Now it is time to head to the library and find the information to ground your claims and back your warrants. Chapter 6 will make that trip much easier.

Learning Activities

1. Select a topic with which you are familiar. Create four arguments for that topic corresponding to the four types of claims: fact, definition, value, and policy. For each unit of argument provide and label each of the following elements: grounds, warrant, backing, and claim. When you have finished, examine your arguments. Do any of them require qualifiers or rebuttals? If so, provide and label appropriate qualifier or rebuttal statements. Concentrate on developing each part of the argument rather than on the use of evidence in establishing the grounds, warrant, and backing.

2. Find three examples of claims that use qualifiers. Develop a complete Toulmin model of each and label each part of the argument.

3. Find three examples of claims that use rebuttals. Develop a complete Toulmin model of each and label each part of the argument.
4. Select an argument, such as an editorial, letter to the editor, or an opinion column. Complete the following:
   A. In a single sentence, state the proposition for argument.
   B. Identify the contentions used in developing the proposition and the claims used to develop each contention.
   C. Classify these claims as to type: fact, definition, value, or policy.
   D. Of the parts of argument, identify those that the author uses and those that are left to the reader to supply.
5. Classify the following claims as to type, and identify those claims that use qualifiers and/or rebuttals. Be sure to identify the part of the claim statement that serves as qualifier or rebuttal.
   A. Argumentation is the process of arriving at conviction through the use of reason.
   B. For good performance through a severe winter, front wheel drive vehicles are best.
   C. Most restrictions on trade and imports will not solve America's economic problems.
   D. Discretion is the better part of valor.
   E. Evolution and Creation are opposing theories of the development of life on earth.
   F. Professional sports just aren't the same now that many players are paid such huge salaries.
   G. If you want to develop confidence in your ability to communicate with others, take a public-speaking course.
   H. We should intervene in the affairs of Central American nations since they are geographically close to the United States.
   I.. Laughter is the best medicine.
   J. White tigers are a separate strain of Bengal tigers with recessive genetic characteristics that cause the white coat and blue eyes.
   K. In the absence of more equitable proposals, many Americans favor a policy of flat rate taxes.
   L. For those who would gain insights into the future, study the past.

Suggested Supplementary Readings

Ehninger, D. (1974). *Influence, Belief, and Argument.* Glenview, IL: Scott, Foresman. This book is full of excellent examples that have not become outdated. The fundamentals of argumentation are discussed in terms of the Toulmin model.
Toulmin, S., Rieke, R., & Janik, A. (1984). *An Introduction to Reasoning* (2nd Ed.). New York: MacMillan.
   For the most comprehensive discussion of the Toulmin model, turn to the source, particularly Chapters 2 through 13. This book is clear and understandable for the beginner. It also examines several fields—law, science, the arts, and management—in depth.

Chapter Six

How Do I Prove
My Argument?

In some situations, proving your arguments will be a matter of drawing on your own knowledge or that of your audience. In most situations, you will need to research the topic thoroughly. You will need evidence, the term commonly used to describe the grounds for an argumentative claim or the information that backs its warrant. In this chapter, we are concerned with the discovery of evidence and the assessment of its quality in a larger sense.

> By definition, **evidence** is information taken from material of fact or opinion used to establish the probable truth of a claim.

The kinds of information necessary to establish the grounds or back the warrant in your argument are determined by your analysis of the issues in your proposition. Standards for determining the quantity and quality of proof necessary for building good units of argument result from applying accepted tests of evidence. Since proof is the foundation of argument, you will need to learn how to discover and apply it. This chapter discusses types of evidence, standards for evaluating its quality, and techniques for finding it.

Types of Evidence

As our definition of evidence suggests, there are two general classes of evidence, *fact* and *opinion*. Equally, there are two sources of evidence, your own observations and the recorded observations of others. The most reliable source of evidence is personal observation and experimentation. Consider the experience of buying a new car. The question, "Which car should I buy?" may ultimately lead to argumentation on a policy proposition.

That proposition might be argued through a number of fact and value claims about the quantifiable performance and qualitative evaluations of a series of automobiles. The most reliable evidence would be obtained through your own road tests of these vehicles. However, even in something as personal as buying a new car, performing your own tests is not always feasible. You may not have the time or ability to conduct as sophisticated a series of tests as those reported in *Car and Driver* or *Motor Trend*. Beyond saving time, reliance on printed sources relieves you of the need to be an expert in a number of fields. It is also often advantageous to add the credibility of expert opinion or research to your own ideas. By using published facts and the opinions of sources in the know, you strengthen your argument and increase the credibility of its rational appeal.

Evidence of Fact

Facts are those things that can be verified as true or false. By verification we mean observation, either our own or that of someone whose ability to make such an observation we respect.

Factual evidence is information obtained from direct or indirect observation that describes or reports what exists—events, objects, places, persons, phenomena.

Factual evidence does not attempt to explain or evaluate, it merely reports what was observed. Direct factual evidence is observed by the arguer. Indirect factual evidence is obtained from the reported observations of others. Indirect evidence is used more frequently than direct evidence in many fields of argument, except for the field of law. Because we live in an age of relatively easy access to a variety of published materials, using evidence obtained from the research of others has almost as much validity as evidence obtained through our own observations.

Examples and illustrations report or describe events and phenomena; they tell us what may be observed in a given situation. This type of evidence may be a brief statement or a detailed description. Compare the following:

In January 1991, a 3-year-old Seattle toddler found his mother's .38-caliber revolver under her pillow. The toddler then accidentally shot his 2-year-old brother in the stomach.

In May of this year, while his parents slept upstairs, a Chicago 3-year-old found a loaded .25 caliber semiautomatic handgun on a closet shelf, with which he fatally shot himself a few minutes later.

Last Saturday in Brooklyn, NY, a 9-year-old playing with an automatic handgun he thought was empty and had found in his house, fatally shot his cousin, age 12, in the head. (Children Carrying Weapons, 1992, p. 10)

With me today is Dorethia Pugh, the woman behind that case and who was the target of that intimidation. She overcame her fears and had the courage to testify in four separate trials.

This case started in January 1993. Ms. Pugh witnessed a cabdriver being shot by two of the Merriweather triplets. Although only 15 years old at the time, the brothers were well known in the Avalon Apartment complex where this occurred and they were feared by many people.

Ms. Pugh never told the police what she knew about the shooting, but one of the brothers involved decided otherwise and decided to silence her. On February 20, 1993, that brother, Jermaine Merriweather, became the mastermind behind a scheme to fire bomb Dorethia Pugh's apartment. He solicited four other youths to help him. They were all aged 15 to 17.

That evening at approximately 10 o'clock p.m. they went down to the Pugh apartment. Jermaine Merriweather looked into her patio window to make sure she was home and perhaps to let her know before she died who was behind it and why.

Minutes later, a firebomb went through that back bedroom window killing the sleeping 1-year-old baby girl. That fire not only destroyed her apartment but the whole building and part of the building next door. Approximately 40 families were displaced and left homeless.

Other witnesses in the case expressed similar fears. Most witnesses still lived in the Avalon Apartments and wondered if the Merriweathers or those associated with them would come after them next.

One witness received a call from the jail from Jermaine asking if she planned to testify. In fact, he called on more than one occasion. Another witness had to take his daughter out of school because of threats made against her and again Jermaine called him at home threatening him. This last witness was an adult witness and even adult witnesses expressed fear of this 15-year-old offender. They had to return to the Avalon Apartments and I did not, and it was their safety that was in danger.

This case, along with the cabdriver shooting, were not resolved until July of this year. During this year-and-a-half before each trial the fear resurfaced and I was never sure if all the witnesses would show, and if they did, if they would tell all they knew. During the trial involving the firebombing, the judge had to advise friends and relatives of the defendants not to make faces at a 17-year-old female witness while she testified. (Witness Intimidation, 1994, p. 13)

These two reports differ in both subject matter and degree of detail. The discussion of the tragic consequences of children finding loaded handguns lists a series of brief, specific instances. It amounts to a series of examples. The more detailed account of one instance of witness intimidation is longer and more informative. It possesses the characteristics of an illustration.

Statistics present descriptive and inferential information about people, events, or phenomena numerically. While an example often describes people, events, or phenomena in isolation, statistics can place such information in context. This gives the reader or listener a sense of the significance of the thing described.

In New York City, it is estimated that poor people spend more than 30 percent of their annual income on food, compared to the national average which is less than 13 percent, and in our study we found that a family will spend, depending on the size of the family, between $350 and $1,000 more a year, and you are talking about the poorest people who have the least access to funds, if they do not have a decent supermarket to get to. (Urban Grocery Gap, 1992, p. 17)

This is an example of a *descriptive statistic*, in which the entire population of people, events, or phenomena of a particular kind are observed. The researchers looked at spending patterns and other available information and reported what they found. Descriptive statistics can be reported in any number of ways. Averages or percentages are sometimes used to reduce raw numbers to a more manageable form and provide standards for comparing one group of people, events, or phenomena to another. The following example of statistical evidence employs ratios.

The Noedecker Report states that in the United States of America we have the highest teen pregnancy rate of any developed country; 96 out of 1,000 teenage girls become pregnant. (Record Labeling, 1985, p. 11)

For statistics to have meaning, they must be interpretable. The advocate aids our ability to interpret these numbers by including comparison groups, other developed countries, for her listeners to use as benchmarks. What we do not know from the advocate's presentation is precisely how the estimate "96 out of 1,000 teenage girls become pregnant" was made. Is this statistic descriptive or inferential?

An *inferential statistic* is one in which data concerning a sample of the entire population of people, events, or phenomena of a particular kind are observed, and the researcher infers that what is true of the sample is true of the population from which it was drawn. The way the data is reported suggests that the researchers may have looked at public health data on the total number of reported teen pregnancies in developed countries and computed the average number of pregnancies per 1,000 teenage girls. However, this data could also report the results obtained from asking 1,000 teenage girls in each developed country whether they had ever been pregnant. If that were the case, the statistics would be inferential rather than descriptive.

Regardless of whether statistical information is descriptive or inferential, it can be misleading. When a source reports results as an *average*, that term may refer to the mean, median, or mode of a set of data. The mean is the arithmetic average of a set of numbers, the median is the middle score in that set, and the mode is the score that occurs most frequently. Given the following data, 98, 57, 23, 11, and 11, a source could report its average to be 40 (the mean), 23 (the median), or 11 (the mode). Be sure you understand what kind of statistics your sources are using to avoid misleading your audience.

Artifacts are actual exhibits of objects, audiotapes or videotapes, or photographs presented for verification by the audience. If you have ever watched "Court TV" or a courtroom drama on television, you are familiar with the use of artifacts as evidence. In a courtroom, artifacts or exhibits constitute real evidence as distinguished from the testimony provided by witnesses. The use of artifacts as evidence enhances argumentation on certain topics. Consider how the use of an artifact in Representative Charles Schumer's opening statement at the hearings on witness intimidation might have enhanced his persuasiveness.

> In some neighborhoods, criminals are brazen enough to hang posters warning that those who cooperate with the police will be killed. In case anybody misses the point, lists of suspected witnesses are also posted.
> I have here in my hand threatening posters, lists of witnesses that were displayed in a neighborhood in this very city.
> These are the names. It says witness X just finished testifying in Maryland. And then it talks about things that might happen to them and a list of other witnesses. (Witness Intimidation, 1994, p. 2)

Premises are factual evidence accepted because they reflect human belief or experience. There are some statements, which may technically be considered claims, that are so widely believed as true that they are accepted as fact without further verification. A premise is accepted because there are many previously recorded or reported instances of its being true. Premises are gathered through your own observation of people's statements about what they believe or from print and electronic sources of information and opinion.

Laws of nature, such as, "water seeks its own lowest level," and rules of thumb or folk wisdom, such as, "monkey see, monkey do," tend to be accepted. A premise is an expressed belief of those in a field and is used as proof to save time and effort. Because premises are predictions or projections based on experience, they can be verified like facts of other kinds, but they seldom are. In theory, an audience could suspend belief until a premise is verified. But when you can predict which premises an audience will accept, it becomes unnecessary to verify them. To do otherwise might insult the intelligence of your audience. Nevertheless, persons learning argumentation should verify premises by providing the warrant and its backing. Even those experienced in argumentation follow this suggestion. As Senator Paul Simon noted,

> We imitate from television, [a form of the folk wisdom premise "monkey see, monkey do"] whether it is a 30 second commercial for soap or violence from entertainment television. And I would like to make a distinction here between entertainment violence and news violence. News violence doesn't glorify violence. Entertainment violence does. And that is a very important distinction. (Violence on Television, 1992, p. 5)

Many premises are the product of, or are tested by, the scientific method. When we encounter a problem—perhaps our car won't start one morning—we attempt to explain it. Our explanation takes the form of a hypothesis, a guess about what might be the source of the problem. "My car won't start because the battery is dead." The hypothesis states the dependency of one thing, our car's ability to start, on the variability or independence of another, the level of charge in the battery. We would test our hypothesis that the battery is dead by seeing if the lights, radio, or horn will work. If they work, this informal measure of the charge in our battery suggests our hypothesis is false, and we would test other explanations such as blown fuses, loose wiring, or a defective starter. What you have just done is roughly equivalent to what researchers in the physical and social sciences do in laboratory and field settings. Published reports of their findings can be used to support your claims.

Scientific evidence reports the results of controlled experiments on the inferred effect of one variable on another. For example, a researcher might feel that prescribing a certain drug for heroin addicts might reduce their addiction. The first variable, the prescription drug, is called the independent variable. Changes in it are hypothesized to produce changes in the second variable, heroin addiction, which is the dependent variable. A third class of variables, nuisance variables, include those things that could minimize or maximize the predicted effect. Examples of possible nuisance variables might be the length of time a person has been addicted to heroin or whether a person abuses other drugs in addition to heroin.

In *laboratory experiments*, the researcher has greater control over the manipulation of the independent variable, measurement of the dependent variable, and the presence of nuisance variables. A laboratory experiment testing the effect of a drug in reducing addiction might manipulate the independent variable, by selecting two groups of addicts and administering the test drug to one group and a placebo to the other. These constitute the treatment conditions of the independent variable, and subjects in the experiment would be randomly assigned to one group or the other, unless the desire to control for one or more nuisance variables required modifying group assignment in some way. The researcher could measure physiological indications of addiction to measure the dependent variable. Finally, the researcher would conduct the appropriate statistical test on the resulting data to compare the test group and the placebo group.

> In one study, patients who were being treated with buprenorphine for heroin addiction, and who were also cocaine addicts, were observed to reduce the abuse of both substances. In another study, recently published in the journal *Science*, monkeys that had been self-administering cocaine virtually stopped using it once they had been treated with buprenorphine. Remarkably, they stopped using it even though it was still available to them. (Drugs in the 1990's, 1989, p. 170)

In a *field experiment*, the independent variable is frequently manipulated by the marketplace or social forces rather than by the researcher. The researcher must find a way to measure the dependent variable as well as find out what treatment condition the subject has been assigned to. If a researcher was interested in assessing the impact of AIDS education campaigns on the beliefs and behaviors of intravenous drug users, a field experiment might be the logical choice.

> Clients interviewed ranged from 18 to 44 years of age: 5 percent were 10-19 years; 50 percent were 20-29; 40 percent were 30-39; and 5 percent were 40–49. There were 35 males (63 percent) and 21 females (37 percent)

interviewed; 89 percent of clients in the study were white and 11 percent were black. There were no Hispanic or Asian clients interviewed. . . .

All participants in the study considered themselves to have been dependent upon or addicted to methamphetamine. The average age at first use of methamphetamine was 20.6 years; it was younger for males (18.7 years) and slightly older for females (23.6 years). . . .

Intravenous (IV) use of methamphetamine was the preferred route of administration by 62 percent of the participants. IV use was reported by 74 percent of males and 43 percent of females. . . .

All IV users interviewed knew the connection between needle sharing and transmission of the HIV virus. Most had learned about needle cleaning within the last 6-12 months. However, only a few stated that they always used a clean needle once they had learned how to clean their equipment. Most believed that the person with whom they shared did not present a risk to them. Some reported cleaning needles a few times, but then expressed that since they hadn't always done so, it wasn't worth the effort. One subject reported a rumor that bleach residue in the needle would decrease the potency of methamphetamine. (Drugs in the 1990's, 1989, pp. 92–93)

When used to ground an argument, scientific evidence may not seem that different from other types of evidence of fact or opinion. Because it sometimes employs statistical tests of significance, scientific evidence differs from other types of evidence of fact in that its statements of direct or indirect observation carry with them an estimate of the probability that the inferred cause-effect relationship could have been produced by chance or coincidence. Scientific evidence also differs from evidence from opinion in that its credibility derives from the rigor of its method of observation rather than the prestige of the person drawing conclusions about those observations.

Evidence from Opinion

While factual evidence describes without judgment or evaluation, opinions are judgments and interpretations, someone's perception of the facts. Anyone may render an opinion, but in argumentation, evidence from opinion usually refers to the use of the opinions of experts in the field you are arguing.

> Opinion evidence consists of the interpretive and evaluative statements made by an expert in a given field in regard to factual material pertinent to that field.

The opinions of authorities in a field provide the arguer and audience with access to their expertise. If we were discussing the constitutionality of imposing term limits on the members of the Senate and House of Representatives, who better to turn to than the men who wrote the document, whom Thomas Mann of the Brookings Institution paraphrased in his testimony.

> The Framers explicitly rejected mandatory rotation. They debated it, they thought a lot about it. The anti-Federalists supported it, and they lost. Madison, Hamilton, and the Federalists wanted not to deny ambition, but to

channel it; not to take Congress out of the political system, but to put it very much into it; not to have a temple for government, but a forum. (Term Limits for Members of the U.S. Senate and House of Representatives, 1994, pp. 9–10)

If we are discussing the economy, we might turn to nationally known and respected economists like Milton Friedman and Paul Samuelson for their opinions. Not all experts, however, are nationally recognized. To find an expert, we seek persons with credentials in the field we are discussing.

Because opinions perform the function of evaluating and interpreting factual information, they often appear to be claim statements. The only real difference between a claim you might make in constructing an argument and the opinion of an expert is that the expertise of the source of the opinion is a kind of proof in and of itself. The qualifications of the source give the opinion probative value. Representative Norman Mineta quoted such an expert witness to support a claim that the internment of Americans of Japanese ancestry during World War II was motivated by racism and fear rather than military necessity.

> Gen. John L. DeWitt, head of the Western Defense Command and a key figure in the internment, actually managed, in speaking of the fact that no disloyal acts had been committed by Americans of Japanese ancestry, to say, "The very fact that no sabotage has taken place to date is a disturbing and confirming indication that such action will be taken." (Japanese-American and Aleutian Wartime Relocation, 1984, p. 75)

To the extent that we are impressed by the general's historical role in the events under discussion, his statement supports Representative Mineta's claim of racism and fear without further verification.

When the qualifications of the source are omitted, the probative value of the opinion may rest solely on their similarity to those of the listener or reader.

> The problem I stress is not to make Congress closer to the people or to make it more responsive. It is, if anything, too close and oversubmissive at the moment. Rather, it is to open up what Professor Mansfield of Harvard calls a constitutional distance between the people and their representatives so the representatives may indeed deliberate, thinking—as the slogan goes—not of the next election but of the next generation. (Term Limits for Members of the U.S. Senate and House of Representatives, 1994, p. 209)

We have no idea what Mansfield is a professor of, only where he teaches. In the absence of credentials, opinion is accepted as proof only by a listener or reader whose opinions are not contrary to it. In essence, the opinion of an uncredentialed source functions as proof only when it is viewed as a premise by the audience.

This raises an interesting problem. In magazines, such as *Time*, or national newspapers, such as the *Washington Post*, the credentials of the author are not provided. In some instances, the author is not even identified. Can you use such material as if it were an expert's opinion? Yes. In this instance, nationally recognized news sources such as those mentioned are acknowledged as reputable sources of information. The publication's own reputation becomes the credential backing the opinion. However, news sources are not infallible. It is usually wise to check the opinions they contain against those of acknowledged experts when you discover what you think might be worthwhile opinion evidence.

Often a news magazine or newspaper article will serve as a secondary source for the authoritative opinion of an expert, as in the following example:

> In *The Uses of Enchantment*, [Bruno] Bettelheim shows how irrelevant to the real needs of children the pro-social enterprise turns out to be. "Since the child at every moment of his life is exposed to the society in which he lives, he will certainly learn to cope with its conditions, provided his inner resources permit him to do so." In concentrating on mere outward behavior (cooperating, helping others), proponents of the pro-social neglect the child himself—the fearful, struggling child "with his immense anxieties about what will happen to him and his aspirations." The difficulties a child faces seem to him so great, his fears so immense, his sense of failure so complete, says Bettelheim, that without encouragement of the most powerful kind he is in constant danger of falling prey to despair, "of completely withdrawing into himself, away from the world." What children urgently need from children's stories are not lessons in cooperative living but the life-saving "assurance that one can succeed"—that monsters can be slain, injustice remedied, and all obstacles overcome on the hard road to adulthood. (Karp, 1984, p. 43)

In this instance, the credibility of the opinion derives as much, if not more, from the source Mr. Karp cited as it does from his own qualifications. While it would be best to read Bettelheim and quote him firsthand, the use of secondary-source material is acceptable.

In using opinion evidence as proof, remember that it does not provide facts but interprets or explains them. Expert or authoritative sources provide interpretations or judgments about facts and are always one step removed from the objects, statistics, and events that comprise their factual basis. Expert opinion is accepted by the listener or reader only when the expert is believed qualified to offer the interpretation or make the judgment or when the expert states what the listener or reader already suspects or believes.

Summary of Types of Evidence
1. *Examples and illustrations* describe or report events or phenomena that exist. Examples are brief statements. Illustrations are more detailed accounts.
2. *Statistics* represent information about people, events, and phenomena numerically; they may be expressed in raw numbers or summarized in percentages or averages.
3. *Scientific evidence* reports the results of field and laboratory experiments on the effect of one variable on another.
4. *Artifacts* are actual exhibits of such things as objects, audiotapes and videotapes, photographs, and diagrams.
5. *Premises* are factual claims that exist as evidence on the basis of their being accepted as reflections of human belief or experience.
6. *Opinions* are interpretive and evaluative statements made by an expert in a field regarding factual information relevant to that field.

Tests of Evidence

In addition to recognizing the types of evidence, you must be able to evaluate their reliability. There are specific tests that can be applied to each type of evidence and general tests of evidence, both of which you should be familiar with. Tests of evidence give us the minimum requirements our proof must meet before it will be accepted as credible by our listeners and readers.

Tests of Facts

In testing evidence of fact, we are concerned with the accuracy and reliability of the observations being reported. In each category—example and illustration, statistics, scientific evidence, artifacts, and premises—certain tests can be performed to determine their factual accuracy and reliability.

Tests of examples and illustrations concern the observations made. These tests ask questions about the accuracy and reliability of the report and the reporter.

Source Qualifications. Was the observer capable of making the observation in terms of the necessary physical and mental ability? A blind witness, for example, may have difficulty describing an automobile accident but may be able to describe minute variation in the sound of an automobile engine. Did the observer have the training and experience necessary to make the observation? Someone who has never driven, for instance, will have difficulty in describing the differences in handling between a front-wheel drive and a rear-wheel drive car.

Data Accuracy. Is the information reported in a straightforward manner, or has it been manipulated to give it more or less importance? Some of the early reporting on the evidence found at the scene of the murder of Nicole Brown Simpson and Ronald Goldman stated that the police discovered a ski mask, which later turned out to be a hat. While this is an example of a lapse of accuracy that was discovered and corrected, the early reports made the artifact the police had found seem more sinister than it actually was. Because information may be interpreted by the source reporting it, you must take care in checking the reliability of the interpretation.

Originality of Observation. Is the source's information obtained from firsthand or secondhand data collection? It is possible to make observations on the basis of someone else's data, but more reliable reports of fact are obtained from firsthand observation. This does not mean that you should never rely on a source that reports secondary information; in some situations, collecting data firsthand is difficult.

Recency of Observation. In general, the more recent the information, the more reliable it will be. Some things remain relatively stable over time; however, many things do not. In using examples and illustrations taken from the reports of others, the recency with which the reporter made the observation can be very important. How easy is it for you to remember what happened last week or last month? The time that passes between when an observation is made and when it is reported serves as an additional filter through which a reporter's account must pass. Arguments dealing with economic matters are a classic example of the need for up-to-date information. You need only examine the economic history of the United States over the past decade to appreciate how much inflation, unemployment, or the Dow-Jones average may vary in a short period of time.

Attitude of the Observer. Ideally, the best sources of factual reports should have a neutral attitude toward what they have observed. Since each person sees the world through unique perceptual filters, prejudice, emotion, and ambition may color the reporting of facts. Thus, a final test of examples and illustrations concerns the reporter's attitude toward what is reported. Try to find unbiased reports framed in relatively neutral language.

Tests of statistical evidence reflect our concern with verifying the reliability of our evidence. While statistics furnish us with an economical form of proof on a variety of subjects, they are more prone to distortion and misrepresentation than are other forms of proof. Statistical proof, you will recall, has a certain psychological appeal. The use of numbers seems somehow credible, but you must take care that your statistics come from reliable sources.

Source Reliability. The first test of statistics is to identify the source of the information. Certain agencies and institutions are in the business of gathering statistics. The U.S. Bureau of the Census, for example, may be regarded as a highly credible source of demographic information about the United States. The Bureau of Labor Statistics might be regarded as a worthy source regarding information on employment. By comparison, the *TV Guide* is a less likely source of information on either population or employment although it is credible source of information about America's television-viewing habits because it reports data collected by the Annenberg Foundation.

Statistical Accuracy. In addition to knowing who collected the information, we also want to know how it was collected. Statistical information is frequently collected by sampling techniques. Did the counting procedure fairly select a representative sample? If a statistic claims to representatively sample the entire country, it should draw information from each state or region. Along with the process of data collection, accuracy is also influenced by the length of time during which data was collected. Conditions change, and it would be a gross misrepresentation to claim that inflation went down last year based on statistics for December that report a drop in inflation, if inflation increased during the months of January through November.

Comparable Units. Since statistics frequently inform through comparisons, it is important for the units being compared to be really comparable. Common sense tells us we cannot compare airplanes and microwave ovens because they don't have enough in common to render such a comparison meaningful. The same caution is necessary when dealing in statistical comparisons because statistics can appear to have been gathered on comparable entities. If you want to argue about technology in industrialized societies, for instance, before citing statistical information about the use of *robotics* in Canada, the United States, and Japan, be sure the term robotics has been defined in the same way by the agencies that compiled each nation's statistics.

Data Significance. Statistics are often expressed in terms of means, modes, medians, percentages, or standard deviations, and data may be created, concealed, or distorted by the method used to report it. Stating that the price of a loaf of bread increased from fifty cents to one dollar and fifty cents in the last decade may not seem significant, but reporting a 200 percent increase in the cost of a loaf of bread in the last ten years does. Statistical measures can provide useful information, but that same data can yield different conclusions depending on who interprets it.

Tests of scientific evidence are primarily concerned with the appropriateness of the methodology used in the experiment and the possible effect of the laws of probability on its outcome. For that reason, you should always understand the methodology of any scientific evidence you use and be able to explain it to your listeners or readers. Three tests of scientific evidence should always be performed.

Generalizability of Setting and Subjects. Laboratory experiments offer researchers greater control over the variables of interest than field experiments. Some, however, question the generalizability of laboratory findings to most settings. If a subject behaves aggressively while alone in unfamiliar surroundings after exposure to televised violence, are we safe in inferring that same person would behave aggressively after seeing the same show at home, possibly in the company of parents or more likely siblings or peers? In addition, some experiments are performed on nonhuman subjects, such as mice or monkeys, for ethical reasons. If a certain food additive produces disease in a laboratory animal, are we safe in inferring it will produce the same disease in humans? Applying these tests does not mean you should exclude all scientific evidence from laboratory studies or all research using nonhuman subjects. Persons conducting such research often address these questions in describing their methodology and discussing the limitations of their study. Examine the arguments they present before dismissing their findings.

Variable Control and Manipulation. Whether in a laboratory or a field setting, scientific researchers should take care to control as many of the variables that could confound their results as possible. If they have reason to believe that members of one sex may be naturally aggressive or more easily influenced by television, they should make sure that members of both sexes are assigned equally to each treatment condition of the independent variable. However, it is impossible to control all possible nuisance variables. Your own investigation of a topic will give you insight into whether the researchers attempted to control the important nuisance variables.

In addition, you should look at the independent variable and the way it is manipulated. Is it capable of influencing the dependent variable, and is it manipulated in a meaningful way? Is seeing a program on the laboratory's thirteen-inch monitor likely to produce the same effect as seeing that same show on a big screen TV with surround-sound at home? If researchers manipulate the treatment groups in a way that takes this into account and a difference is found, does the methodology allow the researchers to determine whether it was a consequence of image size, sound quality, the setting in which viewing took place, or the interaction of two or more of these variables? Fortunately, much scientific research is published in refereed journals in which the editorial board, composed of top professionals in that field, screens and rejects methodologically flawed submissions. Know your source's editorial policy, and apply some common sense.

Consistency with Other Findings. While external consistency is discussed under the general tests of evidence, it requires special attention in regard to scientific evidence. The conclusions of laboratory and field experiments rely on the application of statistical tests of significance to assess whether the independent variable may have had an impact on the dependent variable. When a researcher states that the effect of X on Y was significant at the .05 level, she or he is saying that there are less than 5 chances in 100 that a phenomena of the magnitude observed could have occurred by chance or coincidence. The findings are tentative and conditional on others repeating the experiment and getting similar results.

The ability to replicate is at the heart of the scientific method, and the need to do so is why researchers publish their methodology along with their results. Even if the findings were true, probability theory suggests that if we replicated a study 100 times, randomly selecting a new set of subjects from the available population each time, our statistical test of the effect of X on Y might yield insignificant results on three or four occasions. If the conclusion of a piece of scientific evidence is inconsistent with other findings, you must be able to account for the difference. Was a different methodology used, or have relevant changes in the population from which samples were drawn taken place during the time between when the studies were performed? If you are unable to find a reason for inconsistent findings, be extremely skeptical of them.

Tests of artifacts are usually performed by having the readers or listeners employ their own senses. There are only two tests of artifacts to consider.

Artifact Genuineness. In an age when the ability to edit audiotapes and videotapes has benefited from astonishing technological advances, the authentication of artifacts used as evidence is a concern. Artifacts should be tested to determine their authenticity. Has a document or photograph been altered? The photographic and audiotape evidence supporting the claim that Elvis Presley is still alive offers a clear indication of the importance of document authentication.

Artifact Representativeness. Artifacts are often used in value arguments concerning the worth of a product. Since it is usually impossible to examine all examples of a given item, a representative sample is used. When confronted by a large luscious hamburger in a television commercial, you probably ask yourself why it is not typical of the burgers you get at the local fast-food emporium. What you are applying is a test of the representativeness of the video-burger as an artifact.

Tests of premises are difficult because our belief in a premise is based on the notion that things will continue in the future as they have in the past. Since premises are valid because of the assumption that nothing will occur to invalidate them, you test premises by looking for indications that circumstances, or our interpretation of them, will not change. The decision to intern thousands of Americans of Japanese ancestry after the bombing of Pearl Harbor was based on the publicly stated premise that they represented a threat to the nation's security. The performance of Army units composed of the sons of these internees in the European Theater of World War II invalidated that premise. This example indicates the danger inherent in making policy on the basis of premises.

Summary of Tests of Factual Evidence

Examples and Illustrations
1. Was the report of fact made by a qualified source?
2. Was the information reported accurately?
3. Did the reporter make the original observation or is the report based on secondhand information?
4. Was the report based on a recent observation of phenomena?
5. Was the reporter relatively unbiased toward the material being reported?

Statistics
1. Were the statistics collected by a reliable source?
2. Were the statistics accurately collected from a sufficiently large sample over a sufficiently long period of time.
3. Are comparable units used in statistical comparisons?
4. Is the method of reporting the data an unbiased and fair account of what was measured?

Scientific Evidence
1. Are the results of the study generalizable beyond the setting in which the research was conducted and the subjects who were involved?
2. Are nuisance variables controlled and independent variables manipulated in a meaningful way?
3. Are the conclusions consistent with those of other studies conducted at roughly the same time using similar methodologies?

Artifacts
1. Is the artifact genuine or has it been altered in some way?

2. If the artifact is supposed to represent a certain class of items, is it typical of that class of items?

Premises
1. Is there reason to believe that circumstances, or our understanding of them, have not changed in such a way as to invalidate the premise?

Tests of Opinion Evidence

Unlike facts, opinions are not directly verifiable. However, that does not mean that we cannot test opinion evidence. Opinion evidence can seldom be judged true or false in the same sense as factual evidence. Since an opinion is someone's belief about facts, it is subject to contradiction by someone else's opinion of those facts. Keep in mind that some of the best minds of the sixteenth century believed lead could be turned into gold if only the right chemical formula could be discovered.

Source Expertise. In using opinion evidence, we are concerned with what the law refers to as the expert witness. While our opinions might all be of equal worth on some subjects, it is impossible for each of us to have the degree of experience necessary to make sound judgments about all the phenomena we encounter. If you want to know which automobile is most roadworthy, the opinion of a test driver for an independent consumer-testing agency might be more valuable than the opinion of your mother, who drives a twenty-year-old Ford. In testing the expertise of the source, we are concerned with the credentials that give this person the right to pass judgment on something. Investigate the training, background, and experience of the individual in his or her field of expertise. To the extent that your audience will accept those credentials, his or her opinion will have impact.

Source Bias. As a general rule, seek the most unbiased source of opinion evidence. Although it is virtually impossible for experts to remain totally unbiased about their fields, the more objectively the opinion is stated, the more credible it will be. In instances where bias cannot be avoided, it should be forthrightly acknowledged, so the listener or reader is aware of it.

Factual Basis of the Opinion. As in the case of statistical information, the credibility of opinion evidence may be diminished if the opinion is based on second-hand information. Although many opinions on historical occurrences must, of necessity, be rendered long after the fact, the most credible judgments are those made by an expert observer on the scene at the time something is happening.

Summary of Tests of Opinion Evidence
1. Is the source a qualified expert in the field by training, background, or experience?
2. Is the source relatively unbiased?
3. Is there a reliable factual basis for the opinion?

General Tests of Evidence

The *reliability of evidence* as a source of support for your claims is your first general concern in selecting the evidence to include in an argument. The audience determines the reliability of evidence based on its accuracy and recency.

Accuracy. In considering tests of factual information, we stressed that the accurate representation of what was observed was a key factor in choosing evidence. In particular, reports of statistical information and observations of events should represent them as closely as possible. If evidence is to be believed as reliable, it must be as credible as possible. Evidence of both fact and opinion must be tested for accuracy.

When quoting directly, do not take facts, statistics, or opinion statements out of context. Make sure you honestly portray what the source had to say. When paraphrasing, make honest paraphrases. Sometimes, it is neither practical nor desirable to present a source's entire statement verbatim in your argument. When paraphrasing from books, speeches, or articles, do so in a manner that accurately reflects the author's intent or frame of reference. When quoting or paraphrasing, accurately interpret your source; do not distort the information.

Recency. Much argumentation, and claim making of all kinds, is concerned with current events. Using recent sources of information adds potency to your arguments. This does not mean you should not research the history of your topic carefully. Knowing what has happened in the past helps us hypothesize about what will happen in the future. However, relying on out-of-date sources may cause you to miss recent developments.

The *quality of evidence* is also important. There is a temptation to confuse having a large quantity of evidence with having good evidence. Effective argumentation results more from having high-quality evidence than from having great quantities of evidence. Quality results from choosing evidence that best helps the audience understand how you arrived at the conclusions implied by your claim. Quality evidence has the properties of being sufficient, representative, relevant, and clear.

Sufficiency. Ideally, the best argumentation occurs when we know all of the facts and opinions of experts about our topic. But having all the evidence is seldom possible, particularly in our information-intensive society. Nevertheless, it is the arguer's responsibility to research the topic sufficiently and to provide the support needed to make it possible for the audience to accept her claims.

Representativeness. Is the evidence you have selected to support your claims representative of all available evidence? Just as we are concerned that statistical samples should accurately represent the populations from which they were drawn, the evidence of both the fact and opinion you use should be representative of the available evidence on the subject.

Relevance. Is your evidence related to the claim it is supposed to support? In some cases, the relationship between grounds and claim in an argument is not always apparent. The reasoning process of the warrant can help make it more apparent; the use of additional evidence in backing the warrant may be necessary. The important thing to remember is evidence that seems to have little bearing on the claim will be of little use in supporting that claim.

Clarity. Will your audience readily understand your evidence? The importance of defining terms in such a way that they render a subject more understandable to the audience also pertains to the selection of evidence. Facts and opinions that are too technical or in some way beyond an audience's level of understanding may be unsuitable. Vague or equivocal evidence will not contribute to the audience's understanding of the conclusions that you are asking them to accept.

The *consistency of evidence* with itself, with other evidence on the same subject, or with human understanding contributes to grounding your claim making. Evidence that seems atypical, for whatever reason, is likely to cause the audience to disbelieve the claim it supports. Consistency is assessed on two levels, internal and external.

Internal Consistency. Does your evidence contradict itself? Evidence that comes from a single source should not state contradictory positions. Except in instances where a simple explanation can be provided, a piece of information that reports both an increase and a decrease, or a positive and a negative result, may pose serious problems for the arguer who attempts to use it.

External Consistency. Is your evidence consistent with other sources of information on the subject? Although new discoveries are being made constantly and two equally respected authorities in a field may interpret the same event very differently, we generally expect any piece of evidence to be consistent with others on the same subject. There is a natural tendency for a reader or listener to reject evidence that does not seem to fit. A part of our need for external consistency is our expectation that the evidence used in argumentation will conform with what we already know in general. For example, because we expect the president of the United States to support American values and traditions, we might be skeptical when we hear the president quoted as condemning some intrinsic American value.

Audience acceptability is the last general test your evidence should meet. Will your listener or reader accept the evidence? There is little utility in having the best evidence if the audience will not accept it. This does not mean you should be dishonest or distort evidence in such a way that the audience will be forced to agree. It does mean that audience values, predispositions, knowledge of the subject, and technical expertise must be taken into account as you select the evidence to use.

Arguers have the responsibility to address the rationality of their listeners or readers. If you fail to consider the requirements and tests of your evidence, your ability to affect an audience through the process of argumentation may be seriously impaired.

Summary of General Tests of Evidence

1. Is the evidence accurate in its report of fact or statement of opinion?
2. Is the evidence a recent report of fact or opinion?
3. Is sufficient evidence presented to support the claim effectively?
4. Is the evidence representative of the available evidence on the subject?
5. Is the evidence relevant to the claim being made?
6. Is the evidence clearly presented?
7. Is the evidence internally consistent?
8. Is the evidence consistent with other available evidence on the subject?
9. Is the evidence adapted to the requirements of the particular audience?

The Discovery of Evidence

Now that you know the kinds of evidence you can use in supporting a claim and how to determine the viability of evidence as a means of influencing belief or behavior, your next step is to find and record evidence. Your college library will probably be your best available source for locating facts and opinions. Get to know its organizational system and make the acquaintance of the reference librarian. A working knowledge of how your library is organized and the assistance the reference staff can give you will save time and frustration in your search for proof.

The sources of information described in this section are available in most college libraries. The resources of the reference section can be discovered through guides that provide bibliographies of reference materials. *American Reference Books Annual* has been published yearly since 1970. It provides detailed explanations of such reference resources as dictionaries, general encyclopedias, specialty encyclopedias, foreign reference materials, selected government publications, abstracts, indexes, and some journals. It covers new editions of older references and annually describes references published in serial form. A second guide is *Introduction to Reference Work* by William A. Katz. It discusses the types of material common to the reference section of a library. If neither of these sources is available, consult the card catalog, which is now computerized in most libraries, under the subject heading *reference bibliography*.

Books

Books, nonfiction unless you are arguing about literature, are valuable sources of evidence for argumentation. Your library's electronic card catalog lists all books available in its collection. Unless you are looking for the work of a specific author or know the title you wish to locate, begin your search using the subject index. Do not be discouraged if you find nothing listed under the subject you choose. Those responsible for creating the subject headings may not have given your subject the heading you expect. You need to be a sleuth. Think of a variation of, or synonyms for, your heading. If necessary, ask the reference librarian for assistance.

Books are useful because they generally provide a more comprehensive treatment of a subject than a periodical or newspaper has space for. Books provide historical background on a topic, but they have certain limitations as sources of information. First, they have the disadvantage of quickly becoming outdated sources of fact and opinion. The process of researching, writing, revising, and publishing a single volume may span several years. In that time, the factual basis of the book may become dated, or superseded by new discoveries. Second, your library may have only a limited number of books on your topic, and you may be unable to find the quantity of information you had hoped. You can overcome this problem by using the resources of other libraries through Interlibrary Loan if your college library is part of such a system.

If you require an abundance of up-to-the-minute information, you must seek it from other sources.

Periodicals

Periodicals offer access to current fact and opinion and may offer it in quantity. Because they are so numerous and varied, it is impossible to generalize about which periodicals will be of most value to you. Consulting one of several excellent reference guides to periodicals will help you find the ones most pertinent to your topic. A good place to begin is *The Reader's Guide to Periodical Literature*, which indexes what are commonly termed popular periodicals—*Time*, *Newsweek*, and *U.S. News and World Reports*, for example. It indexes by subject heading; the techniques you used in mastering the electronic card catalog can be applied to *The Reader's Guide*.

The Reader's Guide has one important limitation, however. It does not reference many scholarly journals or special-interest publications. If, for example, you are arguing about the unionization of public school teachers, finding out what is in *Newsweek* on this subject may be less valuable than finding out what is available in *The Journal of Collective Negotiation in the Public Sector*. Since the credibility of material from the latter is greater, you will need to examine specialty indexes. Most college libraries have the following indexes to scholarly or special-interest periodicals:

> *Agricultural Index*
> *Applied Science and Technology Index*
> *Business Periodical Index*
> *Education Index*
> *Human Resources Abstracts*
> *Index to Legal Periodicals*
> *International Index*
> *Psychological Abstracts*
> *Social Science Index*
> *Sociological Abstracts*

Once again, indexing is by subject, and many of these indexes are available on CD-ROM and can be searched electronically.

Newspapers

Not all college libraries offer current and back issues of a wide variety of newspapers, but your library will certainly have one or more major newspapers from your state and some national newspapers such as the *New York Times*. The latter is an excellent source of material, not only because of its reputation but also because it is indexed. This newspaper prints the text of major speeches, Supreme Court decisions, and documents such as the Pentagon papers. This is not to say that there aren't a number of other excellent newspapers, but they are not indexed. Beginning in 1990, both the *New York Times* and the *Washington Post* have been indexed, and their full text is available on CD-ROM.

In addition, a service known as NewsBank collects and reprints articles from newspapers of more than 450 U.S. cities. Although not everything in a particular edition of a paper is included, material on a given topic, the controversy surrounding "Beavis and Butt-head" for example, is available. NewsBank organizes by topic, so if your topic coincides with a NewsBank category, relatively recent information from a variety of papers across the country will be available to you. Since the index is available on CD-ROM, it can be searched electronically.

A final note about newspapers in general and NewsBank in particular: Since most college libraries do not have unlimited space, newspapers are typically stored on microfilm or microfiche. Become familiar with how the equipment for reading and photocopying film and fiche works. While the use of CD-ROM technology is broadening to include additional titles, for example, the full text of the the *Des Moines Register* is now available on CD-ROM beginning in 1992, older issues are only accessible through older technology.

Government Documents

If you are interested in nutrition, how to prepare an income tax return, or treaty restrictions on foreign trade, the federal government has probably published one or more documents on the subject. Texts of the hearings of major and minor congressional committees, information bulletins, treaties and agreements, all proceedings of legislative bodies, court decisions, and the like are contained in government documents, indexed in the *Monthly Catalog of United States Government Publications*. This is not the only available index to these documents, nor is it the easiest to use.

As we have already indicated, more and more indexes are being computerized, and many college libraries have not only computerized their card catalogs but have also made various indexes available on CD-ROM. It will take a little time to learn, but the rewards are well worth the effort. We knew that hearings had been held in 1985 regarding rock music. Searching the Government Printing Office (GPO) data base on CD-ROM for "rock" turned up hundreds of documents that might have interested a geologist; "music" also gave us hundreds of possibilities. Asking for "lyrics" produced the following report (Figure 6-1).

This data base, like most others, allows the use of logical operators. AND, OR, and NOT, are logical operators. You can use them to combine and exclude terms from the search you request the computer to perform. Using AND tells the computer to only report on those documents in which the terms to both the left and right of the operator appear. For example, had we asked for "music" AND "lyrics" in the title of the document, we would have gotten the exact document we were looking for on the first try. A search using *or* will report all documents in which either term appeared. Asking for "music" OR "rock" would have gotten us further from, not closer to, the document we were looking for. A search using NOT will report all documents that contain the term to the left of the operator that do not contain the term to the right. Had we asked for "lyrics" NOT "music," we would have gotten a report that included the second document in Figure 6-1 but not the first. Our search would have missed the mark completely. Even with false starts, our search took about as long as it has taken you to read about it.

FIGURE 6-1   SilverPlatter 1.6   GPO on SilverPlatter (7/76–12/89)

1 of 2

AN: 86013575
SU: Y 4.C 73/7:S.hrg.99-529
SU: Y4C737Shrg99529
CA: United States. Congress. Senate. Committee on Commerce, Science, and Transportation.
TI: Record labeling : hearing before the Committee on Commerce, Science, and Transportation, United States Senate, Ninety-ninth Congress, first session, on contents of music and the **lyrics** of records, September 19, 1985.
SO: Washington : U.S. G.P.O., 1985 [i.e. 1986].
SE: United States. Congress. Senate. S. hrg. ; 99-529.
IT: 1041-A, 1041-B (microfiche)

2 of 2

AN: 77016496
SU: LC 3.4/2:67/5
SU: LC342675
CA: United States. Copyright Office.
TI: Poems and song **lyrics.**
SO: Washington : Library of Congress, Copyright Office, 1977.
SE: Circular ; 67.
IT: 802-A

Source: GPO on SilverPlatter (7/76–12/89). New Lower Falls, MA: SilverPlatter Information, 1990.

The *Congressional Record* is a particularly good source for topics on public policy. It is issued daily while Congress is in session and provides complete transcripts of congressional debates and presidential messages. It also includes an appendix containing a variety of materials—newspaper articles, resolutions, excerpted speeches, and anything else that might pertain to business before Congress.

Almanacs, Fact Books, and Other Printed Resources

A variety of sources that compile statistics and other factual information is available in the reference section of your college library. What distinguishes them is that they compile information in condensed form and are organized for quick access. *The Statistical Abstract of the United States* and *The World Almanac* provide statistical information on such subjects as population, demographic characteristics and change, transportation, agriculture, trade, mining, national and international banking, energy use, and more. They are updated annually. *Facts on File* provides a weekly summary of news from major U.S. newspapers and magazines.

Your library probably contains several sources of biographical information that can be used to discover the credentials of authorities and experts. A particularly good source is *Current Biography Yearbook*. Now in its seventh decade of publication, it provides biographical articles about living leaders in all fields, worldwide. These articles are updated yearly.

While the text of important speeches, court cases, or announcements by public officials can be found in a variety of sources, *Historical Documents of (Year)* collects and publishes these important U.S. documents annually. First published in 1972, it contains texts of public affairs documents, court decisions, government reports, special studies, speeches, and statements by public officials on domestic and foreign policy. If you wanted the text of the speech in which Reagan's "Star Wars" defense proposal was first presented, you could find it in *Historical Documents of 1983*, Ronald Reagan's March 23, 1983 televised address, "Defense in Space."

A resource that treats topics in much the same way as arguers do, developing pro and con positions on a topic, is the *Reference Shelf.* Each volume is devoted to a single topic on a subject of public interest. This source contains reprints of articles, excerpts from books, and opinions of experts. It suffers the same limitations as all other books in terms of becoming dated, but it does provide a variety of sources of information. The series, which began in 1922, can be an excellent source of historical background information on how Americans have perceived many issues.

The foregoing is by no means a complete list of available reference sources, just some suggestions to get you started. To discover what else is available, browse through the reference section of your library, consult the librarian assigned to that section, or experiment with the various computerized services available in your library. The 1990 Census data is available on CD-ROM, as is the *Oxford English Dictionary*, and a lot of other useful information. As you become more experienced, you will find the process easier. We want to reemphasize that a good working knowledge of your library is the first step in the discovery of evidence.

The Internet

We are not going to teach you how to surf the Internet although we do suggest some sources at the end of the chapter that will help if you are not already familiar with this resource. If your only exposure to the Internet is what you have read in popular periodicals, you may be surprised to learn there is more available to you than dirty pictures and sex talk. Internet sources can be very useful in proving your arguments.

Worldwide, the Internet links computers at universities, businesses, and government agencies to each other. Each site makes information available for remote access. As a result, we can check the telephone number of a colleague at a Canadian University, the card catalog of the library of a major research university for a source not available in our library, or the schedule of an upcoming professional conference for scholarly papers on a given topic. A number of newsletters and scholarly journals are available in electronic form, as are books and any other form of data that someone has taken the time to create or recreate in digital form. Practically every interest has a news group, or public discussion, devoted to it, from the love of Formula 1 racing (rec.autos.sport.f1) to the dislike of a certain purple creature (alt.barney.dinosaur.die.die.die). Even the White House is hooked into the Internet, and you can get everything from President Clinton's itinerary to a picture of Socks the cat (president@whitehouse.gov).

The Internet gives you access to a worldwide virtual library with many of the same problems of your university library. The first problem is that, just like your library, 99.9 percent of what is available on Internet may not help you prove an argument. Finding what you need in the library is facilitated by learning how to use the card catalog, electronic or otherwise. Finding something on the Internet requires learning to use programs like Gopher and Mosaic, card catalog surrogates for information retrieval.

The second problem is that, just like your library, once you retrieve some information, you have to decide whether you can use it. The same tests of evidence apply, but they may be more important since the Internet empowers voices that traditional media might not. Does an electronic journal impose the same standards of peer review as its print counterpart, or is it a forum to which anyone can post research? Some news groups are moderated, which means someone or some group screens and approves material before it becomes publicly available. Most are unmoderated, and anyone with Internet access and an opinion can post it.

While watching a televised auto race from Italy, we noticed that failure to install a safety device contributed to a driver's fatal injury. We posted our observation on the Internet. About a dozen people posted messages questioning our eyesight. A single post confirmed our suspicion. Our knowledge of the field allowed us to recognize this person as the author of several books on racing. Had we not known this, we might have relied on the weight of public opinion instead. While this illustrates one of the potential problems of using information retrieved from the Internet in grounding arguments, it also demonstrates another use. By monitoring what is being said about a particular topic, you can enhance your analysis of your proposition, particularly if that proposition is drawn from a field in which presumption is determined by natural rather than artificial means.

Recording Evidence

You should know how to record the material you research to render it most useful when the time comes to use it in constructing arguments. It is one thing to discover information in the library; it is quite another to organize that information so that it will be readily accessible. You may function quite efficiently with a notebook full of bits of information or a file folder crammed with photocopied pages. Most of us are not that efficient. What follows is a workable system of note taking based on the premise that an organized system will make you a better arguer. Failure to have a good system for recording and organizing material is one of the most common problems experienced by beginning and seasoned arguers alike.

The first step in efficient research is to have a clear idea of the evidence needed. Your analysis of the topic should help you get off on the right track. In the initial stages of working with a topic, attempt to discover what information is available by skimming summaries, prefaces, and opening paragraphs. Read for ideas as much as for examples, statistics, and opinion statements. Once you have surveyed the available information, look for specific things—a statistic grounding a relationship you want to claim, the opinion of an authority to back a warrant. Later you can become more concerned about the quality of proof, but initially worry as much about quantity. The key concept to keep in mind is that you can only be efficient in looking for proof if you have a clear idea of what arguments you are trying to prove. Reading for ideas initially gives you a feeling for what can be proven with the resources available to you and keeps you from wasting time later looking for proof that may not exist.

Step two in the research process involves keeping an annotated bibliography and is performed in conjunction with step one. As you consider each source, record the title, author, publisher, date, and page numbers (where pertinent) on an index card; we recommend the four- by six-inch size. It is also a good idea to include the call numbers or reference numbers of all library materials so you can quickly find them again. In a few sentences, jot down the viewpoint of the author, a summary of what the source includes, and your personal evaluation of it. The purpose of this bibliography card is to give you a general idea of what a source contains. Make one card per source and have a system for keeping them in order, either alphabetically by author, chronologically by date, or conceptually by topic.

The third step in the research process involves excerpting specific facts and opinions in an organized system that will allow you to find what you need when you are ready to construct your arguments. The mechanics of the system need not be complex. Again, we recommend the use of index cards for recording each separate fact and opinion statement. Include the author, the author's qualifications, title, publication or publisher, date, and page number on the top of each card; then carefully record the fact or opinion. Accuracy is imperative. Omitting a word, punctuation mark, or phrase can seriously alter the meaning of the fact or opinion. Be especially careful in recording statistical information. In a moment of stress 3.6 million is less likely to be misread than 3,600,000. Also be sure the source stated million and not billion. It is easy to become confused when working with statistical information.

Once you have recorded information on a number of cards, arrange the cards in a fashion that will make it easy to find a particular piece of proof later on. If you require a particular opinion to back a warrant, you do not want to shuffle through sixty index cards to find it and then reshuffle through the same sixty cards to find the material to ground the next argument. An organizational system will help you avoid the paper chase.

The fourth step in the research process involves developing a topical heading system to organize your index cards. The system involves placing headings on each card that are brief, simple, and derived from the argument supported. The heading provides a two- or three-word summary of the information the card contains. Suppose you are arguing about drunk drivers. Some appropriate topical headings might include:

State laws—California
State laws—Nebraska
Deaths per year
Injuries per year
Proposed solution—ignition interlock
Proposed solution—random stop

These headings, commonly referred to as slugs, can help you organize large quantities of material into related categories and distinguish at a glance the cards pertaining to one category from all other cards. Slugs should serve your purposes and make sense to you. They reflect your impression of the contents of a particular card. Since you now have a lot of writing on a small card, confusion may be reduced somewhat if you record slugs in a different color of ink.

As a student of argumentation you may be required to both advocate and oppose the same proposition and you may end up with evidence on both sides of the proposition. If you are not careful, the evidence you find that is suitable to one side of the proposition may become mixed up with evidence suitable to the other side. Using different colors of index cards for advocacy and opposition can avoid this situation. If you cannot find different colors, using cards of different sizes will serve the same purpose. If your argumentation course involves working with more than one topic area, the color or size trick can be used to keep evidence for one proposition separate from evidence for another.

Although this may seem needlessly complicated, we assure you it is important. Because evidence is vital in establishing claims, it is at the nexus of effective argumentation. The more systematic your approach to the discovery and recording of materials of fact and opinion and the creation of a means to facilitate its retrieval, the better you will be in building arguments.

Knowing the types of evidence used in building arguments, the tests it must meet, and the means of finding and recording information enables you to begin preparing arguments. The next chapter discusses how to turn your ideas into arguments by considering the relationship of grounds, claim, and warrant in the reasoning process.

Learning Activities

1. Find two samples of each of the following types of factual evidence: example, illustration, and statistic. Explain how each of your samples meets the tests for its type of factual evidence.
2. Choose a topic with which you are familiar. Find three sources that provide authoritative opinion evidence on this topic. Explain why each source is credible in terms of the tests of opinion evidence.
3. Find five examples of evidence based on premises. Consider each premise in terms of how it came to be held as true without needing further proof. Is there any reason to believe these premises might become invalid?
4. Review the definitions of fact and opinion in this chapter. Decide which of the following statements are facts and which are opinions.
   A. The Supreme Court has decided that legal counsel will be provided for those who cannot afford to pay for it.
   B. Humans are primates descended from earlier forms of primates.
   C. College tuition costs have stabilized.
   D. The Pacific Rim will dominate world trade in the twenty-first century.
   E. Many professional educators believe that studying a foreign language will help students become more proficient in the structure and grammar of the English language.
   F. Railroads played an important part in the North's ability to win battles during the Civil War.
   G. Simply by visiting the Smithsonian, all may enjoy our nation's treasures.
   H. Natural-habitat zoos are more interesting than traditional caged-exhibit zoos.
5. Begin researching the topic area you have selected for future assignments concerning propositions of fact, value, and policy. Your evidence file should meet the following criteria:
   A. All sources of information should be identified on bibliography cards.
   B. Each item of evidence should be classified by type.

C. Each item of evidence should be evaluated for its credibility—does it meet the tests of evidence?

D. Each piece of evidence should be slugged according to the topic you have selected.

Suggested Supplementary Readings

Broudy, H. S. (1981). *Truth and Credibility: The Citizen's Dilemma.* New York: Longman.

Harry Broudy addresses the question: When two equally respected experts disagree, how does the ordinary citizen know which one to believe? Broudy examines the variety of evidence that experts offer to ground arguments about the facts, values, and policies that affect all Americans. He explains how to judge whether someone is an expert, why experts disagree, and what role our personal sources of belief play in how we judge the expertise of others.

Kazoleas, D. C. (1993, Winter). A Comparison of the Persuasive Effectiveness of Qualitative Versus Quantitative Evidence: A Test of Explanatory Hypothesis. *Communication Quarterly,* 41, 40–50.

This article is an example of argument from fact, testing a hypothesis, and a formal study of the persuasiveness of evidence. The research compares audience responses to statistics (quantitative) and narrative (qualitative) used in argumentation. Kazoleas found that audiences tend to recall, and consequently may be more influenced by, the qualitative narratives found in examples, especially illustrations.

Kimble, G. A. (1978). *How to Use (and Misuse) Statistics.* Englewood Cliffs, NJ: Prentice-Hall.

Statistical and scientific evidence is used extensively in argumentation. This book provides useful insight into the scientific method and a thorough discussion of statistics, particularly the kinds used for significance testing in laboratory and field experiments. Its aim is the development of statistical literacy rather than computational ability. We recommend it to students who foresee a specific need to develop greater understanding of this form of analytical thinking or who are particularly interested in the use of statistical and scientific evidence.

Levine, J. R., & Baroudi, C. (1993). *The Internet for Dummies.* San Mateo, CA: IDG Books Worldwide.

For those who can't make sense out of the manual that came with their computer software and are intimidated by the other after-market books, the . . . *for Dummies* series has been their salvation. This book covers the basics. It explains what the Internet is, how to use it to send electronic mail, how to log onto and retrieve files from another computer when you already know where something you want is, and how to find it and retrieve it if you do not.

Levine, J. R., & Young, M. L. (1994). *More Internet for Dummies.* San Mateo, CA: IDG Books Worldwide.

This volume picks up where the previous year's edition left off. It provides a clear explanation of how to gain access to the Internet through commercial services like America Online and how to install and use graphically oriented

Windows software like Mosaic and Trumpet to search for and retrieve information. There is also a nice discussion of how to access census data, weather information, and stock prices, along with what the authors describe as fun and silly stuff, such as how to access the Juggling Information Service.

J. C. Reinard. (1988). The Empirical Study of the Persuasive Effects of Evidence: The Status after Fifty Years of Research. *Human Communication Research*, 15, 3–59.
As the title suggests, students of human communication have long wanted to know what makes evidence effective or ineffective in persuading an audience to change a belief or behavior. Reinard summarizes the research findings of the studies done in the field of communication in the last five decades. This is an excellent synopsis because Reinard compiles research findings into tabular form that is easy to understand and easy to use in evaluating the persuasive potential of different kinds of factual evidence.

Tolhurst, W. A., Pike, M. A., & Blanton, K. A. (1994). *Using the Internet, Special Edition*. Indianapolis: Que Corporation.
For the techno-literate, this almost 1,200-page book has it all, including a piece of software that provides Internet access through a commercial service along with an index of more than 3,000 news groups and mailing lists. Beginning with the history of the Internet, the reader is introduced to its structure and resources, as well as legal issues from copyright to privacy that surround its use. The chapter concerning the law is more than 100 pages long while the chapter on using various programs to find and retrieve information is less than 35, not that it takes more than that to explain Gopher searches. You can learn a great deal about the Internet and its resources from this book, but it may be more than you want to know.

Wright, E. T. (1990). *Evidence: How and When to Use the Rules to Win Cases*. Englewood Cliffs, NJ: Prentice-Hall.
Many of our tests of evidence are derived from those used in the legal field. Edward Wright explains for laypersons the law's rules of evidence. Especially useful for students of argumentation are his discussions of relevancy, opinion testimony by the nonexpert witness, and the bases of opinion testimony by the expert witness.

Chapter Seven

How Do I Reason with My Audience?

A rgumentation is a process of drawing inferences. As you discover information on a topic, you make guesses about how it fits together and how it might
support or fail to support your own ideas about the topic. You become concerned
with creating viable arguments. But what makes an argument viable? In part, an
argument is viable because the evidence used to ground the claim has been tested
for validity, but there is more to the viability of an argument than the validity of
the evidence that supports it. The relationship between evidence and the claim it
supports is established through reasoning. In studying the reasoning process, you
are concerned with the logic of the inference drawn when you ask your listeners
or readers to agree that the evidence you provide warrants accepting your claim.
In Chapter 5 we indicated that this inferential relationship is established by the
warrant, which can be tested for validity. When it passes the test, we say that the
argument is viable.

The reasoning process is based on recognizing common patterns of experience. Consider a not uncommon experience of dormitory life: You encounter
Dennis and Paul. Dennis has an empty bucket and Paul is dripping wet. What
goes on in your mind? Since you were not on the scene to observe firsthand how
Paul got wet, you probably inferred the cause of Paul's wetness. Experience suggests that the claim, "Dennis dumped a bucket of water on Paul," is viable. How
reliably do the grounds, Paul's wetness and Dennis's empty bucket, support the
claim? How probable is it that your claim describes what really happened? You
do not know with any degree of certainty based on the grounds and claim alone,
but a warrant increases your certainty of the relationship between grounds and
claim. This chapter is about the reasoning process, the warrant step in the Toulmin model of argument.

In using the Toulmin model to create units of argument, remember that it
is an idealized blueprint for creating and testing arguments. It graphically depicts

111

the process of reasoning from evidence to a conclusion. The form an argument takes in the model may not represent the best way to articulate it in a speech or an essay. The actual wording of an argument for presentation depends on such factors as communicator style, audience needs, and how individual arguments combine to shape your speech or essay. As we guide you through understanding how the reasoning process works, we will provide examples that show how arguments are typically authored. Chapter 12 addresses the question of how oral arguments are best presented, as we discuss effective language use, delivery, and brief writing.

While you are learning about argumentation, we strongly suggest that you employ all four elements—grounds, warrant, backing, and claim—in creating your arguments. As you develop skill, you may find it unnecessary to articulate all of them all of the time, you will elect to use all of them only when your audience is likely to require them or want them supplied.

Reasoning is the inferential leap from grounds to claim made through the warrant. In earlier chapters, we noted that arguments may be developed in many different fields. Although the subjects about which inferences are drawn and the pattern of inference drawing that is favored may differ from field to field, the reasoning process does not change because it is based on patterns of common human experience. In this chapter we consider the forms of reasoning and the rules for testing the validity of warrants. In the chapter that follows, we will consider what happens when these forms and rules are not observed and fallacies in reasoning, appeal, and language use occur.

Six major forms of reasoning develop the relationship between grounds and claim: cause, sign, generalization, parallel case, analogy, and authority. In addition, a minor form of reasoning, dilemma, is useful in certain circumstances. As you study these forms of reasoning, it is important to remember that reasoning, the warrant, is used to infer that *because these grounds exist, believing this claim to be true or probable is justified.*

Argument from Cause

Argument from cause is one of the most prevalent forms of reasoning in argumentation. When things are happening to us and around us, it is human nature to infer connections between them.

> As a form of reasoning, **argument from cause** suggests a temporal connection between phenomena.

We claim that an event or condition of one kind is the cause of an event or condition of another. Consider these phenomena.

Phenomenon 1: A student does not read his assignments.
Phenomenon 2: The student receives an F on an exam.

It is useful to conceptualize events as existing on a time line (Ehninger, 1974). Phenomena along it may be connected, and it may be traveled in either direction. A present effect may be connected with a preceding cause; a presently existing cause may be identified to predict some future effect.

Argument from cause is based on the premise that things occur in an orderly fashion for some reason. Since neither the affairs of humanity nor nature are random, we assume we can rely on the premise, "Everything has a cause." In an argument from cause, the grounds, warrant, and backing must validate the claim on the basis of their temporal connection. If we are careful in researching phenomena, we can support claims that events or conditions of one kind are the cause of events or conditions of another.

As an illustration of how argument from cause works, consider the written testimony of James Hall of the Up Front Drug Center in Miami.

> "Smoking" methamphetamine causes drug problems even more serious than those associated with crack cocaine. Methamphetamine may be vaporized ("smoked") in its crystal (salt) form and need not be converted to a base form like crack. When "smoked," its extreme volatility delivers a highly concentrated dose of the drug instantaneously to the brain, even more intensely than with crack. The drug's rapid tolerance means that smoking methamphetamine accelerates compulsive abuse and addiction. Its long duration of action contributes to the probability of toxic and fatal reactions. Brain damage is expected to be more severe from methamphetamine "smoking" than from crack as is the violent, paranoid behavior associated with either drug. (Drugs in the 1990's, 1989, pp. 80–81)

Put yourself in Mr. Hall's position for a moment, and suppose that because of your own observations or research you knew the following things to be true of methamphetamine when it is "smoked."

GROUND 1: It is easier *because* it "need not be converted to a base form like crack."

GROUND 2: It packs a bigger, faster wallop than crack *because* of "its extreme volatility."

GROUND 3: It hooks users faster *because* of "the drug's rapid tolerance."

GROUND 4: It is more likely to harm or even kill users *because* of "its long duration of action."

Notice that in every case, something inherent in the nature of the drug's consumption or pharmacological impact causes its effects to be worse than crack as forecast in the paragraph's opening and closing sentences.

CLAIM: "Smoking" methamphetamine causes drug problems even more serious than those associated with crack cocaine [including] . . . brain damage [and] the violent, paranoid behavior associated with either drug.

In arguing causality, some precautions must be taken to ensure that our inferential leaps are justified. The most important question to ask is: Are the grounds sufficient to bring about or cause the conditions specified in the claim? Focusing on the grounds is an important first step in testing the strength of the argument from cause. Examine your arguments from cause using the following questions as guidelines:

1. Are other grounds likely to lead to the effect?
2. Is the asserted relationship between grounds and effect consistent, or are there instances in which this effect has not followed from these grounds?

When using causal reasoning, you are generalizing about the relationship between phenomena along a time line: In the presence of phenomenon A (cause), we can always find evidence of phenomenon B (effect); or if we can find evidence of phenomenon B (effect), it is likely to have been the consequence of phenomenon A (cause). The regularity with which this has been true in the past warrants speculation about causes or effects that are undocumented or undocumentable. This is particularly useful when arguing about things that have not yet happened, such as brain damage, paranoia, and violent behavior. We look at a drug that is easier to get, more potent, longer lasting, and more lethal than crack, and we can reasonably expect it will have the worst effects on its users. This same strategy can be used in speculating about the consequences of a policy change, taking that course of action as a cause and forecasting the effects, both good and bad, that it is likely to produce.

We also want to examine the arguments produced by cause and effect reasoning to make sure they are really a cause and its effect, not simply two phenomena that happened to occur sequentially. Just because phenomenon A is followed by phenomenon B does not make A the cause of B. Many superstitions are based on this notion of false cause. Knocking on wood to ward off a run of bad luck, which was never going to happen in the first place, is a prime example.

Causality requires proof of more than chronological occurrence. When two things happen sequentially, and you suspect a cause-effect relationship, consider whether the alleged cause is capable of producing the effect. Is the cause potentially strong enough to do so? If a drug is easier to get than crack because it requires no preparation, does that mean it will produce worse problems than crack?

Avoid being trapped by superficial connections between events by looking for alternative explanations of what happened. In both interpersonal and public relations, few things happen as the result of a single cause. The argument on smoking methamphetamine is a good example of the identification of multiple causalities: It is not only easier to get but also more potent, addictive, and longer lasting than crack, making the problems it produces more serious. For any given set of events, before placing too much faith in any single cause-effect relationship, look for possible alternative or multiple causes for the effect.

A cause may be discussed in terms of its being necessary and sufficient. A cause is said to be *necessary* if, without its presence, the effect will not occur. However, this cause may not be *sufficient* to bring about the effect all by itself. The difference between necessary and sufficient cause is illustrated by the relationship between HIV and AIDS. Millions of people who are HIV-positive do not have AIDS, so apparently the virus alone is not a sufficient cause for the disease. The discovery that some AIDS patients are not HIV-positive suggests the virus may not even be a necessary cause. In the case of smoking methamphetamine, none of the four causes are sufficient to make the effects worse than they are for crack cocaine. Taken together, the facts that it is easier, more potent, addictive, and longer lasting constitute a series of necessary causes that, taken in toto, are sufficient to make the effects worse.

Why is this distinction important? In determining whether a cause produced an effect, sufficient causes can always be counted on to produce predictable effects. The distinction between causes that are necessary and causes that are sufficient helps to emphasize the importance of always looking for alternative and multiple causes.

Summary of Argument from Cause
1. Argument from cause suggests a temporal connection between events in which one produces the other.
2. When we can document effect, we may reason as to its cause; when we can document cause, we may reason as to its effect.
3. A necessary cause is a factor that must be present to bring about an effect but will not in and of itself produce the effect.
4. A sufficient cause includes all factors needed to produce a particular effect.
5. Causality involves more than chronological order and may be tested by asking the following questions:
   A. Is the cause capable of producing the effect?
   B. Is the effect produced by the cause or does the effect occur coincidentally to the cause?
   C. Are there other potential causes?
   D. Has this effect consistently followed from this cause?

Argument from Sign

Unlike arguments from cause, which link causes to their effects,

arguments from sign connect phenomena with conditions that merely exist.

Signs are indicators—observable symptoms, conditions, or marks—that tell us what is the case. Would-be naturalists often study the behaviors of animals and connect those behaviors to other events. Consider the following examples of sign reasoning in which the sign has no causal connection to the events they are used to predict:

When the squirrels store extra nuts, it means we're in for a hard winter.
If the groundhog sees its shadow on February 2, spring is still six weeks away.

What kinds of things serve as signs? Events are often seen as signs of attitudes or activities. We observe that a certain product is selling well and take this as sign evidence of the product's quality or the effectiveness of its advertising. Statistics are often interpreted through sign reasoning. High employment and low inflation are signs of a healthy economy. Public opinion polls signify attitudes about policies, activities, and persons. William Hopkins, Chief of the Ethnography Section in New York's Division of Substance Abuse Services, used a series of examples in presenting a sign argument before a Senate Committee.

> I just wanted to make a comment on the paranoia. We see it regularly on a full-scale basis. The types of things we see relating to paranoia are almost unbelievable.
>
> I know a woman who locked herself in a closet, kept a gun in one hand because she was afraid somebody was going to get after her. She would actually urinate in her clothing in the closet because she was afraid to come out. She wouldn't go anywhere and she put food in the closet, and this is the actual way we live.
>
> I could rattle about paranoia cases, extreme paranoia, almost steadily, and it is mainly from people who smoke crack on a regular basis. We find when people smoke crack, they smoke it in binges. They smoke and smoke and smoke until they don't have any more crack or any more money to buy it, and then they will do anything, but anything, in order to get it.
>
> I have actually seen a woman have oral sex with seven men for one rock of crack, one rock, and then there was an argument of whether they should give her the rock first or the crack [pipe]. And as I watched her having oral sex, she is holding the rock of crack up in her hand and one of the men was holding the pipe.
>
> I have seen a woman take an infant which was hers and just take it and heave it over her shoulder up against a wall behind [her], and [she] sat down and smoked her pipe, not even realizing what she did. Somebody had to take the baby out and rush it [to the hospital]. We see all kinds of violence and paranoia directly related to it. It is serious. (Drugs in the 1990's, 1989, pp. 60–61)

Mr. Hopkins wants to convince the Senators that both regular crack users and those who binge have serious problems. In order to do this, he advances two claims supported by sign reasoning from examples. He can rely on his position. He has been called as an expert witness, which implicitly backs his unstated warrant that these women's behavior reflects the paranoia and lack of concern for self and others present in crack users. He can also rely on the fact that the Senators have a full agenda. This may lead them to believe he could provide more examples or back his warrant in some other way if they gave him the time to do so.

CLAIM: Regular crack users become paranoid.
GROUND: "I know a woman who locked herself in a closet."
WARRANT [implied]: This woman's behavior is a reliable indicator of the
   behavior of regular users.

CLAIM: Crack users who binge will do anything to themselves and others to get their fix.

GROUND 1: "I have actually seen a woman have oral sex with seven men for one rock of crack."

GROUND 2: "I have seen a woman take an infant . . . and heave it over her shoulder up against a wall."

WARRENT [implied]: These women are behaving in ways that reliably indicate behavior of binge users.

What would you rely on if you were in his shoes? For insight into building and maintaining credibility with an audiece, turn to Chapter 12.

There are some cautions to observe in arguing on the basis of signs. The most important is to be sure the sign you use is reliable. We have longed for spring months after the groundhog's first appearance. The problem with finding a reliable sign is that signs are only circumstantial evidence in many instances. Things we observe as signs may not really warrant any claim unless backing for the warrant can be found.

A second caution regarding sign reasoning is that signs should not be confused with causes. A good rule to follow in distinguishing sign from cause is this: *A sign tells what is the case, while a cause explains why it is the case.* Arguments from cause attempt to analyze events in terms of antecedents and their consequences. Arguments from sign concern themselves with what the sign will signify. They tell us what we can expect to observe as a result of having first observed the sign. Mr. Hopkins's arguments do not explain why regular users and binge users have different kinds of problems, only that they do have different problems.

A final caution about sign reasoning is that we must be concerned with the strength of the sign. Sign arguments lead to conclusions about what was, is, or will be. Sign reasoning is presented as a factual claim about the sign and what it signifies. It must be tested the way we test any factual claim, by examining its grounds. We want to know if the grounds, the sign, always or usually validate the prediction of what it signifies, the conclusion drawn in the claim. Examination of the grounds might include asking if sufficient signs are present. After all, one robin does not constitute spring, but a flock of robins and other species, buds on trees, and the absence of snow may reliably lead us to conclude that spring is at hand.

Summary of Argument from Sign

1. Signs are observable symptoms, conditions, or marks used to prove that a certain state of affairs exists.
2. Signs should be reliable so that the grounds point to the conclusion drawn, not to some alternative conclusion.
3. Sign reasoning must not be confused with causal reasoning. Signs describe the situation; causes analyze the situation.
4. Sign reasoning is assessed on the basis of the presence of a sufficient number of signs or the certainty of an individual sign's strength.

Argument from Generalization

Generalizations, based on sampling populations to draw conclusions about wholes, are very common. Much social science research studies a small sample of people or events and generalizes about the group the sample represents. A generalization states that what is true in some instances is true in all or most instances.

Generalizations are a form of inductive reasoning in which one looks at the details of examples, specific cases, situations, and occurrences and draws inferences about the entire class they represent.

Generalizing may be the form of reasoning you have experienced most frequently in forming your attitudes, values, and beliefs. If you have had a negative experience with a course in Department X, you may reason that no course offered by Department X is worth taking. Prejudices against people and nations are often formed on the basis of generalizations. This does not mean, however, that generalization is not an effective and efficient form of reasoning.

What we see on commercial television is determined on the basis of reasoning from generalization. The Nielson ratings of the popularity of various television shows are based on sampling the viewing habits in a few American homes and generalizing that what is true of the viewing habits of the sample is true of the viewing habits of all Americans.

Suppose you wanted your readers to accept a claim that armed violence occurs too frequently in schools. You have found an example, but unlike Mr. Hopkins from New York your readers are unlikely to accept it as a reliable sign on your word alone. If you could find some other examples from cities across the nation, your readers might be willing to accept the generalization that what is true in these cities is probably true in cities nationwide. Despite the fact that he is executive director of the National School Safety Center, this is precisely what Ronald Stephens did in his written testimony.

Reading, writing and retaliation has become a common theme on many of our nation's campuses. Far too often this retaliation involves ducking bullets and serious violence. . . .

September, 1992, Palo Duro High School, Amarillo, Texas—Teenager shoots 6 in school after a fight; 2 seriously hurt.

May, 1992, Lindhurst High School, Olivehurst, California—Four slain, 11 injured as ex-student enters high school campus and opens fire; 59 students and teachers were held hostage during the eight-hour siege.

March, 1992, Largo High School, Washington, D.C.—Sixteen-year-old girl was stabbed in the abdomen with a 3-inch paring knife by a female classmate.

March, 1992, McAuliffe Elementary School, Chicago, Illinois—Eight-year-old boy brings gun to school in his book bag, thinking it is a toy and shoots and paralyzes an 8-year-old girl in the classroom.

February, 1992, Thomas Jefferson High School, Brooklyn, New York—Two students are fatally shot in school hallway by a ninth-grader while students are changing classes.

February, 1992, Roland Park Elementary/Middle School, Baltimore, Maryland—Seventh grader shoots a school police officer for confiscating his pager. (Children Carrying Weapons, 1992, pp. 30–31)

Since the claim and the grounds that support it are so transparent, focus your attention on the warrant and how the choice of examples subtly provides backing.

WARRANT [implied]: What is true in these instances is probably true in other instances nationwide.

BACKING 1: This is not a regional problem; the examples are drawn from five states and the District of Columbia.

BACKING 2: This is not a high school problem; two of the examples are drawn from elementary and middle schools.

BACKING 3: This is not an exclusively male problem; one of the assailants and at least two of the victims were female.

The one limitation on the generalizability of the claim that Mr. Stephens's development of this unit of argument does not address is that the warrant and its backing leads to the conclusion that this is an urban, or at least a large city, problem. He addressed this in his next unit of argument, claiming "school crime is not simply a big-city problem. It encompasses rural, suburban and urban communities" (Children Carrying Weapons, 1992, p. 31).

Generalizations may be restricted in nature, arguing from some to more. Notice the qualifiers "many" and "far too often" in the opening statement. Mr. Stephens does not assert that all disputes on all campuses result in armed violence; it is left to the reader to determine exactly how often "far too often" and how many "many" really is. The use of qualifiers in claim statements facilitates generalization when the behavior of an entire population, or the qualities of an entire class of objects, cannot be validly predicted. You may have owned three cars made by The Motor Car Company, experiencing great dissatisfaction with each, but would it be warranted for you to generalize that "The Motor Car Company produces lemons"?

Generalizations may also be universal, arguing that what is true of some members of a group will be true of all members of that group. In making a universal generalization, the arguer needs to be careful that the sample on which the generalization is based is adequate to warrant the conclusion. Much of what we discussed in Chapter 6 about the verification of factual and statistical evidence applies to generalizations. There are four generic tests to apply to arguments from generalization to determine whether a generalization should be universal or restricted.

First, sufficient cases or instances should be cited as grounds to assure a reliable generalization. It would be unreasonable to argue on the basis of what happens in one state that armed violence in our schools is a nationwide problem. A sample composed of states from each region might be needed to show a national trend. How large must the sample be? Large enough that the addition of more instances does not change the conclusion. Ultimately, the audience is the final arbiter of how many cases are needed to support the claim. The more familiar your audience is with the topic, the fewer instances you will need to cite.

The second test of generalizations is sample representativeness. Do the individuals or items cited in the grounds fairly represent the group or class about which the generalization is made? Items or individuals must be typical of a class if they are to represent it. All items must actually come from the same class, and it makes a difference how you define the class. For example, generalizing about a class of objects called schools may be problematic if your definition allows the inclusion of institutions, such as reform schools or alternative schools, to which children who have already had trouble with the law are sent.

The third test of generalizations is that instances must be taken from random samples of populations. If in attempting to generalize about school violence you include schools from only the most violent urban areas, distortion may occur. The schools you have selected may have more violence and thus fail to accurately represent a national trend.

The final test of generalizations asks if negative instances have been accounted for or explained. A generalization will not hold up if too many instances exist that contradict it. Including a rebuttal statement to modify such a claim is absolutely necessary. If in preparing an argument on school violence you discover that religiously affiliated schools do not share this problem with their publicly funded counterparts, you would use a rebuttal to account for the difference.

Summary of Argument from Generalization
1. Generalizations argue that what is true of some members of a group will be true of more or all members of the same group.
2. Generalizations should be based on a sufficiently large sample of cases if a conclusion about an entire group is being drawn.
3. Instances cited in making the generalization should be representative of all members of the group.
4. Instances should be randomly selected to avoid distortion.
5. Negative instances should be explained or accounted for.

Argument from Parallel Case

Argument from parallel case is used when we have all the particulars about a given case and we reason from it, comparing the known case to a similar unknown case.

> Arguments using **parallel case** involve reasoning on the basis of two or more similar events or cases.

Government policy makers and organizations such as universities often use argument from parallel case to frame their thinking. Those who set academic policies and regulations governing graduation requirements may study what is happening at other similar schools, reasoning that what is appropriate at college$_1$, college$_2$, and college$_3$ should be appropriate at our college.

In arguments based on parallel case, grounds involve the case (or cases) that is in some critical way similar to the case about which the claim is made. The warrant, backed by additional evidence when necessary, explains how the case described in the grounds and the case identified in the claim are truly parallel cases. An example of an argument reasoning from a parallel case is found in former Judge Frank Orlando's testimony on the juvenile justice system.

> The public, I believe, is badly misinformed about today's juvenile court, largely due to the secrecy and confidentiality that surrounds the court.
>
> Let me make a brief parallel to amplify my opinion and conclusions. Imagine, if you will, the finest hospital in this city, or any hospital. This hospital's mission is to treat seriously ill and injured patients. Now imagine, if you will, that the clientele from other systems that are failing miserably arrive and line up at the hospital's admissions office.
>
> Let us assume the homeless, school dropouts, abused and neglected children, and many persons inflicted with minor physical ailments are admitted in large numbers to the hospital. Little or no concern is given to the hospital's ability to provide appropriate or necessary care for such problems.
>
> It would not take long before the hospital would begin to fail to meet its stated objectives, and the public would lose confidence. My question is whether the loss of the confidence is the fault of the hospital, or the fault of the other failing systems.
>
> This, in my opinion, is precisely the situation in the juvenile court. The hospital example is easy to understand, and the court's is not. Simply put, the court "admissions office" is being overloaded with the many inappropriate clients whose needs would be more appropriately met by these other social institutions. With these problems, the court is destined to fail. (Juvenile Courts, 1992, pp. 4–5)

Judge Orlando's point is not that a court is like a hospital but rather that the public has lost confidence because it "is badly misinformed about today's juvenile court." Using the hospital as a parallel case serves as a vehicle for remedying misunderstanding since "the hospital example is easy to understand, and the court's is not." To the extent that his listeners perceived fundamental similarities between a hospital and a court, Judge Orlando's argument demonstrated his point. Those similarities are established in whatever grounds the arguer provides.

GROUND 1: Just as a hospital has a mission, "to treat seriously ill and injured patients," the juvenile court system has a mission.

GROUND 2: Just as a hospital is not capable of functioning effectively if "many persons inflicted with minor physical ailments are admitted in large numbers," the juvenile court system cannot function if it must also deal with "the homeless, school dropouts, abused and neglected children."

GROUND 3: Like a hospital, the only reason that people with problems beyond the scope of the juvenile court's mission and "ability to provide appropriate or necessary care" would bring them to juvenile court is that they are "the clientele from other systems that are failing miserably."

GROUND 4: While "the public would lose confidence" in a hospital or a court system for failing "to meet its stated objectives," their attribution of fault should more properly be placed on "other failing systems," which are the real cause of the problem.

There are two tests to apply to arguments from parallel case and both involve scrutinizing the similarities between the cases cited. First, ask yourself, "How similar are the cases cited?" If we hear that we can better understand the problems of the juvenile court system by comparing them to those of a hospital that is asked to provide service beyond its stated mission, we must be able to find enough similarities between the court and the hospital to make the comparison hold up in our minds. Are there dissimilarities, such as the hospital's ability to charge on a fee-for-service basis, that might suggest the hospital is not only different from the court system but also different in a way that might enable it to cope better with the exigency?

The second test to apply to arguments from parallel case is to ask, "Are the similarities cited key factors?" In general, the more critical the factors common to both cases, the more force the argument will have. In particular, the similarities cited must have relevance to the claim being made in the argument. Judge Orlando claimed that the juvenile court is misunderstood. A hospital is offered as something more easily understood. It is similar to the court with regard to having a mission that is clientele-specific and in having to face the possibility of taking on additional responsibilities when other entities in the social system fail to fulfill their clientele-specific missions. Are these the key factors, or are they such things as our media-informed impressions of hospitals as the place where doctors rush to save lives and of courts as the place where lawyers engage in seeming interminable cross-examinations of witnesses and sidebar discussions with each other and the judge?

Summary of Argument from Parallel Case
1. Argument from parallel case reasons on the basis of two or more similar events or cases; because case A is known to be similar to case B in certain ways, we can appropriately draw inferences from what is known to what is unknown.
2. For the argument from parallel case to be valid, the cases must not only be similar but their similarities must also pertain to important rather than trivial factors.

Argument from Analogy

Analogies represent a special form of comparison in which the cases compared do not have a sufficient degree of similarity to warrant argument from parallel case.

Arguments from analogy assume some fundamental sameness exists between the characteristics of dissimilar cases.

The argument proceeds much as it would if it were an argument from parallel case. A claim that is true of case$_1$ should be expected to be true of case$_2$ because both share a sufficient number of relevant characteristics. The essential difference between an analogy and an argument from parallel case is found in their forms of comparison. Analogies are figurative, often used as rhetorical devices to add style to an argument, while arguments from parallel case are literal.

Consider the following from Representative F. James Sensenbrenner's statement during the hearings on witness intimidation.

> And now, if I may descend into politics for a minute, I couldn't help but think of witness intimidation this week as I watched the Whitewater hearings. There was that poor kid, Joshua Steiner, who wrote one thing in his diaries in February and completely changed his story before the Senate Banking Committee on Tuesday.
>
> I was reminded of the scene in *Godfather, Part Two*, which also took place in a Senate hearing room where Frankie Pentangelo suffers sudden memory loss as he is about to testify against Michael Corleone. It looks like witness intimidation is going on at the Treasury Department and perhaps even at the White House. It is not in the same league as the drug gangs, but it might be almost as important because we expect the leaders of our country to set a moral example.
>
> How can you tell the street punk that witness intimidation is wrong when he can turn on his TV set and see the white-collar version occurring at the highest levels of government? (Witness Intimidation, 1994, p. 3)

Comparisons in analogies are based on the functional equivalence of very different entities. Starting with a premise that "life imitates art" as its implied subtext, Representative Sensenbrenner's argument from analogy refines and sharpens that point as he "descends into politics for a minute."

BACKING 2: Life imitates art.

BACKING 1: Because some of life is politics, and some of art is the movies, some of politics is like the movies.

WARRANT: Because some movies are about the criminal behavior of gangsters, it should come as no surprise that some politicians behave like gangsters.

GROUND: Joshua Steiner behaved the same way in changing his story when he testified at the Whitewater hearings that Frankie Pentangelo behaved in refusing to testify against Michael Corleone in *Godfather, Part Two*.

CLAIM: Bill Clinton is like Michael Corleone.

QUALIFIER: "It is not in the same league as the drug gangs."

REBUTTAL: Then again it may be worse because "how can you tell the street punk that witness intimidation is wrong when he can turn on his TV set and see the white-collar version occurring at the highest levels of government?"

We do not normally think of analogies in terms of the Toulmin model of argument. If you are going to use them yourself, you need to think them through, and the Toulmin model provides the framework for doing just that. Ask yourself what might cause your analogy to be accepted or rejected by your audience, and where the likely points of attack might be for those who are arguing against you.

Because of its figurative nature, analogy has been classified as the weakest form of argument (Eisenberg & Ilardo, 1980; Toulmin et al., 1984; Ziegelmuller et al., 1990). It is said that the comparison of dissimilar cases is a rhetorical device and cannot actually warrant a claim. The analogy's usefulness is primarily confined to illustrating, clarifying, or making an argument more memorable or striking. Frankly, we have been unable to get the image of Bill Clinton sitting in the Oval Office saying to some staff member, "Why do you come to me with this on the day of my daughter Chelsea's wedding?" out of our heads since we first read Representative Sensenbrenner's argument.

As Ehninger (1974) suggests, the position you ultimately adopt on the use of analogy will be determined by how you define argument and by the degree of probability you expect an asserted relationship to possess before you are willing to regard it as proven. If your definition of argument is restricted to instances where the relationship between grounds and claim produce conclusions that have a high probability of truth, you will probably not be satisfied with arguments from analogy.

Argument from analogy can be useful in communication. Since rendering the form of an argument understandable to the audience is a requirement for effective communication, there will be times when an analogy is the most appropriate argumentative choice. Analogy fulfills several critical functions in argumentation (Wilcox, 1973). It helps organize and clarify thought by relating terms, it enables us to learn new information, and adds style to our reasoning.

Should you choose to argue from analogy, there are two tests to apply to determine its viability. First, the cases alleged to be similar must be sufficiently similar in function in all important ways. An analogy will not hold up if the functions compared are so dissimilar that the analogy is incomprehensible to the audience. Second, the dissimilarities between the cases compared must not be so great as to adversely influence perception of implied similarities. Since analogies compare things that are essentially dissimilar, those dissimilarities must not overshadow their similarities.

If you decide to use this form of argument, search for analogies that will add force to your argument. While there is probably a point of diminishing returns in the use of analogy, it is possible to use more than one analogy to help your audience make connections between the available evidence and the claims you wish to advance.

Summary of Argument from Analogy
1. An analogy is a comparison of fundamentally dissimilar cases that draws attention to the common function they perform.
2. Analogies are commonly used as rhetorical devices, providing figurative rather than literal comparisons.
3. The dissimilarities between the cases should not be so great as to nullify the validity of the comparison being made.

Argument from Authority

In Chapter 6, we said arguers often use the opinions and research of experts as evidence. Society has become so complex that we are no longer confident of our own expertise on many subjects, so we rely on the knowledge of authorities. Textbooks, including this one, are examples of reliance on authority to shape inferences about the nature of things. Watch the news on television, read an article in a magazine, or listen to the opinions of friends; it will not take long to discover how reliant you are on authorities.

Who are these people we turn to for opinions and interpretations of fact? We label as an authority any person or group determined to possess expertise in a given field. Their expertise may come from education or experience, from having published in their field, or from being a well-known professional, scientist, physician, jurist, artist, or the like. In addition, leaders, public figures, government officials, and spokespersons for well-known institutions, groups, and organizations are acknowledged as authorities.

In an argument from authority, the inference is that the claim is justified because it is consistent with the opinion, interpretation of fact, or research findings of an authority.

As a form of reasoning, **argument from authority** relies on the credibility and expertise of the source to warrant acceptance of a claim.

Since authorities use the same patterns of reasoning as the rest of us, an argument from authority may appear to be an argument from cause, sign, generalization, parallel case, analogy, or dilemma. What distinguishes argument from authority is that the warrant identifies why the audience should regard the authority as credible rather than drawing some other inference linking grounds and claim.

Earlier in this chapter, you read William Hopkins's sign argument on the paranoia of regular crack users and the willingness of binge users to do anything to themselves or others to obtain the drug. One reason his implied warrant—that the sign evidence he offered was a reliable indicator of behavior patterns—was probably accepted by those listening was the argument from authority with which he began his testimony.

I am the chief ethnographer for my agency, the New York State Division of Substance Abuse Services, and I bring you greetings from our director, Julio Martinez, and I personally consider it an honor to appear before you and the committee.

I think it is very important that I start off by spending a minute or two to tell you what I do. I think it is extremely important so that you would know where my information comes from, and I might add I am not attempting to promote myself. I already have my retirement papers in, but I think it is important you know where our data comes from. I spent 20 years with the New York City Police Department and I have been with my current agency, the New York Division of Substance Abuse, for 21 years.

About 10 years ago, Julio Martinez said to me that he needed to know what was going on in New York City as far as drug activity was concerned, and he created a unit that is unique. He created what is today known as the street research unit. . . .

The kinds of things that we learn in our street work, and we have been doing it now for 10 years, is new drug mixtures, drug-dealing methods, drug trends, attitudes of the people on the street, those both selling drugs and the communities. We learn all about street terminology, drug paraphernalia, drug gangs, drug violence, and the role of children in drugs.

We are usually the first to learn in the city what is going on in the streets, and I might add that we were the group that was credited with first finding crack in New York City and I was one of those involved in breaking the first story to the media when we saw that it was getting out of control. (Drugs in the 1990's, 1989, pp. 14–15)

If we examine the basis in fact that Mr. Hopkins lays out in his argument, we gain insight not only into how he established his own credibility but also into how you might structure your arguments from authority using evidence of fact and opinion from credible sources. In establishing personal credibility, as Mr. Hopkins does, the crux of the argument lies in the grounds that are offered.

GROUND 1: I have been doing this job for a long time: "20 years with the New York City Police Department and I have been with my current agency, the New York Division of Substance Abuse, for 21 years."

GROUND 2: I am where the action is: "To know what was going on in New York City as far as drug activity was concerned," you have to be in the streets.

GROUND 3: I learn about a number of important things, such as "new drug mixtures, drug-dealing methods, drug trends, attitudes of the people on the street, those both selling drugs and the communities."

GROUND 4: I am in a position to be the first to know about things like "crack in New York City and I was one of those involved in breaking the first story to the media when we saw that it was getting out of control."

WARRANT: [implied premise] The voice of firsthand experience is to be trusted.

CLAIM: [implied] You should believe everything I tell you.

In arguments from authority using evidence of fact and opinion that you might author, the locus shifts to the backing for the warrant that establishes the credibility of the source of fact or opinion used to ground a claim. Your own arguments from authority can be structured in one of two ways. In the first form, state your own opinion as the claim. The reason for your reader or listener to accept the claim is warranted because an authority, established by backing the warrant, provides the factual grounds for it. In a sense, this is the form nearly all arguments in academic argumentation take. Through research, you discover as much as you can about a topic, determine the opinions you hold on it, and decide how those opinions will be formed into claim statements. Then you find evidence from credible sources to ground your claims.

In the second form of argument from authority, you take an authority's opinion, restate its main point as the claim, and use evidence taken from the authority's opinion as grounds for the claim. As in the previous form of argument from authority, the warrant states that the authority should be considered credible, and backing applies one or more of the tests of argument from authority to establish that credibility.

Because argument from authority involves evidence that expresses an opinion, interprets fact, or reports research findings, many of the tests of evidence discussed in Chapter 6 may be appropriate. The specific tests of argument from authority seek answers to the question: Can the authority be regarded as credible?

The first test of argument from authority is to determine whether the source is a qualified expert in the field by reason of training, experience, or background. The academic degrees a person holds, the length of his or her experience, and the nature of his or her background are all ways of verifying that an alleged authority is indeed an expert. To be recognized as an authority, some demonstration of expertise must be made.

The second test of argument from authority examines the context in which the source offered an opinion or presented information. Is the statement made within the context of the alleged authority's area of expertise? Public figures express a variety of opinions that may not necessarily be within their field of expertise. For example, prominent members of the entertainment industry have expressed opinions about the environment, but are ecology and industrial policy within the context of their field of expertise?

The third test of argument from authority examines the source's degree of involvement. Is the alleged authority relatively unbiased? The office or position a person holds may induce bias in a certain direction, and a person who is trying to protect tenure in an office or position will reflect such biases. We would expect the president of the American Medical Association to reflect some bias in expressing an opinion about government regulation of physicians' fees or the cost of malpractice insurance. While all authorities have a vested interest in their fields, the important thing to look for in examining their biases are obvious conflicts of interest or self-serving statements.

The fourth test of argument from authority examines the source's statement in relation to those of acknowledged experts in the field. Does the alleged authority reflect a majority or minority view? In legal argument, each side may have its own expert witnesses, amply qualified, who express diametrically opposite views. Experts often disagree with each other on subjects inside and outside their fields of expertise. Just because a view is different, it is not automatically invalid. However, an alleged authority may also express a totally isolated point of view. Many accepted principles were once minority opinions. If you cite an authority whose view does not reflect majority opinion, be prepared to establish the credibility of that view by providing the backing for the warrant in your argument.

The fifth and final test of argument from authority examines the factual basis on which the source's statement rests. Is there a reliable factual basis for this opinion? Remember, it is not the image or stature of the alleged authority that grounds the claim but the factual basis on which the opinions are offered. When someone with prestige, office, or an academic reputation offers an opinion, we assume there is some basis for it. This may not be the case. The person may be bluffing, expressing a point of view that is contradicted by the evidence, or speaking outside his or her field of expertise, relying on reputation alone to support the view (Wilson, 1980).

Because of the special nature of this pattern of reasoning, we offer a final caution about argument from authority. Arguments from authority can be used to circumvent the reasoning process when authority is cited to prevent further consideration of a matter. In Chapter 8 this error in reasoning is discussed in more detail.

Someone is properly regarded as an expert because the person possesses special knowledge not because of fame or status. The warrant in an argument from authority should reassure the listener or reader that this is so. Backing is used to verify the basis of the alleged authority's expertise. It is important to include both steps in creating arguments from authority.

Summary of Argument from Authority
1. Argument from authority relies on the credibility of the source of information to warrant acceptance of the claim it grounds.
2. The source should be a qualified expert in the field by reason of training, experience, or background.
3. The statements of authorities are only credible within the context of their fields of expertise.
4. The authority should not be unduly biased.
5. If the authority expresses an opinion at odds with those of the majority of experts in the field, the arguer should establish the credibility of that view.
6. The authority's opinion should have a basis in fact.

Argument from Dilemma

This final type of reasoning deals with choice making and the consequences those choices bring. For that reason, arguments from dilemma are built with two or more arguments from cause that embody undesirable consequences.

> An **argument from dilemma** forces a choice between two unacceptable alternatives.

Economic policies are common sources of arguments from dilemma. Consider the international financier's dilemma: Which alternative causes the least amount of harm, renegotiating lower interest rates on loans to Third World countries on the verge default or allowing them to default on billions of dollars in loans? Many of us face unpleasant choices in our own lives.

Before his descent into politics, Representative F. James Sensenbrenner eloquently described the dilemma faced by those who witness crimes. On the one hand, they have an obligation help preserve the fabric of society by testifying. On the other, their obligation to self-preservation may discourage them from doing just that.

On the subject of this hearing, witness intimidation is one of the toughest issues we have discussed this year. In the twisted mind of a gang member, murderer, he has little to lose if he kills witnesses. Since he has already killed one victim, he could face the death penalty or live in prison and there is little more that the criminal justice system can do to him. That makes this problem tough to solve and puts a lot of pressure on the good people, on the police and prosecutors to protect innocent people who are witnesses, people who are trying to do their duty as good citizens and trying to help take the killers off the streets.

Imagine being the witness to one of these murders. One day you are leading a normal life at home with your family, going to work, the next day you see a murder. And all of a sudden, due to no fault of your own, your life and the lives of your family are threatened by the gang members. How outrageous that these decent people must change their habits, homes and identities simply because they are doing the right thing and they are doing their duty as citizens of this great democracy. (Witness Intimidation, 1994, p. 3).

Regardless of the number of alternatives suggested in the argument, the validity of a dilemma depends upon its identification of a true either-or situation. The grounds presented must identify the options available, and these alternatives must indeed be different, mutually exclusive, choices. An argument from dilemma can either point toward the one suitable, or least objectionable, choice among the alternatives that the arguer favors, or it can suggest that, in the absence of change, no suitable alternative exists.

Representative Sensenbrenner's argument takes the form of a forced choice between remaining silent, being silenced if you testify, or having to go into a form of custody if you enter a witness protection program so you can testify. The warrant indicates these are true either-or choices, since the criminal's lack of inhibition to kill again explicitly backs the warrant. No matter what choice the witness makes, adverse consequences occur. Maximizing the societal value by testifying minimizes personal values of safety or freedom or both. Minimizing the societal value may not raise the level of personal need satisfaction since the criminal will still be at large in the witness's neighborhood.

Reasoning makes the connection between claims and the evidence used to ground them. Although in actual argument the warrant and its backing are seldom stated, it is only through the presentation of the warrant that your reasoning is explicitly stated to your reader or listener. In your early attempts to frame arguments from dilemma, we suggest you include at least four elements of the Toulmin model—grounds, warrant, backing, and claim—as a means of developing facility with this technique of reasoning.

When you reason, you make an inference that establishes relationships between observed or known facts and the probable truth or validity of a claim. The purpose of reasoning is to assist in determining that probability. In the process, warrants are offered in the form of argument from cause, sign, generalization, parallel case, analogy, authority, or dilemma. Each form has some specific tests associated with it that help determine the validity of the reasoning process. However, these tests do not identify all the potential errors in reasoning that can occur in argumentation. In the next chapter, these errors are discussed as we consider some of the common fallacies that can impair the quality of your arguments.

Learning Activities

1. Conduct a discussion of argument from cause on one or more controversial topics such as gun control, abortion, euthanasia, or a campus controversy. What necessary and sufficient conditions establish cause in each case? Are these instances in which multiple causality may apply? What would be necessary to prove cause in each case?
2. Find examples of public opinion polls on an issue such as gun control, pollution, or presidential popularity. Construct an argument from sign based on the statistical information. Explain the strengths and weaknesses of this sign in establishing the probable truth of your claim.
3. Examine the text of several speeches from a recent issue of *Vital Speeches*, or other similar sources, for examples of the use of analogies. Share your examples in class. Which analogies succeed in creating comparisons that make the unknown more easily understood? Which seem to fail, and why do they fail? On the basis of this experience, are analogies a useful reasoning technique?

Suggested Supplementary Readings

Golden, J. L., Berquist, G. F., & Coleman, W. E. (1992). *The Rhetoric of Western Thought*. Dubuque, IA: Kendall/Hunt.

Chapter 13, Stephen Toulmin on the Nature of Argument, describes each form of reasoning in terms of the Toulmin model. The authors make extensive use of the model to visualize the thought process we use in each type of reasoning. Particularly useful is their discussion of how the warrant creates validity for each type of reasoning.

Patterson, J. & Kim, P. (1991). *The Day America Told the Truth*. New York: Prentice-Hall.

James Patterson and Peter Kim conducted one of the most extensive survey projects ever undertaken to determine what Americans believe in and reported their research techniques and results here. The value of this work is that it provides you with a series of excellent examples of how researchers make generalizations. The subjects include surveys on beliefs about sex, drugs, family life, what we keep secret, crime, patriotism, the work ethic, and other topics. The authors explain how Americans differ in their beliefs about these subjects on the basis of geographic region and other variables.

Shinn, R. L. (1991). *Forced Options,* 3rd. Ed. Cleveland, OH: Pilgrim Press. Roger Shinn explains how the decisions that we make in the present create dilemmas for the future. He considers the forced choices all humans will face on issues of social justice, preservation of the ecosphere, feeding world populations, advances in genetic engineering, and war in a post–Cold War world. Particularly useful to learning how to argue dilemmas is Chapter 11, Living with Risk. Shinn points out that the risk posed by a forced choice may have good points as well as bad ones.

Walton, D. N. (1989). Reasoned Use of Expertise in Argumentation. *Argumentation,* 3, 59–73.
Douglas Walton evaluates the strengths and weaknesses of arguments that reason on the basis of source expertise. He explores the logic behind the idea of expertise, what it is, and how we came to value it in a technological sense. He makes some interesting predictions about how the potential for artificial intelligence will influence what we think of as an expert source in the future.

Chapter Eight

What Should I Avoid?

The strength of your arguments is determined by the use of reliable evidence, sound reasoning, and adaptation to the audience. In the process of argumentation, mistakes sometimes occur. At this point, it is important to distinguish between those made deliberately to distort or deceive and those made in error. The message appears the same, whether the mistake is the product of intentional deception or the honest error of an arguer who has failed to examine his or her arguments critically. These mistakes are generically termed *fallacies*.

Rather than identifying all possible ways in which deliberate distortion and deception can occur, focusing on errors to avoid will better serve your development as an arguer. This chapter suggests how you can not only improve your skills as an advocate or an opponent of change but also hone your critical thinking skills to become a more discerning consumer of argument.

Since most errors in logic result from faulty reasoning or problems in language choice, we want to emphasize the need to pay careful attention to the structure of arguments, the nature of the appeals they make, and the language used to phrase them. Consider these problems from the following perspective:

> The study of fallacies can be thought of as a kind of sensitivity-training in reasoning. It should attune the student to the omnipresent dangers to which we are exposed as a consequence of imprecise expressions—vague, ambiguous, or misdefined terms—students should also be alert to unarticulated assumptions and presumptions. (Toulmin et al., 1984, p. 132)

Fallacies in Reasoning

Hasty Generalization

When you make a hasty generalization, you have committed the error of jumping to a conclusion. Recall the two tests of argument from generalization: The

132

generalization must be made on the basis of a sufficient number of cases and the cases must comprise a representative sample of all cases. The fallacy of hasty generalization occurs when the claim is not warranted, either because insufficient cases were used or because they constitute a nonrepresentative sample.

Representative Albert Bustamante asked Dr. Ronald Cotterill, director of the Food Marketing Policy Center at the University of Connecticut, about U.S. Department of Agriculture studies that indicate the poor do not pay any more for groceries than the average consumer. Dr. Cotterill's response indicates that even scientific research can lead to hasty generalizations if either the methodology, or its means of operationalization, is flawed.

> [T]here was a study in 1988 with regards to whether the poor pay more that purports to show that, in fact, inner-city, low-income residents do not pay any more than anyone else. The study is fundamentally flawed by the nature of the price indices used.
>
> The study does not control for quality as clearly as they could, and it is a very complicated process. In respect for the people that worked on the study, they had hoped to get a full-scale sample, a statistically valid sample for the United States, and they had to use Pinkerton Agency employees to go into stores in 26 cities and gather several thousand prices from several stores at each of these areas.
>
> Quite frankly, the Pinkerton Agency's employees in my opinion, were not up to the task of doing this. Consequently the data was very, very sporadic and with a lot of missing data, and as a result their aggregation procedures produced quite flawed price indexes. (Urban Grocery Gap, 1992, p. 14)

The scientific method imposes rigorous standards for data collection and analysis that must be met if valid generalizations are to be drawn. In the field of scientific argument, those reporting results are also expected to report any limitations that would restrict their generalizability. These limitations constitute the deficiencies in the backing available to support warrant implicit in all scientific research, that the results are generalizable beyond the sample from which they were derived because the scientific method was employed.

No similar tradition exists in academic argumentation. Avoiding the fallacy of hasty generalization underscores the importance of our earlier suggestions that arguers include all elements of the primary triad in the Toulmin model of argument and that they back their warrants. "If we are forced to spell out the warrants on which our arguments rely and the backing on which those warrants depend, it will usually become clear at once when our grounds are based on too small a sample of cases or on examples that are quite *untypical*" (Toulmin et al., 1984, p. 154).

Many fallacious generalizations occur when arguers are tempted to squeeze more from an argument than is actually warranted. Arguing an unqualified claim grounded on insufficient or atypical cases, rather than one qualified to conform to the limitations of your research, is a mistake. Since generalization is one of the most frequently used forms of reasoning, you are well advised to examine the generalizations you make and hear very carefully.

Transfer

Transfers extend reasoning beyond what is logically possible. There are three common types of transfer: fallacy of composition, fallacy of division, and fallacy of refutation.

Fallacies of composition occur when a claim asserts that what is true of a part is true of the whole. In testifying before the Senate Committee on the Judiciary's Subcommittee on Patents, Copyrights and Trademarks, Mr. Ralph Oman, Register of Copyrights and Associate Librarian for Copyright Services of the Library of Congress, made precisely that error in reasoning.

> Your bill, Mr. Chairman, cuts with what I see as a surgical precision. It does not overreach. It does not cramp the taping habits of teenage America, who still use the analog format. These teenagers have little disposable income anyway, so it's harder to make the case that home taping displaces sales. They would not always buy prerecorded tapes if they couldn't copy.
> But that's not the case with digital audiotapes, Mr. Chairman. We're dealing here with a very expensive, high-end technology. Only a serious audiophile with a large disposable income will buy the machines at $800 a copy. Only he or she has the money to pay $25 per prerecorded DAT tape. He or she insists on the best quality. With the DAT machines, the serious music lover can make perfect copies for the digital tape deck in the Mercedes. Without the DAT machine, he or she would buy the extra tape. So in the digital format, copying does displace sales. (The Audio Home Recording Act of 1991, 1991, p. 7)

Before you start thinking hasty generalization, because this argument certainly is one, notice the whole lifestyle asserted to accompany the part that represents differences in disposable income between teenagers and the rest of humanity. As a class of citizens, teenagers are poor and unable to afford high-quality stereo equipment or even prerecorded tapes some of the time. The inferior sounding analog copies they make do not hurt the profits of the recording industry or artists. A trip to Tower Records or Musicland to observe the merchandise and the clientele exposes the fallacy of composition. Teenagers may be strapped for cash, but the kind of music that is produced and sells in quantity suggests the industry wants and gets their business. Since music is an important part of teenage culture, young people discuss it, share it, copy it for each other. These copies, even if they are inferior sounding analog ones, hurt profits because money is being spent on blank tapes rather than prerecorded ones.

Equally fallacious is the characterization of audiophiles. They have enough money for a high-end stereo, and a high-end car with a high-end stereo in it. Is the transfer from part, spending money on a high-end stereo, to whole, being wealthy enough to own a Mercedes, warranted? Audiophiles can afford to buy one tape to have at home and another to have in their car, so when they make a perfect DAT copy the industry loses money. Is the transfer from part, they are clever or industrious enough to be wealthy, to whole, they are too stupid or lazy to use one tape in both places, warranted? When claims assert that what is true of a part is true of the whole, the warrant and its backing must be carefully examined since they are what justifies the inferential leap from part to whole. Mr. Oman's argument fails to justify this leap for either teenagers or the rest of humanity.

Fallacies of division are the opposite of fallacies of composition. The error arises from arguing that what is true of the whole will be true of its parts. When you break a whole into its parts and attempt to make claims about them, you may create an unwarranted transfer from the whole to its parts. "Speech courses are fun, and argumentation is a speech course; therefore, argumentation is fun." This may be true, it may be false; but the transfer from whole to part is not sufficiently warranted.

Mr. Neil Hickey, senior editor for *TV Guide*, committed the fallacy of division in responding to Representative Charles Schumer's question about whether networks program to the lowest common denominator, violence, to get better ratings and make higher profits.

> Now we are hearing about the possibility of there being 500 channels into the home. What does that mean if everybody is doing the same kind of eye-catching and occasionally violent programming that we have seen samples of today?
>
> It is not realistic to suppose that suddenly all of those programs, all those program creators are going to get religion and start doing Shakespeare.
>
> So we have to deal with the real world, we have to deal with the available world. In the available world, program producers use violent, eye-catching programs, really cheaply produced violent activity as an eye-catching movement, as a ratings builder. (Violence on Television, 1992, p. 60)

Whenever we speak of all members of a group as having uniform motives or behavior patterns, we risk committing the fallacy of composition. When the group is composed of members of an industry such as television, they compete with each other for customers. Since differentiating from one's competitors may be as commercially advantageous as emulating them, the warrant for a claim such as the one Mr. Hickey makes should be carefully examined. Even in an area where only forty-six channels are available on cable, the groundless nature of his claim, that every channel ends up carrying similar, violent programming, is obvious.

Fallacy of refutation is the final transfer fallacy, also known as the *straw man* argument. It occurs when an arguer attempts to direct attention to the successful refutation of an argument that was never raised or to restate a strong argument in a way that makes it appear weaker. It is called a straw man argument because it focuses on an issue that is easy to overturn. It is a form of deception since it introduces a bogus claim, one that was not part of the argument, or misrepresents the original claim.

In her written testimony, Ms. Susan Lamson, director of the Federal Affairs Division of the National Rifle Association of America's Institute for Legislative Action, commits the fallacy of refutation by arguing that a bill that would prohibit juveniles from possessing handguns will fail to solve broader social problems.

In 1982 there was a murder committed by a juvenile approximately every 40 days. In 1992 a murder was committed by a juvenile every 12 days. In 1982 a juvenile committed a rape every 26 days; by 1992 it was every 5 days. The statistics on violent behavior may partially include every race and income group, but those who ignore the fact that there is an overwhelmingly disproportionate impact on poor, black and hispanic inner city youths are not focusing on where the problem lies.

The pathologies of the inner city cannot be remedied by creating stronger laws, unless of course we can pass laws that every family has two caring parents; unless we can pass laws that reverse the pernicious effects of drugs and widespread alcohol use in our inner cities; unless we can pass laws outlawing poverty; unless we can pass laws that give young people stability and knowledge that they can reach their goals by hard work and perseverance—and that the goals are worth reaching.

Last year, Professors Joseph Sheley, Zina McGee and James Wright published "Gun-Related Violence in and Around Inner-City Schools"—the results of a cross-sectional survey of ten inner-city high schools in several states. Noting that "nearly everything that leads to gun-related violence among youths is already against the law" the researchers' prescription was neither more gun restrictions, metal detectors, nor shake-downs of students, but "a concerted effort to rebuild the social structure of inner cities." (Children and Gun Violence, 1993, p. 73)

Fallacies of this sort are relatively easy to commit. We often raise a series of questions or call attention to things related but not central to the issue at hand, thinking they constitute a sufficient response to the arguments of another. Ms. Lamson is correct in claiming that the fundamental problems of the inner city would remain if juveniles were prohibited from possessing handguns. Denying juveniles access to handguns as a tool for coping with their frustrations, with the very real problems she identifies, would result in fewer people being shot and killed. Her carefully prepared argument refutes a point that was never raised by the bill's advocates, whose goal was to reduce the level of gun violence.

It is easy to accidentally shift the focus of argumentation in an inappropriate direction. When we are uninformed or ill prepared, we may unintentionally create straw man arguments. Carefully examine the degree of similarity between the things compared in an analogy or the number of cases used to support a generalization. Responding to an argument perceived to be weak with a strong argument of your own does not mean you are necessarily creating a straw man by magnifying a minor issue into a major one. Remember, the quality of individual units of argument can vary, depending on both the competence of the arguers and the availability of evidence.

Irrelevant Arguments

An irrelevant argument is one that does not seem pertinent in terms of the claim it advances or the basis of the proof it offers. Such fallacies are also known as *non sequiturs*, Latin for "it does not necessarily follow." Winston Cox, CEO of Showtime Networks, and Representative Charles Schumer engaged in an interesting discussion of the relative offensiveness of sexually oriented versus violent television programming. Dean-emeritus of the University of Pennsylvania's Annenberg School for Communication, Dr. George Gerbner punctuated their conversation with a classic non sequitur.

MR. COX: I think in our country, I ask friends, and I would ask any member of this panel, are you more uncomfortable having your child watch a movie with an adult sexual content or with violence? In most cases the people will say, the sexual stuff should not be on.

MR. SCHUMER: I agree, except that is because the violence is so much more prevalent that you expect it. If every day the morning cartoons show the Ninja Turtles in sexual acts with one another and never show violence, who knows how they might feel? I don't know enough about turtle physiology.

DR. GERBNER: None of the Ninja Turtles are women.

MR. SCHUMER: I see. (Violence on Television, 1992, pp. 135–136)

Perhaps Dr. Gerbner's comment was only made to reduce Representative Schumer's uncertainty or in jest. If it was, it misses the point that the turtles could engage in sexual acts with each other despite the fact that none of them are women. The only way in which his comment is anything other than a non sequitur is if it is taken as extreme shorthand for the following unit of argument.

CLAIM: [Implied] Viewers would be more troubled by the depiction of homosexual than heterosexual acts on television.

WARRANT: [Implied] Because the United States is a homophobic nation.

GROUND: "None of the Ninja Turtles are women."

Since the discussion went off in another direction, there is no way of knowing for certain what Dr. Gerbner meant. If it is your intention to advance an argument, do so completely by stating your claim, the grounds that support it, and the warrant that links them so that you do not appear guilty of speaking or writing in non sequiturs.

Circular Reasoning

Also known as begging the question, arguments that are circular support claims with reasons identical to the claims themselves. In testimony that took place before the colloquy on turtle sexuality, Mr. Cox noted that people choose to subscribe to a premium service, such as Showtime, and then argued in a perfect circle around the issue of unwanted exposure to violence.

There are thus no premium network subscribers who find themselves unwittingly exposed to programming they did not ask to receive and pay to receive.

Our research has indicated that people subscribe to Showtime's premium services primarily to view recent Hollywood motion pictures. Many of these pictures, including many Academy Award winners for best picture—for example, "Platoon," "The Godfather," or "Silence of the Lambs"—contained depictions of violence as part of their plots.

Movies that are hits in the theaters are usually hits on our services as well. In March of this year, the premiere exhibition of "Silence of the Lambs" on Showtime received the highest viewership rating of any program ever to appear on Showtime up to that time. The rating was surpassed last August by the premiere showing of "Terminator 2," another picture containing episodes of violence. Our subscribers clearly have a preference for feature films, including those containing adult themes and violence.

This is not to say that violence on television, and in all other media, is not an important concern for our society. However, at least with respect to premium television, the protections offered to viewers by the subscription process itself, coupled with the scheduling and communication efforts of the premium networks, safeguard against unwanted exposure to the programming we offer. (Violence on Television, 1992, p. 103)

In this example, the meaning of grounds and warrant are equivalent to the meaning of the claim itself.

CLAIM: Unwanted exposure to violence is not a problem on the premium channels.

GROUND: People choose to subscribe and watch the programming that they want to see, some of which is violent.

WARRANT: The act of choosing to watch a violent program causes the viewer to not be exposed to any unwanted violence.

Strictly speaking, this is a nonargument, since it makes no inference from grounds through warrant to claim. It is an example of a fallacious attempt to support a claim by simply repeating the essential aspects of the claim using different words.

Avoiding the Issue

Any attempt to shift attention away from the issue at hand is an error because ignoring an issue rather than discussing it denies the integrity of the reasoning process. While we suspect that some avoidance behaviors are intentional, it is more likely that arguers pay insufficient attention to the task at hand. Monitor your own behavior and that of others for these common errors.

Simple evasion is the first type of avoidance. Changing the subject for no apparent reason, or bypassing a critical issue, diverts attention from the issues central to the argument. This error is most likely to occur when insufficient time has been spent analyzing the topic to determine which issues are inherent to the proposition. In some instances, evasion represents a conscious attempt to avoid confronting an unpleasant fact.

Critics of the death penalty often cite the execution of innocent people as one basis for their opposition. Since human systems have some residual level of error in them, no matter how many safeguards are built in, this could well be the case. In his statement opening the Senate Judiciary Committee's hearing on the death penalty, Senator Howard Metzenbaum charged the Supreme Court with simple evasion on this point.

In *Herrera*, the Supreme Court rules that the Constitution does not require that a hearing be granted to a death row inmate who has newly discovered evidence which, if proven, could establish his innocence. It was appalling to me that the Chief Justice, Justice Rehnquist, in his opinion for the Court was unable to clearly and unequivocally declare that the Constitution forbids the execution of innocent people. Instead, as the *National Law Journal* put it, his, "opinion puts forth the novel idea that innocence is not a necessary bar to carrying out a death sentence." (Innocence and the Death Penalty, 1993, p. 2)

It should be noted that those on the other side of the issue argued Senator Metzenbaum and the *National Law Journal* misconstrued the meaning of the Court's decision.

Attacking the person not the argument is the second avoidance behavior. Known as an *ad hominem argument*, it shifts attention to the personality or appearance of the arguer, her ability to reason, the color of her skin, or the values she holds, all of which tell us nothing about the validity of her arguments. "Jane, you ignorant slut," the phrase with which Dan Aykroyd began his part in "Saturday Night Live"'s parody of the *Point-Counterpoint* segment on "60 Minutes," is an example of invective used for comic rather than argumentative purposes, unless you assume the show's writers were using it to deride the conservative agenda that Aykroyd articulated.

It is essential that the worth of ideas behind claims be given primary consideration in the argumentative context, and the ad hominem argument subverts this. Former President Carter wrote a book of poetry that was well received by critics. An ad hominem attack dismissed it briefly, without presenting sound reasons why it was not worth reading. "He's written a book of poetry. I think that I shall never see/a poem as lovely as a goober pea" (Mullen, 1995, p. 10). White House Chief of Staff Leon Panetta used a similar tactic with regard to incoming Speaker of the House Newt Gingrich. "He's not the editor of a cheap tabloid, he's not just an out-of-control radio talk-show host. He's the speaker of the House of Representatives, and he's got to learn to behave as the Speaker of the House of Representatives" (*Republicans*, 1994/1995, p. 60).

There is one circumstance in which attacking the person is appropriate and does not commit any fallacy. That is when the qualifications of a source of information are called into question. So long as the argument focuses on factors relevant to the disputed issue and avoids irrelevant personal attack, no fallacy of reasoning takes place. In a written response to the Senate Judiciary Committee, Professor Michael Radelet of the University of Florida and Professor Adam Bedau of Tufts University attacked the tactics of a witness who appeared before it and the expertise of a source of information used by that witness.

> Mr. Cassell also presented the Committee with a distorted discussion of the research that has been done on the deterrent effect of capital punishment. Again, the belief that only sources that support his conclusion should be cited is seen. Mr. Cassell argues that the death penalty has strong deterrent effects, and cites a study done by Stephen Layson, a young economist, not a criminologist, and published in a regional economics journal, as support. He

ignores the fact that a meticulous critique of this study has been published since 1989 that showed that Mr. Layson's conclusions do not follow from his data. In addition, Mr. Cassell ignores the fact that no criminologist or sociologist in the country today claims to have data that show the death penalty has a better deterrent effect than long imprisonment. He ignores the fact that virtually every study done on deterrence in the United States in the last sixty years has found no deterrent effects. He ignores such authority as the National Academy of Sciences, whose study on this topic in 1978 concluded that a study similar to that cited by Mr. Cassell had no relevance for public policy. Even Stephen Layson, author of the study cited by Mr. Cassell, acknowledged in his 1985 Congressional testimony that his results were an artifact of the 1960s, when few executions occurred, and thus the findings could not be generalized to other years in the irresponsible way done by Mr. Cassell. By ignoring the problems with the work on deterrence he cites, as well as by ignoring numerous other studies that conflict with his preset conclusions, Mr. Cassell misleads this Committee about the status of modern research on deterrence. (Innocence and the Death Penalty, 1993, p. 158)

What Radelet and Bedau did differs from the three previous examples because they offer a series of arguments indicting the tactics of Mr. Cassell and the qualifications of Mr. Layson. They apply tests of proof, source credibility, and sound reasoning rather than attacking the personhood of either the opposing arguer or his source. They apply the rule of that noted practitioner of argumentation, Don Vito Corleone, the Godfather, "It's not personal, it's business."

Shifting ground is a third fallacy of avoidance. Shifts of ground occur when an arguer abandons his or her original position on a particular argument and adopts a new one. It is probably one of the easiest errors to commit. In everyday communication, most of us do not decide on what we plan to say in advance. There is a tendency to adapt, to modify our thoughts and the manner of their expression, to those around us. This becomes a problem when we are involved in argumentation because shifting ground gives the impression of evasiveness. We need to be careful to stick to our claims. This does not mean you can never change your mind or admit an error in argumentation. However, if you find it necessary to move away from your original claims, take special care to explain what has caused you to shift ground.

Notice how Mr. James Fendry, legislative director of the Wisconsin Pistol and Rifle Association, moves from a position of saying we are all in agreement to a position that is precisely the opposite. He justifies this change by arguing that while he can agree with reasonable regulation, he cannot accept an outright ban.

Perhaps my most favorite saying by a philosopher is that conflict among men is seldom a conflict of good versus evil; rather it's varying ideas of good. Everybody in this room, and I think in this nation, concurs with what you want. I agree with what you want, I agree with what Attorney General Doyle claims to desire, but if everybody listened very closely and looked for the Freudian slips, we'd see there's a little more. This isn't an issue of guns and gun control. This is an issue of civil rights and personal freedoms and whether your descendants are going to have the ability to own guns. General Doyle has proposed and has introduced legislation that doesn't reasonably regulate firearms. It strongly bans firearms acquisition on the way to further bans. And the speaker that will follow me will talk about the need for reasonable regulations. But Sarah Brady's organization, Handgun Control, Inc., continues to donate large sums of money to communities and to states that attempt to ban the possession of handguns and of semi-automatic rifles and shotguns, and that's not a reasonable regulation. That is a ban. And even in one of the most liberal cities in the United States, Madison, Wisconsin, when the voters had an opportunity to decide whether they wanted to lose the right, the money that was put in by Sarah Brady wasn't enough and the issue failed. And this is the slippery slope that we're concerned about, Senator. (Children and Gun Violence, 1993, pp. 151–152)

Seizing on a trivial point is the final error of avoidance. When you locate another's weak or indefensible argument and magnify it out of all proportion to discredit his entire position on the proposition, you have committed the fallacy of seizing on a trivial point. Since Mr. Fendry referred to Sarah Brady, let's see how her testimony almost committed the fallacy of seizing on a trivial point. At one point, she responded to Senator Herbert Kohl's question about the claim that the existence of 22,000 gun laws proves that legislation cannot reduce gun-related violence.

OK. First of all, I would say, no one has ever been able to figure out where this 22,000 figure comes from. According to the Justice Department we can only figure out close to 15 or 16,000 laws, most of which are very local, some very antiquated. (Children and Gun Violence, 1993, p. 159)

The accuracy of factual information is of great importance, but focusing all of your attention on minor inaccuracies and trivial points is unsound argumentation. Had her response stopped at this point, Mrs. Brady would have seized on a trivial point. Even using the lower range of the Justice Department estimate, 15,000 laws is a lot. It should be enough to reduce gun-related violence if laws were a necessary or sufficient cause to produce that effect. The remainder of her response to Senator Kohl's question is what enabled her to avoid the fallacy of seizing on a trivial point.

They are certainly not federal laws. And it points out what we need are effective, national, uniform laws that are enforceable and that are enforced. And we need effective laws, and that's what we're working toward with the Brady Bill, that's with your bill, which would be put in place federally, what Wisconsin already has in place, would do, would make it uniform so that you can't go to other states and traffic guns back in, so that everybody across the country is on an even footing. (Children and Gun Violence, 1993, p. 159)

Forcing a Dichotomy

A forced dichotomy is one in which listeners or readers are presented with an oversimplified either-or choice, phrased in such a way that it forces them to favor the arguer's preferred option. The fallaciousness of the forced dichotomy rests on its failure to consider alternative choices fully. The forced dichotomy is also known as the false dilemma. Because argument from dilemma involves clustering two or more arguments from cause, forced dichotomies or false dilemmas are produced when arguers fail to account for the possibility of partial or multiple causality. The forced dichotomy is a fallacy in reasoning because the choice making that it forces is too simplistic.

Notice how Representative Charles Schumer rejected a false dichotomy, that television is either the cause of all social problems or has no effect on them whatsoever, in his statement opening the hearings on television violence.

> At a recent symposium on television violence sponsored by *TV Guide*, Neil Hickey pointed out that, in 1940, the seven top problems in public schools identified by teachers were: talking out of turn; chewing gum; making noise; running in the halls; cutting in line; dress code infractions; and illiteracy.
>
> In 1980, the top seven problems in public schools were: suicide; assault; robbery; rape; drug abuse; alcohol abuse; and pregnancy.
>
> Now, of course, television is not to blame for all of this dramatic change, but it is just as wrong to say it has had no effect at all. It has, and that is why we are here. (Violence on Television, 1992, p. 2)

The either-or rhetoric of a forced dichotomy in this instance would have forestalled consideration of too many potential issues. In human affairs, truth about causality is seldom an either-or proposition, a simple choice between two alternative explanations. Examine your own reasoning and that of others to avoid being trapped into arguing or accepting forced dichotomies.

Summary of Fallacies in Reasoning

1. *Hasty generalizations* offer conclusions based on insufficient information, for example, on too few instances, atypical examples, or overstatements that claim more than is warranted.
2. *Transfer fallacies of composition* result from the unwarranted assumption that what is true of the part is true of the whole.
3. *Transfer fallacies of division* result from the unwarranted assumption that what is true of the whole is true of its parts.
4. *Irrelevant arguments*, non sequiturs, make assumptions that do not follow from the information provided.
5. *Circular reasoning* offers as warrants and grounds statements equivalent in meaning to the claims they are supposed to support.
6. *Avoiding the issue* is an error in reasoning that shifts attention from the issue under consideration. It commonly takes the form of a simple evasion of the issue, an attack on the arguer rather than the argument, a shift of ground, or seizing on a trivial point rather than the central issue.
7. *Forcing a dichotomy* puts the listener or reader in the position of having to choose between oversimplified either-or options.

Fallacies of Appeal

When you construct an argument, you do not do so in a vacuum. You have an audience in mind and develop your arguments accordingly. This can lead you to commit a series of fallacies based on the appeals you decide to make. In particular we must be careful when appealing to emotion rather than the ability to reason. There is nothing intrinsically wrong with emotional appeals, but problems can arise when you use these appeals to avoid arguing the issues at hand. Appeals that bypass reason are usually based on the feelings, prejudices, or desires of the audience. The fallacies of appeal we shall discuss are some of the more commonly occurring lapses arguers experience that reduce the rationality of their arguments. Again, we emphasize that emotional appeals are an important part of the process of persuasion and caution that in argumentation emotion should not supplant reason.

Appeal to Ignorance

Appeals to ignorance, known by the Latin term *ad ignoratium*, ask the audience to accept the truth of a claim because no proof to the contrary exists. Something is true simply because it cannot be proven false. Often the appeal to ignorance is couched in terms of a proposal to study the problem further or to suspend judgment until the results of a study already in progress are available. When asked by Representative Charles Schumer if cable wasn't more violent than network television, Mr. Winston Cox, CEO of Showtime Networks, was both evasive and appealed to ignorance.

> As I said, we are in the final stages of having Dr. Gerbner actually conduct a study for us on violence in the original programming created for cable. A lot of the programming on cable is a product that is acquired or that has played somewhere else first, in the case of Showtime, theatrical feature films. In the case of other networks, it is product they may have acquired from places like the broadcast networks themselves. When USA Network licenses, for example, "Miami Vice," it is what we characterize in the business as an "off-net" piece of product.
> But I think the areas we can be most directly responsible for, and can exercise some control over, are programs that we create specifically for our networks. I think we need to wait until the results of the study are finished to see just how cable networks stack up against other forms of television. (Violence on Television, 1992, p. 134)

His response was evasive because it asserts that cable should not be accountable for the violent content of material produced elsewhere, even though cable chooses to license and broadcast it. His response appealed to ignorance by playing for time until the results of a study of cable content, which will ignore material produced elsewhere, become available.

Even more troublesome is the technique of claiming that because we cannot prove something has not happened or does not exist it therefore must have happened or must exist. "The inability to disprove the existence of flying saucers and extraterrestrial visitation to earth confirms the existence of the former and the occurrence of the latter."

Can you make nonfallacious claims about what the absence of proof may mean? Yes, to a certain extent. An absence of evidence suggests the possibility of a claim's validity in certain fields of argument. For example, drugs are tested for side effects and are presumed safe when none occur. The problem with using this type of reasoning in other fields of argument is that backing for the warrant becomes the assertion that the lack of evidence is, in and of itself, evidence. This tends to trivialize the meaning of evidence as a concept (Toulmin et al., 1984).

There is one important exception that would extend the medical paradigm to other fields of argument: Artificial presumption may be assigned in such a way that failure to prove something leads to the conclusion that its logical opposite is true. When the prosecution fails to present a prima facie case against the accused, we conclude the accused must be innocent. In other fields that do not rely exclusively on artificial presumption, the absence of contrary evidence may strengthen a claim, but it in no way proves it. The absence of evidence may simply mean that research regarding the phenomenon has not been very thorough.

Appeal to the People

Also known as the bandwagon appeal, or an *ad populum argument*, appeals to the people address the audience's prejudices and feelings rather than the issues. When a claim is justified on the basis of its alleged popularity—we should do or believe something because the majority of people do or believe it—an appeal to the people is being made. Mr. Norman Ornstein of the American Enterprise Institute for Public Policy Research explicitly rejected the idea of relying on ad populum arguments when he testified on the issue of term limits.

> Dave Mason mentioned public opinion. Of course, there is no question that a clear majority, a vast majority of Americans now like term limits. Term limits has struck a chord connecting with the anger, angst, and antipathy that a majority of voters feel toward politics and politicians. But I think it should be noted that Americans in large majorities like the idea of abolishing the electoral college, they like the idea of a constitutional amendment to ban flag burning and we have a variety of surveys over the years that have shown clear majorities willing to repeal various parts of the Bill of Rights.
>
> I don't think most of the members of this subcommittee would support all of those ideas, and I think in the end few would argue, although some proponents of term limits do, that simply the support of the American people for an idea through surveys is itself a sufficient condition to pass a law or change the Constitution. It is clearly a good reason to examine this issue in depth, and I think Mr. Mason is absolutely right in this regard, but that is all. (Term Limits for Members of the U. S. Senate and House of Representatives, 1994, pp. 48–49)

On the one hand, common sense suggests that when matters concerning "the people" are discussed, their will should be taken into account. In the case of a future law, this allows us to forecast whether it would likely be obeyed or violated. On the other hand, to make popular opinion the sole criterion of a claim's worth, and to appeal to this opinion in order to discourage consideration of pertinent facts, cannot help but result in less informed and less thoughtful decisions.

As Mr. Ornstein suggests, critical consideration of the issues should take precedence over popular opinion.

Appeal to Emotion

As we suggested, the use of emotional appeals is not necessarily bad, nor is it possible to be entirely rational. Nevertheless, strong appeals to emotion are no substitute for careful reasoning. Any emotion may be a source of appeal; here, we will concentrate on the two used most frequently in poor argumentation, appeals to pity and fear.

Traditionally, the use of the appeal to pity was taught as a means of creating audience sympathy for an individual or group. Such appeals are common on topics that address the suffering of those unable to overcome misfortune without the aid of others. No fallacy is committed when such appeals are used in conjunction with sound reasoning. However, when pity is the only basis on which an alteration of belief or behavior is justified, argumentation has been abandoned in favor of exclusively emotive persuasion.

The appeal to fear is another form of emotion seeking, arousing concern over potential consequences. As with appeals to pity, the use of appeals to fear is a matter of appropriateness and balance. There are occasions when a little fear is needed to move people to action, but appealing to fear alone may produce disastrous consequences. When fear dictates behavior, rash decisions may result, such as the blacklisting that destroyed careers during the McCarthy era.

James Fendry employed appeals to both fear and pity in his testimony opposing legislation that would prohibit juveniles from possessing handguns. His use of these appeals is fallacious because his argument makes a hasty generalization about the dangers faced by an indeterminate number of farm boys, young gay people, young single mothers, and college co-eds who would be denied access to handguns.

> [O]ne doesn't have to go to Wyoming to find people under the age of 18 carrying handguns. If we take a look, we'll find that some of the farm boys in the hills of Baraboo carry handguns while working their family farm because of the abundance and the dangers of rattlesnakes that reside in the area. The question then, is would it be prudent or even practical to make that type of activity a Federal violation? Of course, it's the cities where all the problems lie. Even if S-1087 was limited to cities of a certain population, then what about the safety of those under 18 who live alone? How do we tell a young gay person, thrown out of their home by homophobic parents, that if they possess a handgun for protection from murderous gay bashers, that this possession would become a federal offense? How do you tell a young single mother, living alone, the type of women who often won't have enough money to buy a handgun better than one that was pictured here before, that if she decides to possess one to protect herself and her child that she will then have violated Federal law? And how do you tell the female students at the Florida University, where so many numerous classmates have been raped and

murdered, that if dad and mom give them a handgun to keep them from being next, the entire family, then, could end up in Federal court? (Children and Gun Violence, 1993, p. 149)

In the absence of someone arguing the other side of the issue, pointing out that most college students are over eighteen years old and that the potential harm to farm boys, gays, and young mothers cannot be assessed because these claims are ungrounded, it would be left to the members of Mr. Fendry's audience to guard against being swayed by a fallacious emotional appeal by engaging in critical listening.

Appeal to Authority

An argument from authority that utilizes the opinions and testimony of experts is a legitimate form of reasoning. However, care must be exercised to ensure that the argument from authority does not become a fallacious appeal to authority. An appeal to authority is fallacious when a seemingly authoritative source of opinion either lacks real expertise or prevents a fair hearing of the other side of the issue. Instead of being used to ground a claim or back a warrant, the authority is characterized as infallible and is used to shut off further discussion of the issues. Abuses of authority commonly involve the Bible, the Constitution, revered persons, or testimonials by celebrities in advertising.

Senator John Chaffee noted how fallacious appeals to authority sometimes find their way into arguments over gun control.

I noticed that the NRA is going to testify later, and I just wanted everybody to fully understand the second amendment. The second amendment, as quoted by the NRA, is "The right of the people to keep and bear arms shall not be infringed." What they don't mention is the first part of the second amendment, which says, "A well-regulated militia being necessary to the security of a free State, the right of the people to keep and bear arms shall not be infringed." That has been universally interpreted by Federal courts to mean that the right of the people to keep and bear arms deals with those who are in a well-regulated militia.

Frankly, I have no argument with the National Rifle Association because my bill doesn't deal with rifles. It deals solely with handguns. And I think it is important for everybody to understand what the second amendment does say and mean because it is not fully explained frequently. I receive lots of letters on this, saying, oh, you are monkeying around with the second amendment of the Constitution. But not at all. (Children and Gun Violence, 1993, p. 10)

Besides avoiding the use of authority to short circuit the process of argumentation entirely, be prepared to defend your choice of experts. Unknowingly, your choice may represent a fallacious use of authority if you cite someone outside her or his acknowledged field of expertise. While we might take Joe Montana's advice on football, is he likely to be an expert on soft drinks? Making this distinction is sometimes difficult because an individual may be an expert in more than one field. At one time, comedian Bill Cosby appeared in a series of computer commercials. We might acknowledge his expertise on issues of comedy or acting, but what about education, the major claim advanced in these commercials? In fact, Bill Cosby has advanced degrees in psychology and education, has produced several educational films, and has also lectured on race relations and motivation. This illustrates why it is always important to provide information documenting the qualifications of those you cite.

Appeal to Tradition

We normally have strong ties to tradition, and learning the historical background of a topic is a good way to prepare to argue it. However, asking an audience to accept something because it is customary rather than because of the reasons that justify it commits the fallacy of appeal to tradition. A discussion of the circumstances under which it might be appropriate for a juvenile to be able to use a handgun between Senator Carol Moseley-Braun and Susan Lamson of the National Rifle Association culminated in an appeal to tradition.

MOSELEY-BRAUN: Ms. Lamson, I am a little perplexed by part of the testimony. You testified that you wouldn't want to interfere with the lawful use of handguns by juveniles, and I can't think of an instance in which a child should ever have a handgun. I was confused as to what you meant by the lawful use of a handgun by a juvenile.

LAMSON: The issue at hand is the lawful use of firearms under supervision, and there are certainly target ranges, and so forth, that allow juveniles, young teenagers who are juveniles within the age limitation who are quite capable of learning target shooting—

MOSELEY-BRAUN: Well, that is exempted under the bill.

LAMSON: That is right, that is correct, and that is why we recognize there is a lawful use there. As I mentioned in the testimony, one other area we would like to discuss is the ability to have an exception for hunting because most States provide an age for hunting that is less than the Federal standard in terms of possession of guns.

MOSELEY-BRAUN: Well, in terms of hunting specifically, I used to hunt with my daddy when we were growing up and he never used a handgun to hunt. Do people use handguns?

LAMSON: They do for varmint hunting as an example, yes.

MOSELEY-BRAUN: Wouldn't it be alright to say, for hunting for juveniles, we would restrict that to long guns?

LAMSON: Well, the thing is what we are talking about is lawful use, and I think as long as there is an exception—

MOSELEY-BRAUN: Well, we make the laws. That is why we are here. . . .

LAMSON: Well, I would say that we would like to look at this legislation not restricting uses that have been traditional in this country, you know protected and covered by State law, as well as Federal law, and that is why we raised the subject of hunting. We can provide additional information to you on that as it relates to handguns. But, again, we have recommended under consideration because the draft legislation already speaks to or already has underscored that there is firearm use by juveniles that has been legal and that is legitimate.

MOSELEY-BRAUN: Thank you. (Children and Gun Violence, 1993, pp. 76–77)

The argument that since young people have been able to do something in the past they should be able to do it in the future is a fallacious appeal to tradition. It suggests the existence of any practice sanctioned by law is sufficient in and of itself to justify its perpetuation. On that basis, women should not have the right to vote, and African Americans should not have the opportunity to learn to read, because giving these rights to either group violates a tradition that was legally sanctioned at one time.

Comparisons that reference tradition are not necessarily inappropriate. Value claims often involve matters of taste derived from tradition. A thorough analysis of the reasons behind a tradition provides a valid basis on which to argue its future violation or veneration. However, it is important to realize that arguing on behalf of a belief or behavior solely on the basis of tradition gives the audience insufficient understanding of the issues that justify opposing a proposed change in that belief or behavior.

Recalling our discussion of presumption, you may think something is amiss. Doesn't presumption favor tradition, that which is already in existence? Yes, and opponents in argumentation find themselves arguing on behalf of the benefits of continuing to believe or behave as we have in the past just as Ms. Lamson does. However, when the opponent uses such argument, she must provide good and sufficient reasons to justify maintaining that tradition and not merely appeal to tradition alone.

Appeal to Humor

Appeals based on humor can be problematical for several reasons. The arguer who resorts to a series of jokes about women drivers to refute criticism of auto safety standards uses humor to entertain rather than enlighten. When humor is used to such an extent that it becomes the focal point of the discussion, the point of argumentation is lost.

An ongoing dispute during hearings on term limits was the issue of how long it takes new representatives to learn enough about how the government works to be able to accomplish anything meaningful or worthwhile. Advocates of term limits argued newcomers could be effective on their first day in Washington, while opponents such as Representative Henry Hyde claimed it took them eight years to get up to speed. That led to the following exchange between syndicated columnist George Will and Representative Hyde.

WILL: I am fascinated by Mr. Hyde's eight-year threshold for competence. Before sending my crack staff back to study the first silent years of Henry Hyde's tenure to see if he was silent and demur, which I doubt—

HYDE: I was noisy, but ignorant. (Term Limits for Members of the U. S. Senate and House of Representatives, 1994, p. 291)

Fortunately, the discussion returned to a more serious-minded consideration of the performance of newly elected and appointed officials at the federal and state levels. Had it continued in this lighthearted manner, little would have been accomplished to advance rational consideration of an important issue of public policy.

Humor is also misused when it takes a claim to its most extreme and, therefore, absurd meaning. This is known as *reductio ad absurdum*. Reducing a claim to absurdity is a particularly troublesome kind of fallacy because it sometimes occurs in an effort to employ style. What it mostly does is decrease the discussion's rationality. One of the premises of the National Rifle Association is frequently seen on bumper stickers: "I support the right to bear arms." This claim is reduced to the absurd by another bumper sticker: "I support the right to arm bears!" While such a turn of phrase may be witty, it has the effect of trivializing a serious issue.

This is not to say that humor cannot be an effective device. Humor can have a positive effect, creating good will or lessening tensions in a heated situation. During the summer of 1980, President Carter had the unpleasant task of informing farmers in the southwest that the economic aid they desired would not be forthcoming. Just before his helicopter landed in the drought-stricken Dallas–Fort Worth area, there was a sudden rainfall. President Carter began an address to a group of farmers saying, "Well, you asked for either money or rain. I couldn't get the money so I brought the rain" (Boller, 1981, p. 346).

Summary of Fallacies of Appeal

1. *Appeals to ignorance* ask the audience to accept a claim solely because no proof exists to deny its validity.
2. *Appeals to the people* ask an audience to accept a claim because it is supported by majority opinion.
3. *Appeals to pity* arouse sympathy for individuals or groups to encourage the redress of some wrong or misfortune they have suffered.
4. *Appeals to fear* attempt to gain the audience's acceptance of a claim by arousing concern over the consequence it alleges.
5. *Appeals to authority* encourage reliance on some ultimate source of knowledge in place of reasoning as the basis of a claim.
6. *Appeals to tradition* ask an audience to accept a claim because it represents a customary belief or course of action.
7. *Appeals to humor* either fail to make a serious point or reduce another's claim to its most absurd level.

Fallacies in Language

Since language is the vehicle of your argument's meaning, you must be cognizant of how you use it in constructing arguments. We have already indicated some concerns about the way in which claims are phrased and stressed the importance of defining terms. We now discuss the care that must be exercised in choosing language appropriate to all aspects of argumentation. In any use of language, but especially in using it to alter belief or behavior, it is important to remember that meanings are in people, not in words. The meaning we attach to the words of others is a consequence of their passing through our own perceptual filters. Become aware of your own language habits and biases to avoid falling victim to the fallacies of language described here.

Ambiguity and Equivocation

The ambiguity of language interferes with effective argumentation when a term is used differently by both parties to the dispute. This "meanings are in people" problem may occur unintentionally, with both arguers operating on the basis of legitimate, but entirely different, meanings for a term. If you have ever handed a paper in late and the professor, emulating Benjamin Disraeli, has told you, "I shall lose no time in reading this," you have experienced the uncertainty that ambiguity engenders.

Like the errors resulting from the ambiguity of language, errors of equivocation occur because words have multiple legitimate meanings. An error of equivocation occurs when we use ambiguous words in order to conceal the truth or avoid committing ourselves to a position. When you shift the meaning of a term in an argument, you are equivocating. When you use language to try to step around an issue rather than face it head on, you are equivocating. The statements of candidates for public office are frequently and intentionally equivocal as they attempt to avoid offending part of the electorate.

Following World War II, our government authorized a number of studies of the effects of radiation on human beings. Many of the subjects were on active duty in the military or were seeking treatment at hospitals operated by the Veterans Administration. Some were children who were fed or injected with low doses of radioactive material. In all cases, adult subjects and the parents of children included in the experiments were not made fully aware of the nature of the experiments. As a result, they could not give their informed consent to participating in these experiments.

Hearings before the Senate Committee on Labor and Human Resources afforded Austin LaRocque, one of the children in the experiment at the Fernald School in Waltham, Massachusetts, the opportunity to confront Dr. Bertran Brill, research director and professor of nuclear medicine at the University of Massachusetts. In earlier testimony, Dr. Brill indicated his own participation since the late 1950s "in the conduct of studies such as we are talking about from the Fernald School" (Human Subjects Research, 1994, p. 13).

LaRocque: To this gentleman here. Nothing personal. But if you had your son here, would you have allowed this to happen, knowing what you know about radiation.

Brill: Well, I have, you know, many of us in medicine, when we are investigating new phenomena will take radioactive tracers and study ourselves. I've done it so many times.

LaRocque: But you didn't answer my question directly. I want to know, if it was your son, would you have accepted it?

Brill: Knowing what I know now, I would. But at the time, I don't know. At this time, I think the radiation risks from the kinds of doses that were being used are in the noise [*sic*] in terms of biological effect. I don't think any hazard in terms of radiation damage would occur from the kinds of doses that were received. And if I was—the way I think I am, I'd say yes, honestly, yes. (Human Subjects Research, 1994, p. 22).

Since the audience is a part of the process of argumentation, it will be impossible for you to avoid all instances of ambiguity. However, by exercising care in phrasing arguments and defining key terms, you can avoid many errors of equivocation. You should be cognizant of language in the arguments you construct and scrutinize the language used in the evidence these arguments contain, especially when it is opinion evidence.

Emotionally Loaded Language

The arguments of everyday life are frequently condensed to what fits on a bumper sticker, a T-shirt, or a picket sign carried at a march or rally. "War is unhealthy for children and other living things." "Abortion is murder." "A boy of quality is not threatened by a girl of equality." In addition to serving as a vehicle for the denotation of ideas, language is a powerful instrument for the expression of attitudes and feelings. Your choice of language can reveal your attitude toward a topic. There can be little doubt how Marvin Kitman, television critic for "Newsday," feels about the issue of violence.

> The networks are like serial killers. Their programs are the equivalent of writing with lipstick on the mirrors in our home, "Stop me before I kill again." They have won the disrespect and distrust of the Nation in dealing with the violence problem. It is time TV was made to end the killing fields of violence. (Violence on Television, 1992, p. 16)

In various forms of imaginative or creative speaking and writing, language that fully expresses feeling or attitude is highly prized. Indeed, if language did not possess the power to express and elicit feelings, most of the world's great literature would not exist. In arguments, however, emotionally loaded language, which exceeds the natural warmth that marks a sincerely expressed belief and earnestness of purpose, becomes an impediment to rational decision making and represents a poor choice.

Technical Jargon

The use of the technical terminology of a field becomes a problem when it so confuses listeners that they lose sight of the issues or when it is used in place of reasoning on the issues. Beginning arguers frequently become so involved in their topic that they forget that not everyone is as conversant with its jargon as they are. Technical terminology may be important in explaining the issues involved, but it is possible to send an audience into semantic shock if you ask them to deal with too many new terms at once.

Audience analysis is critical in determining what needs further explanation and what does not. Some of the discussion of the bill prohibiting possession of handguns by juveniles centered on the wisdom of passing a law that would create, for the first time, a federal status offense. For those in attendance, the issue was not clouded by jargon. As lawmakers and lobbyists, they all knew a status offense is one in which behavior is only an offense (an illegal act) for persons of a certain status (under eighteen years old). A minor caught with a beer is a status offender. A minor caught with marijuana gets busted just like the rest of us.

In some cases, problems with jargon are less a result of the failure to analyze our audience than they are a failure to refrain from making word-salad when we speak or write.

> One of the concerns that we had in our preliminary review of the bill is that it doesn't state an interstate nexus to it, and you have a situation of possession with intrastate, and so we just would want to address what we need to do in terms of the Federal Government's role as the nexus in interstate commerce. (Children and Gun Violence, 1993, p. 75)

The best way to avoid problems with jargon is to say what you mean, and mean what you say, plainly.

Summary of Fallacies of Language

1. *Ambiguity* occurs when a term is used in legitimate but different senses by two or more persons involved in argumentation.
2. *Equivocation* occurs when an individual uses a term in different ways in the context of the same argument.
3. *Emotionally loaded language* is a problem when we use terms that show more about our feelings on the issues than about the rational basis from which those feelings derive or when we use emotion as the sole means to alter the belief or behavior of others.
4. *Technical jargon* becomes a problem when the audience is overwhelmed with too many new terms or when it is used to impress the audience or replace sound reasoning.

The foregoing are the sorts of errors in reasoning, appeal, and use of language that you should avoid in constructing your own arguments. Use them as a yardstick as well in evaluating the arguments of others. You should now be able to construct valid arguments, patterns of proof and reasoning that are sufficient to support claims. You are ready to begin putting it all together. In the next chapter, we will look at how advocates and opponents argue propositions of fact.

Learning Activities

1. Discuss current examples of advertising in the mass media. Which seem to have fallacies? What kinds of fallacies are they? Which examples of advertising, if any, employ sound reasoning according to the tests in Chapter 7?
2. Each of the following statements represents a fallacy of the types discussed in this chapter. Identify the type of fallacy in each statement and explain why the reasoning, appeal, or use of language is in error. Some statements contain more than one error, so be sure to identify all fallacies.

   A. In reference to high levels of defense and social spending, the government should have learned from the Vietnam experience that you can't have guns and butter at the same time.
   B. By definition, since a housewife is someone who doesn't work, it follows that all housewives are unemployed.
   C. When you've seen one zoo, you've seen them all.
   D. The Democratic party has always been the party of the working man and woman. It makes no sense for the AFL-CIO to endorse a Republican candidate.
   E. Obviously, the authors of this book want to make us schizophrenic. They want us to learn how to both advocate and oppose a proposition on the same topic.
   F. Your argument that drunk driving causes death and injury is very interesting, but what about all the people who weren't wearing their seatbelts at the time of the accident? Aren't you assuming that every person involved in an automobile accident has been drinking? You can't really make that claim until you look at some of the other information.
   G. We outlawed prayer in schools and look what happened! Within ten years of that sacrilegious court's decision, the divorce rate approached 50 percent, students are becoming functionally illiterate, drug abuse abounds in our schools, and juvenile crime is increasing.
   H. Cheating on exams must surely be acceptable. After all, most college students cheat on an exam at least once.
   I. The advocate has obviously misanalyzed the situation. The Supreme Court ruled in favor of freedom of choice in the matter of abortions in 1973, not 1972.
   J. The Motor Car Company's new V-Body designs have had serious problems with their brake systems. I'd be suspicious of all their products.
   K. Rolling Valley Vineyards must produce good wines. Their commercials state that they are the only American winery that doesn't use pesticides to control insect damages to the crop. We should all be concerned about pesticides in what we eat and drink.

L. The chairman of the rules committee says that our bylaws have been incorrectly developed. He ought to know. After all, he's the chairman of the rules committee.

M. We shouldn't be surprised that State University's basketball team was cited for recruiting violations. Recruiting players has always been a matter of which college could offer a prospect the best deal.

N. Professional athletics is a hotbed of drug abuse. Why just last week, three more football players were arrested for using cocaine.

Suggested Supplementary Readings

Fearnside, W. W., & Holther, W. B. (1959). *Fallacy: The Counterfeit of Argument.* Englewood Cliffs, NJ: Prentice-Hall.
This is one of the most comprehensive sources on the nature of fallacies. The authors provide an excellent classification system to cover fallacies of logic, emotional appeal, and language use. Despite its age, this book remains usable since most of the examples are taken from well-known historical sources or common communication situations.

Tindale, C. W., & Gough, J. (1987, Winter). The Use of Irony in Argumentation. *Philosophy and Rhetoric,* 20, 1–17.
The authors distinguish between the inappropriate use of humor to reduce reasoning to the level of absurdity and the potential for an appropriate use of the humorous technique of irony. Irony is a legitimate, and frequently used, literary device for offering social criticism. Tindale and Gough suggest that irony used for negative commentary is not necessarily committing a fallacy. Their discussion of the audience's receptiveness to ironic forms is particularly good.

Walton, D. N. (1980, Fall). Why Is the Ad Populum a Fallacy? *Philosophy and Rhetoric,* 13, 264–278.
Walton considers when the appeal to the people, the *ad populum* argument, is a fallacy and when it may be a legitimate use of reasoning techniques.

Walton, D. N. (1988). Burden of proof. *Argumentation,* 2, 233–254.
The fallacies of begging the question and appealing to ignorance can undermine an advocate's ability to meet her or his burden of proof. Walton suggests that begging the question "begs for" the audience to accept an argument rather than proves it. This is not argumentation; for something to be an argument, proof must be supplied. Walton suggests that the appeal to ignorance may not be as much a fallacy as simply a poor argument in which the arguer fails to meet his or her responsibility to ground claims with valid evidence.

Woods, J. (Ed.) (1987). *Argumentation,* 1, 209–349.
This entire issue of the journal, *Argumentation,* is devoted to discussing fallacies. Eight articles consider the nature of fallacies, how we might revitalize fallacy theory, fallacies of statistical use, and other topics that point toward a reconsideration of the nature of fallacies.

Chapter Nine

How Are Factual Propositions Argued?

Because their cultures placed such a high value on the legal field, the ancient Greeks and Romans became experts in factual argumentation. As the practice of being your own lawyer gave way to hiring a professional, textbooks on argumentation began to pay less and less attention to arguing propositions of fact. In the twentieth century, most argumentation textbooks have considered learning how to argue a factual proposition a stepping stone on the way to arguing about values and policies. And, it is a valid point that the ability to successfully argue propositions of value and policy is greatly enhanced by learning how to argue those of fact. The complexities of the twentieth century, however, have created a new interest in factual argumentation. The complicated relationships of our personal and public lives, the explosive development of technology, the pursuit of new knowledge, and the interpretation of existing knowledge in every field have revitalized argumentation theory and awakened our interest in arguing factual propositions in their own right.

Beyond the legal field's use of factual argumentation to determine probable guilt or innocence, we encounter factual propositions in many other fields. In the sciences, researchers and lay persons want to answer questions about the nature of things: What kind of diet contributes to healthy living? Is the inability to lose weight or the recurrence of migraine headaches a result of life style or one's genes? Is our physical universe expanding or contracting? And why won't my stupid computer do what I want it to? In the business field, our economic vitality depends upon finding the answers to such questions as: Will interest rates rise? Will the new product line sell? Are health care benefits going to bankrupt the retirement fund? Is the union likely to engage in a strike? The humanities, social sciences, athletics, religion, and every other field you can think of has its own factual questions to answer.

Answering factual questions is often a matter of arguing a factual proposition. Many fields see factual, as well as value and policy, argumentation as central to the production of knowledge in response to such questions. Argumentation is more than a process of advocating and opposing prima facie cases and asking an audience to render a decision as to which side wins. The new interest in factual argumentation suggests that we consider argumentation as critical thinking that questions how we use the knowledge and practices of each field. "Argumentation is no longer solely the articulation and testing of claims, it is also the understanding, critique and creation of the means of legitimation of knowledge" (Sandman, 1993, p. 101).

You may best understand the renewed interest in factual argumentation by thinking of your own experiences as a student.

> A physicist or biologist who argues, in a lecture in a course, by giving reasons for believing a particular scientific hypothesis is not typically trying to persuade his or her students. The teacher is often trying to see what the weight of the reasons for believing the hypothesis is. (Meiland, 1989, p. 186)

In this description of factual argumentation as a college lecture, Jack Meiland reveals a new perspective on the use of argumentation: Some practices of argumentation are less persuasive and more informative. Although we told you in Chapter 1 that argumentation is a subset of persuasion, our classification of human communication into uses is commonly divided into three: to inform, to persuade, and to celebrate ceremonial rituals.

Pragmatically, your authors subscribe to the philosophy that all human communication has persuasive potential. Even the college lecturer in physics or biology makes choices from the available knowledge in the field about what to include in a lecture. He or she will most likely choose the most accepted theories, a choice that "persuades" students to accept the prevailing viewpoint. If his or her personal viewpoint differs from accepted theory, the teacher may offer the prevailing viewpoint counterposed against his or her dissenting viewpoint. This latter version of teaching often makes for the most interesting class sessions and is a good example of factual argumentation. Whichever version of lecturing a professor might subscribe to, both have persuasive dimensions as he or she chooses what to include and exclude in the prima facie case for what the student should believe about the nature of physics or biology.

Learning how to argue factual propositions also has practical applications for you—a student who must write term papers and answer certain kinds of test questions. If you have ever written a research paper or an essay on a topic such as "The invasion of Grenada was an illegal use of presidential war powers," "The Union blockade of Confederate ports was the decisive factor in the South's defeat," or "The Monroe Doctrine justifies U.S. intervention in the political affairs of Latin America," you have developed argumentation on a factual proposition. What you learn in this chapter, and the chapters on value and policy argumentation, can be used as the basis for writing term papers and essays.

How can argumentation make you a more proficient paper writer or test taker? Meiland (1989) believes that when we approach argumentation as a process of inquiry, where we do not already have a predetermined role as advocate or opponent in mind and are free to choose our role, "the process of discovering what (if anything) it is rational to believe about a topic" (p. 187) is the essence of argumentation as knowledge seeking. Like scientists who seek truths through application of the scientific method, argumentation as knowledge seeking follows this pattern:

1. Decide what question or problem involving a fact may be found in the factual proposition.
2. Formulate a primary inference on the subject by defining terms or clarifying what the question or problem asks you to answer or solve.
3. Discover those issues and their supporting arguments that support the primary inference as probably true.
4. Discover those issues and their supporting arguments that deny the primary inference as probably true.
5. Decide whether support or denial is the more rational explanation of the factual proposition.

Although argumentation as inquiry, or knowledge seeking, can be used for value or policy argumentation, its most common application is in arguing about facts. We want to know what is happening, what something means, or how to interpret information that contains contradictions. We also turn to experts for their interpretations of this information.

Although scholars and lay persons in a field often have great passion for the interpretations they make of facts in their field, argumentation as knowledge seeking can be more emotionally neutral. Because much formal knowledge seeking is done to test hypotheses, researchers take pains to try to remain as emotionally neutral as possible. Nevertheless, factual argumentation can involve strongly held positions and very passionate explanations of how to interpret information. Two professors arguing over whether the "pop quiz" causes students to read assignments in advance of a class meeting can produce a heated exchange over that factual proposition. Whether your participation in factual argumentation is done from the more neutral position of seeking knowledge or from a strongly held position on one side of a proposition, the techniques of advocacy and opposition will assist you in case building.

Advocating Propositions of Fact

Construction of a prima facie case for a proposition of fact begins with analysis of the proposition, using the steps we identified in Chapter 4: locating immediate cause, investigating the history, defining key terms and making the primary inference, and using the stock issues for factual argumentation to determine the actual issues you will argue.

In locating immediate cause, look for examples, illustrations, or other information of fact and opinion that emphasize or signify something about the topic. New data from the Hubble telescope leads theoretical physicists to hypothesize about the composition of the universe. The discovery of paintings in a cave in France leads archaeologists and artists to interpret the civilization of our early ancestors. These are immediate causes that involve people in factual argumentation. Look for instances of unusual discoveries, data collection, or an authority's statement that we need to know more about something as the source of an immediate cause.

As you investigate the historical background of your topic, collect published research that investigates the topic, look for repetitions of events, search for government hearings or fact-finding reports by both government and private sources. For arguments focusing on the interpretation or investigation of past fact, public documents, biographies, specialized histories, and periodicals devoted to historical subjects are useful. In some argumentation about past fact, investigating the history and applying the stock issues of fact blend into a single analytical step.

Defining key terms and making the primary inference is important in factual argumentation, even when the proposition seems to point to only one possible inference. Suppose that you were involved in a controversy over where to place the strongest main point of your argumentative case. Your classmate says, "Place it first," but you think placing it last might be a better strategy. You both agree to solve the controversy by testing it as a hypothesis: "The strongest argument in a case should be presented first." Two key terms will be defined to clarify the inference in this proposition: "strongest" and "presented first." The definitions need not be complex, but a clear idea of what is meant by a "strong" argument and exactly what "first" means need to be clarified.

The stock issues for analyzing factual propositions are used to decide what main points to use in developing the primary inference. You will recall that the stock issues point you in the direction of finding what information and reasoning is available to prove the primary inference.

1. What information confirms (or denies) the alleged relationship between the subject and the predicate of the primary inference?
2. What techniques of reasoning should be used to demonstrate this relationship?

Again suppose you are seeking to resolve your disagreement with your classmate about where to place your strongest argument. To test the probable truth of your classmate's proposition that it should be placed first, you ask:

1. What information will confirm that placing the strongest argument first increases the persuasiveness of a case?
2. What kind of reasoning technique should we use to interpret this information?

The two of you decide that sufficient information to confirm or deny the proposition can probably be found from two sources: literature in the speech communication journals on the persuasiveness of different organizational patterns and your own experiment to see what happens when you test the hypothesis.

After collecting the information, you and your classmate may decide that the most appropriate reasoning techniques are sign and authoritative reasoning to interpret your findings from the review of literature and generalization to draw conclusions from your original research.

If you and your classmate presented your arguments orally to your class or wrote them up as a report of your original research for a journal, the speaking time or writing space available to you might be relatively short. Some factual argumentation can be briefly stated. Other kinds of factual argumentation take place at great length. Consider that arguing the factual proposition, "A sustained nuclear reaction can be controlled," involved thousands of scientists and technicians, occupied several years in the 1940s, and cost a substantial amount of money.

Whether your case is brief or voluminous, advocating and opposing a prima facie case is based on developing one or more contentions. Each contention uses the stock issues of asking what information and reasoning are available to affirm or deny the probable truth of the contention. We will next discuss how an advocate in factual argumentation meets the burden of proof in case building and what strategies the opponent may choose in denying its probable truth.

Building the Prima Facie Case ✕

Our advocate is building a prima facie case on the proposition: *College professors do not know how to teach.* She has defined the key phrase, "know how to teach," as "have sufficient instruction in teaching techniques." Her immediate cause is an experience she had in a class where her test scores and feedback on assignments seemed inconsistent with the final grade she received. Her investigation of the historical background uncovered information that virtually no college or university requires its faculty to have the kind of certification and teacher-training education mandated for kindergarten-through-twelfth-grade teachers. Her analysis of information and reasoning techniques suggests she should argue two contentions:

1. College professors prepare for a teaching career by getting a doctorate in a specialized area.
2. College professors do not receive training in effective teaching techniques.

A prima facie case supporting the advocate's primary inference, "The educational preparation of college professors does not place sufficient emphasis on teaching techniques," would have to consider her audience's existing knowledge and opinions. It would also respond to the presumption that teaching is effective, because the United States is acknowledged to have some of the best colleges in the world. She must decide how to use the concepts of presumption and inherency in building her case.

The advocate may choose to treat presumption as a way of identifying the common practices used to prepare college teachers to teach, but she should also take her audience into consideration. If the advocate is addressing a student audience, she may draw on her own experiences as a student and consider presumption to be natural—the custom of college-level teaching is that no special instruction in teaching techniques is required. If her audience consists of faculty and administrators, she may treat presumption as a method for analyzing the audience to discover what sources of information and what kinds of reasoning the faculty-administrator audience will find most credible for arguments on this subject.

The advocate then builds her prima facie case by creating units of argument for each of her contentions. How does she develop the individual units of argument? Advocates for factual propositions create units of argument about effect, significance, and inherency to argue why the contention is probably true.

In factual argumentation, *effect* focuses on one or more units of argument that call the audience's attention to the results or consequences of what has happened, is happening, or will happen. In arguing her first contention, "College professors prepare for a teaching career by getting a doctorate in a specialized area," the advocate may develop units of argument proving two claims:

CLAIM 1: Graduate-level curricula focus very narrowly on the subject matter of an academic discipline.

CLAIM 2: Graduate-level curricula do not include courses in teaching methods.

It is not enough to know that something is a result or consequence; building a prima facie case must also explain the *significance* of the thing's happening. The advocate must also tell the audience why the two facts she established as an effect of the existing state of affairs in the preparation of college teachers are important. She might develop a unit of argument proving the claim:

CLAIM 3: No graduate program in our state offers coursework on "how to teach the college course" in its curricula.

Finally, the advocate must consider *inherency* as she provides information concerning why this state of affairs exists in college teaching. She must demonstrate to her audience what causes doctoral programs to neglect training college professors in how to be effective teachers. She might develop units of argument proving the following claims on the inherent nature of doctoral programs:

CLAIM 4: A college professor has always been considered a person who "professes" knowledge on a subject, as opposed to a teacher who "teaches" the subject to others.

CLAIM 5: Standard practice in European and American doctoral programs has been to consider a course in teaching methods as unnecessary.

The advocate would then go on to develop units of argument proving effect, significance, and inherency for her second contention. She does not have to organize her units of argument into a fixed pattern of first arguing effect, then significance, and finally inherency. She may place those units of argument in whatever order she thinks will make the most sense to her audience. Significance is often a way of focusing on an immediate cause—those things that draw our attention to a topic are often what gives it significance. Our advocate might decide to use a unit of argument grounded on her own negative experience with a college professor first, then argue why such negative experiences are inherent to the way college professors are trained, and finally use her units of argument about the effects of this inherency.

Preempting Opposing Arguments

Finally, the advocate is well advised to take a moment to *consider the proposition from the opponent's perspective*. What is the opponent likely to argue, and where are points of clash likely to occur? The opponent may choose to argue that most college professors have been teaching assistants and that experience as a T.A. is a parallel case to the student teaching experience that kindergarten-through-twelfth-grade education majors receive. If so, the advocate may consider including *preemptive arguments* in her case, arguments that respond to the probable objections the opponent will make before he has a chance to raise them. Our advocate might offer a third contention as a preempt, that even though many college professors begin their careers as teaching assistants, they still received no formal instruction in teaching methods. Prudent use of preemptive arguments keeps the discussion focused on the proposition and keeps presumption and burden of proof where they belong.

However, the advocate who chooses to preempt an opponent's arguments must avoid excess, preempting everything but the "kitchen sink" and creating a series of what might be unrelated arguments. Kitchen sink preempts are also a bad rhetorical strategy because they run the risk of weakening, rather than strengthening, the advocate's position in the audience's mind. They create the impression that the advocate's position must be weak if she can find so many objections to it herself.

Argument in Action

Advocates of factual propositions use the areas of effect, significance, and inherency in building cases. In the following example, notice how Cleta Mitchell, director and general counsel of the Term Limit Legal Institute, builds a case to explain why many Americans favor term limits for members of Congress. We have omitted from the text some asides about the charts she used to present statistics and an interruption when someone asked a question.

> What I do want to talk about today is why the American people support term limits. I am trying to appear today and speak on behalf of those people, millions of people, and to let you know what they would say if they were here to talk to you today.
>
> I begin by acknowledging the support of many Members of Congress, but unfortunately, it is still a minority of Members of Congress who do support term limits. Congresswoman Tillie Fowler, Congresswoman Karen Shepherd who led the charge to have these hearings in the first place, Congressman McCollum, Inglis, Coble, Mr. Dornan, Congressman Hoekstra all support term limits.

Unfortunately, there is still and obstinate majority in Congress who refuse to really take this issue seriously; who tell us that term limits for Members of Congress simply will not work. Term limits are not a new idea. The President is term limited. Thirty-six Governors serve under term limits. Sixteen State legislatures, many dozens of statewide elected officials and 16 state legislatures all have term limits.

This is not a new or novel idea. The idea that somehow Congress cannot function under term limits is antithetical to the idea of citizen government all of us grew up believing in. . . .

I think one of the important things to try to understand is why the American people feel that the House is not representative.

Let's start with looking at what the average tenure in the current job is, because we hear a lot about the idea that since we have turnover, we don't need term limits. The average tenure of the American worker according to the Bureau of Labor Statistics in 1994 is 6 years. The average tenure of House Members is 10 years. But the average tenure of the leadership of the House, and by that I mean committee chairmen, the Speaker, majority leader, the whip, is 27 years.

Look at the situation with regard to racial composition of the House and its leadership which is a little better than some of the other areas we are going to look at. 25 percent of the American population is made up of racial minorities; 14 percent of the House Members consist of racial minorities; 21 percent of the House leaders consist of racial minorities.

One thing you need to realize is that almost all racial minorities elected to Congress were elected in open seats. Eighty-seven percent of the black Members of Congress were elected in open seats. Eighty-three percent of the Hispanic Members were elected in open seats. And 79 percent of the women who serve in the House of Representatives were elected in open seats.

In fact, in 1992, the famed year of the woman, 21 of the 24 women elected to the House of Representatives were elected in open seats. Then look at the representation of women in the decisionmaking in the House. Fifty-one percent of the American people are female, 11 percent of the House membership, zero percent of the House leadership.

I think that the next chart probably is the most distressing to the American people. 68 percent of the American people consider themselves other than Democrats. I say this as a registered Democrat who has run for office as a Democrat, served as a Democrat my entire life. Forty-one percent of the House Members are something other than House Democrats, and zero percent of the House leadership. . . .

The fact of the matter is that I don't think most of the people think that is a good system. What we hear from the Republicans, unfortunately, is if you elect us, give us a majority, we will exclude the Democrats from the decision-making. I don't think that is a very representative body.

We hear that power corrupts and absolute power corrupts absolutely—if you look back at those Members of Congress who have been charged with crimes over the last decade, we find that 29 percent of those served fewer than four terms and 71 percent had served 8 terms or more. So that the fact of the matter is that the people in this country suspect that the longer you serve in office, the more potential there is for corruption; and we are not wrong about that, the statistics bear that out.

The final area is one that I think people are extremely concerned about and that is the way incumbents control their own reelection. Forty-five percent of the funds of the total campaign funds for incumbent Members of the House of Representatives during the 1992 cycle came from PAC's.

You compare that to challengers who received 15 percent of their funds from PAC's, and in open seats, an average of 21 percent. People in this country have serious concerns about the way campaigns are financed.

The similar bureaucratic relationship exists between raising money and the very people with whom you do business every day on Capital Hill. We hear you are going to pass a campaign finance bill, but we say to you we do not believe that any bill that is passed by Congress is going to make it easier for you to lose your elections.

We would suggest that it would be far better to pass a term limits bill guaranteeing open seats periodically because that would eliminate a lot of the mischief and the dominance of PAC's in reelection campaigns.

There are lots of problems with Congress. Lots of problems that political scientists have written about. I just point out two or three that I think are particularly startling.

When you tell us term limits will not work, what I say to you on behalf of many, many Americans, is we don't think it is working now. We see bills coming to the House floor with a closed rule, 77 percent of the time in 1993, according to the Heritage Foundation statistics, which means our legislated representatives are not allowed to offer amendments on legislation that is being acted upon by the House of Representatives.

We see bills being passed, laws being enacted from which you are exempt and from which you exempt yourselves; and we have to figure out how to live and make a living under those laws. Then you wonder why we are angry.

We see bills being voted upon so that it allows Members to vote opposite ways on the same issue so you can go back and tell your constituents, "Well, I voted for that," but we know that there are times when you are able to have it both ways; and then you wonder why the American people are cynical.

We see major decisions being made governing our lives, being made behind closed doors in secret sessions and then you wonder why we don't trust you. (Term Limits for Members of the U. S. Senate and House of Representatives, 1994, pp. 229–231)

Summary of Fact Advocacy

1. What is the primary inference identified in the proposition of fact?
   A. Is the primary inference about past, present, or future fact?
   B. What is the nature of probable truth concerning this proposition and how should it be argued?
2. What do the stock issues lead you to discover about this proposition of fact?
   A. What reasoning pattern is sufficient to establish the key issues?
   B. Is sufficient proof available to support this reasoning pattern?
   C What will audience expectations be in regard to proof and reasoning; should warrant and backing be included in establishing the pattern of reasoning?
3. Have the requirements of a prima facie case been satisfied?
   A. Are terms defined where necessary for clarity?

B. Is the interpretation of the proposition topical?
C. Does the development of issues provide good and sufficient reasons for accepting the advocate's inference?
4. Should preemptive arguments be used?
A. Is the opponent likely to be skeptical of the advocate's interpretation of the issues?
B. Will preemptive arguments focus argumentation or create confusion?

Opposing Propositions of Fact

Whether the proposition is one of fact, value, or policy, both advocate and opponent are obligated to follow certain rules. The advocate has the burden of proof and must develop claims that uphold it; the opponent initially possesses presumption. He may choose to question the validity of the advocate's allegations concerning fact in a number of ways. Determining exactly what to argue as an opponent is a matter of using the resources gained while analyzing the proposition and paying careful attention to what the advocate has argued.

The opponent begins construction of his case by examining the advocate's primary inference in interpreting the proposition. The inference established her unique way of describing the relationship between the subject and the object of the proposition. The opponent's task is to determine what strategies to employ in disputing the probable truth of the advocate's inference.

Evaluating the Primary Inference

The opponent's first strategic decision is to determine whether to accept the advocate's primary inference as topical or as unnecessarily restricted. The inference grows out of the advocate's definition of terms and issues discovered while analyzing the proposition. While the opponent is not obligated to dispute the advocate's definitions, it may be advantageous to do so. If the advocate has defined terms in such a way that the primary inference represents an unreasonable interpretation of the proposition, the opponent may wish to argue for a different definition of terms. He should consider whether the advocate has developed a topical prima facie case.

The opponent of the proposition, "College professors do not know how to teach," may choose to argue that the advocate's definition of "know how to teach" does not clarify what teaching means. He may suggest that "have sufficient instruction in teaching techniques" does nothing to clarify the meaning of "know how to teach" and supply his own definition. The opponent may create a unit of argument that defines the key term as "classroom experience." When the opponent chooses to contest the advocate's definition of terms, his case development will begin with an overview suggesting how his definition provides a better understanding of the primary inference of the proposition.

Using Presumption to Dispute the Primary Inference

Because presumption may be considered from a number of different perspectives, the opponent has several options to choose among in deciding how to employ the benefit of presumption in favor of that which exists—the standard practices of doctoral programs in preparing college professors. He may regard presumption as artificially assigned, and his role is to deny the advocate's primary inference as being probably true. He may consider presumption as natural, a description of college teaching practices, customs, values, and so on as legitimate and capable of preparing college teachers. He may also choose to consider presumption as a device for audience analysis and use the beliefs and sources his audience respects as the basis for his arguments about the present practices of preparing college teachers.

Which concept of presumption should our opponent choose in this example? Beginning with the audience may be his best strategic choice. If he and the advocate are addressing a student audience, they may each draw on a common pool of experience that other college students have had in the classroom. The opponent may choose examples, sources, and student evaluations of teaching on campus to create units of argument that suggest the advocate is probably incorrect in her view that college teachers do not know how to teach. He will prove they do. If the audience consists of faculty and administrators, the opponent may choose to use natural presumption to argue that the advocate is mistaken, that faculty and administrators have worked for decades to improve the quality of teaching through the system of teaching assistantships.

Refuting by Denial and Extenuation

Having examined the advocate's primary inference to assess topicality and decided how he will use the benefit of presumption, the third strategic decision the opponent makes concerns how to respond to the units of argument that develop the advocate's contentions. The opponent must determine whether the strategies of denial and extenuation can be used to refute these arguments. He makes this decision after examining how well the advocate's arguments satisfy the requirements of the stock issues for factual argumentation.

First, the advocate will have selected a particular pattern of reasoning to use in constructing arguments substantiating the proposition. The opponent should make sure that this pattern is sufficient to demonstrate the probable truth of the inference made in each of the advocate's units of argument. Second, the opponent may elect to challenge the sufficiency of the proof offered by the advocate. In essence, this strategy asserts that while the advocate's claims in and of themselves would be sufficient to establish the probability of the inference, those claims are not grounded in proof and reasoning sufficient to warrant assent. The two strategies commonly used by opponents to refute the advocate's arguments are denial and extenuation.

In employing a strategy of *denial*, the opponent does not argue that the advocate has knowingly engaged in distortion or deception, but that the arguments offered are nonetheless fallacious because the advocate has:

1. misanalyzed the situation, and the analysis provided by the opponent is proper
2. overlooked certain important facts, which the opponent provides along with an explanation of the significance of their having been overlooked
3. given undue significance to certain facts, and the opponent explains why they lack significance
4. drawn unwarranted conclusions from the proof, and the opponent provides the proper conclusion

Those who disputed the conclusions of the Warren Commission, that Lee Harvey Oswald, acting alone, assassinated President Kennedy, based their arguments on the strategy of denial. Oswald was not that good a marksman, the rifle he was alleged to have used could not be fired rapidly enough to inflict all the wounds, evidence suggested that the shots came from more than one direction, and so on. Denial is a form of refutation in which the opponent argues that the advocate has failed to determine what proof and reasoning would be sufficient to establish the inferred relationship of a contention and its supporting units of argument.

Extenuation is the other strategy commonly used to oppose arguments of fact. Extenuation arguments focus on the circumstances that surround a given fact and its interpretation. In this type of refutation, the opponent argues that the relationship inferred by the advocate is based on a limited understanding of the circumstances surrounding those facts and that a more complete understanding of those circumstances would lead to a different inference. Extenuating or unusual circumstances warrant a conclusion other than the one normally drawn when these facts are present.

The defense team for John Hinkley, Jr., may have conceded that he fired the shots that hit President Reagan, but it did not concede the criminality of the act. Extenuating circumstances, in this case insanity, lead to another inference—a proposition of fact advanced by the nominal opponent. John Hinkley, Jr., was not guilty of shooting the president of the United States by reason of insanity.

Responding to Preemptive Arguments

The final strategic choice the opponent must make concerns what to do if the advocate presents preemptive arguments. Is the opponent obligated to respond to them? No. The opponent has as much right to determine his own strategy and select the arguments he will advance in refutation of the proposition as the advocate has in choosing hers. The opponent must examine the advocate's preempts carefully. Although they may represent a sincere and ethical attempt to keep argumentation focused, they may be nothing more than a collection of straw man arguments cynically and unethically introduced to gain an advantage.

Argument in Action

Opponents of factual propositions have many strategic options in deciding how they will respond to the advocate's arguments and in how they will use the benefit of presumption. In the following example, notice how Linda Fowler, professor of political science, Maxwell School of Citizenship and Public Affairs, Syracuse University, uses her research on historical background to respond to Cleta Mitchell's argumentation on the proposition that Americans favor term limits for members of Congress for a variety of reasons. We have omitted a lengthy transition statement about her use of historical information.

Speaking against term limits as I do today, does not mean that I support the status quo. Like all of you, I read the polls, I read the signs that the public is extremely disaffected with Congress and I worry about that.

I spent 20 years of my life working on the Hill or studying and teaching about it. I think the health of our legislative institutions is a fundamental thing that we have to worry about in this democracy.

Nevertheless, it seems to me that it is hard to make a case that careerism is really the source of the problems that the Congress has both internally and with the public; and I am convinced that term limits are not an effective remedy for these kinds of difficulties.

Let me give you a little historical perspective first. What I want to do is show how high turnover in legislatures of the 19th century and Congress in the 20th century in the States produced something very different from the picture that either George Will or Cleta Matthews [*sic*] would have you believe. Thus—if you look honestly rather than sentimentally—at legislatures in those periods, you will see they were not the great deliberative bodies they have often been portrayed to be. . . .

Certainly, we here at this table are all trying to cloak ourselves in the Founding Fathers. But it seems to me that the best place to look and see what the Framers intended is in Federalist 53.

Madison was seen to be addressing quite specifically the question of the length of term; and you see Madison and Hamilton saying very specifically that the complexity and size of the new Nation demanded people that they called masters of the public business. These were experienced, seasoned people who had the understanding to guide the country in the right direction.

In fact, they went so far as to say that whenever you have a large number of new Members in the legislature, they will be more likely to be led into the snares that unscrupulous people will set for them.

Hamilton was also worried about incentives for talented individuals to enter government if they did not have the opportunity of acquiring real influence over public policy.

We can look at a few giants who served in the Congress of that time; but basically if you look at the Congress of Jefferson's time, you see it was rife with factionalism, parochialism, and procedural disorder.

Let's not forget the citizen legislatures of the 14th Congress refused to raise taxes out of fear of angering their constituents. While the Secretary of State was on horseback looking for the enemy, the Members decamped, left the city defenseless; and the British promptly burned down Washington, DC. Let's not sentimentalize citizen legislatures.

Later Congresses in the post–Civil War era, where turnover averaged 64 percent, were plagued with sectionalism, scandal, and pork-barrel politics to a degree that makes anything you see in Washington today seem positively innocent.

A telling statistic of that time regarding congressional priorities: 73 percent of all statutes passed between 1867 and 1901 were private bills. If you look at the legacy of legislation from that era, one statute has to do with minerals and mineral rights. What you see is an exceptional generosity to various powerful and organized interests.

Indeed, when observers came and looked at out legislatures in that period, both de Tocqueville in the 1830's and Lord Bryce in the 1890's commented on the low caliber of individuals serving in the Nation's legislatures. Lord Bryce noted the problem with American democracy he saw was not in the constitution provisions but in the consequences of "the prominence of inferior men in politics."

I cannot imagine a foreign visitor coming to this distinguished body in this day and age and making a similar judgment.

Again, when you look at the State legislatures, what you see is very high turnover. Most legislatures a generation ago in States were amateur, part-time bodies with low salaries, few perks, few staff and very short sessions. Indeed, in the 1960's, there was a group that organized a citizen's conference on State legislatures that put together a reform agenda to try to improve the performance of State legislatures.

They use as their model a highly professionalized Congress of the United States. Their remedy for what was ailing the legislature were the very thing term limits advocates attack today: high salaries, professional staff support, year-long sessions, and so forth. In other words, people who were reforming State legislatures that at that time and era showed an enormous inability to deal with complexities of modern government, turned to professionalism and careerism that they saw in Congress as the remedy for the problems.

In other words, the claims advocates make that when legislators aren't worried about reelection they will not be so parochial, they will make tough financial decisions, won't traffic with special interests groups, and so forth, I don't think a historical record for either the Congress or State legislatures supports that view.

If we look at this past performance honestly, I think we will see the high turnover and short average tenure among legislators of the past did little to foster the public welfare. (Term Limits for the Members of the U.S. Senate and House of Representatives, 1994, pp. 190–192)

Summary of Fact Opposition

1. Will the advocate's definition of terms be challenged or accepted?
   A. Does the advocate's definition of terms stay within the bounds of the proposition's figurative ground?
   B. What definition of terms does the opponent offer, and why is it a more reasonable interpretation of the proposition?
2. Will the opponent support presumption?
   A. Are there existing interpretations of fact that the advocate has overlooked that the opponent wishes to argue?

B. What is the level of probability that the advocate's arguments are true? Is that level of probability greater than the probability that existing beliefs about ideas, institutions, laws or rules, policies, customs, or practices are worth preserving?

3. How will the advocate's argumentation on stock issues be opposed?

A. Will denial arguments be used to argue that the advocate has misanalyzed the situation, overlooked important facts, given undue significance to certain facts, or drawn unwarranted conclusions?

B. Will extenuation arguments be used to argue that special conditions or circumstances result in interpretations of fact other than those made by the advocate?

4. If the advocate has presented preemptive arguments, how will they be addressed?

A. Are such arguments truly representative of the counterarguments an opponent might be expected to raise? Or are they straw man arguments?

B. Do preemptive arguments reveal significant flaws in the advocate's interpretation of the proposition that the opponent might exploit?

Propositions of fact attempt to establish what has been, is, or will be. Value and policy cases of advocacy and opposition are built on a foundation of issues of factual argumentation. Learning how to argue fact is a necessary step for becoming effective in arguing value and policy, as well as worthwhile in its own right.

Learning Activities

1. Review the text of Cleta Mitchell's arguments that Americans favor term limits for members of Congress. Analyze her advocacy position in terms of the following:

A. What is her primary inference? Does she define any key terms to make this inference?

B. What arguments of effect, significance, and inherency does she argue? What forms of evidence does she use to ground each argument? Do you think her evidence is effective in making her point? What reasoning techniques does she use in interpreting the evidence? Why are these techniques effective or ineffective?

C. Is her case prima facie? Why or why not?

2. Review Linda Fowler's opposition to the idea that many Americans favor term limits for members of Congress. Analyze her opposition in terms of the following:

A. What is her overall philosophy of opposition? How does she approach the primary inference of Mitchell's case?

B. How does she use the benefit of presumption in opposing Mitchell? What concept of presumption does she use?

C. What strategies of denial and extenuation does she use in opposing Mitchell's case? Are they sufficient to overturn a prima facie case?

3. Examine the text of a landmark Supreme Court decision such as *Brown v. the Board of Education of Topeka* (1954) or *Roe v. Wade* (1973). What issues seemed most important in the Court's decision? What interpretations of law were made in deciding the case? What factual inferences form the basis of the decision (and any dissenting view if one was expressed)?
4. Written or Oral Assignment:
   A. Phrase your own proposition of fact about what was, is, or will be. Prepare a prima facie case from the advocate's position.
   B. Respond as an opponent to your advocate's case of factual argumentation, or to that of a classmate as assigned by your professor.

Suggested Supplementary Readings

Meiland, J. W. (1989, May). Argument As Inquiry and Argument As Persuasion. *Argumentation*, 3, 185–196.

Meiland describes two views, that we use argumentation for both informative and persuasive purposes. In particular, he focuses on how we use argument to seek knowledge, an informative purpose. This is an excellent article for understanding new trends in argumentation theory that legitimize the study of factual argumentation as something many of us do on a regular basis.

Sproule, J. M. (1980). *Argument: Language and It's Influence*. New York: McGraw-Hill.

This is a book for the more advanced student, but it provides extensive discussion of argumentation in the larger context of persuasion. Of particular interest here is Chapter 4, Descriptions: Arguments That Draw Issues of Fact, in which Sproule considers the use of examples, statistics, and testimony as the basis for grounding factual arguments. The chapter features an interesting extended example of argumentation on the existence of UFOs.

Walton, D. N. (1992). *Plausible Argument in Everyday Conversation*. Albany: State University of New York Press.

This book focuses on how argumentation is used in relationships, to answer questions, exchange ideas, and make decisions. Walton does not restrict his discussion to factual argumentation, but much of his discussion of argument in ordinary conversations deals with fact. We recommend that, in the context of studying about factual argumentation, you read Chapter 3, Dialogue. In this chapter Walton explores how the process of dialogue as a series of questions and answers is our medium for acquiring knowledge.

Chapter Ten

How Are Propositions of Value Argued?

Where do we find examples of value argumentation? Almost any statement, lengthy or brief, can contain a value judgment. How we describe something or someone will necessarily be colored by our feelings toward what we have described. Throughout this textbook, both implicit and explicit claims are made about the worth of studying and practicing argumentation—they are value judgments. Value argumentation communicates our feelings about something or someone and the standards of judgment from which those feelings derive. Value propositions exist about any subject and are characterized by the use of intrinsic or extrinsic judgmental criteria.

There are some fields of endeavor that deal almost exclusively in value argumentation. Religion and philosophy are both concerned with right and wrong, moral and immoral, and ethical and unethical behavior. Both fields seek to determine standards of socially or doctrinally acceptable behavior. A theologian examines behavior in terms of whether it measures up to a moral code expressed in sacred texts. The philosopher may speculate on the existence of several alternatives for ethical and unethical behavior.

The arts—film, theater, music, sculpture, photography, painting, and dance—concern themselves, in part, with judging artistic works against a set of critical standards to determine whether they are "good art." The critics continually revise these sets of standards to keep pace with trends and changes. We rely on the opinions of the professional critic to help us determine what we will patronize and accept. You have a chance to observe how critical standards for evaluating film, television, and music are developed and applied by reading articles and reviews in such publications as *The Journal of Popular Culture*, *TV Guide*, *Premier*, or *Entertainment Weekly*.

Other fields also engage in value argumentation, particularly regarding standards of ethical behavior. Medicine, law, business, education, public relations, and almost any other field you can name are concerned with determining acceptable behaviors for their practitioners. Is prescribing a certain drug to certain categories of patients ethical? Is a certain sales technique an ethical business practice? Is a certain behavior appropriate for a professional educator? Often professional organizations draw up codes of behavior, such as the codes of ethics of the Public Relations Society of America and the American Bar Association. Such codes provoke extensive value and policy argumentation as individuals and groups seek to interpret and apply them.

The locus of value argumentation is as varied as the groups and individuals who are concerned with standards of excellence and codes of conduct. In academic argumentation, you may be asked to develop argumentative cases about the quality or lack of quality of some institution or practice, the appropriateness of the actions of certain groups of people, or the degree to which something is in the best interests of the nation in general. In this chapter we will examine how arguments are developed for propositions of value.

Value can be a very ambiguous term. Consider how a number of scholars have tried to fix the meaning of something that is a psychological and sociological process:

> Values are intangibles . . . things of the mind that have to do with the vision people have of "the good life" for themselves and their fellows. (Rescher, 1969, p. 4)

> A value is a general conception of what is a good end state or a good mode of behavior. (Rieke & Sillars, 1984, p. 125)

> *Values* are premises which are related to the preference of a particular audience for one thing as opposed to another. (van Eemeren et al., 1987, p. 222)

> A *value* is an enduring belief that a specific mode of conduct or end-state of existence is personally or socially preferable to an opposite or converse mode of conduct or end-state of existence. A *value system* is an enduring organization of beliefs concerning preferable modes of conduct or end-states of existence along a continuum of relative importance. (Rokeach, 1973, p. 5)

> Values may be defined as concepts that express what people believe is right or wrong, important or unimportant, wise or foolish, good or bad, just or unjust, great or mean, beautiful or ugly, and true or false, and that, therefore underlie all choices. (Walter & Scott, 1984, p. 224)

From these definitions, we can understand just what the arguer grapples with in a controversy involving values. In value propositions, controversy exists over opposing evaluations of a person, object, event, or idea. The purpose of argumentation is to decide how we should judge something—a political candidate, a product, a federal program, an artistic performance, or a moral standard.

The demand or desire for a change in values emerges from the collective experience and expanding knowledge of those in a field or in society in general. Advocates and opponents should pay particular attention to Nicholas Rescher's (1969) classic discussion of shifting societal values in terms of those factors that bring about change: changes of information; ideological and political change; erosion of values through boredom, disillusionment, and reaction; and changes in the operating environment of a society.

The value system of a society can change when *new information* is introduced. Consider the impact that the discovery of antibiotics or vaccines against polio and measles had on health or the way in which the development of the birth control pill influenced moral standards. Many of today's changes are brought about by scientific discovery. One of the great unanswered questions that may produce a significant value change if it can be resolved is the determination of the point at which life begins. While it has sometimes been said that there is nothing new under the sun, new discoveries about old things happen with some regularity. As you investigate the immediate causes and historical background of your proposition, be alert for new discoveries, new directions, and shifts in thinking that point to changing values.

A second way in which society is altered is through *political and ideological change*. These can be revolutionary changes as occurred in Eastern Europe in 1989 and 1990. In that situation, both political and ideological changes took place as Communist governments were overthrown and attempts at democracy were begun. Such change is not necessarily abrupt; "it can take the gradualistic form of conditioning, advertising, propaganda, and promotion" (Rescher, 1969, p. 117). For instance, consider the ways in which television commercials and programs articulate what is to be valued. The mass media call our attention to everything from eating habits to controlling wildlife in urban areas and offer us the commentary of experts and those who are affected most by the topic. These commentaries and experiential views give us new or revised thinking on politics and ideologies.

The third way in which societal values change is through their *erosion*, which occurs when large numbers of people resist acting in accordance with a value. This was what happened during the 1960s when thousands of young men refused to register for the military draft. Erosion can also occur as a society experiences gradual change over time and, as a result, a value loses much of its importance. In an age when leisure pursuits are strongly encouraged and widely sold by the mass media, the value of work may have less importance attached to it.

Society may also become disillusioned with a value. In the late nineteenth century, many Americans placed sobriety very high in their personal value systems. The Women's Christian Temperance Union, the very colorful activist Carrie Nation, and religious leaders all advocated abstinence from alcohol. Sobriety was so highly valued that in 1920 a constitutional amendment prohibiting the manufacture and sale of alcoholic beverages was adopted. Disillusionment over the Eighteenth Amendment was such that it was repealed by the Twenty-First Amendment just thirteen years later. The reactions of an earlier generation to the erosion of moral standards about drinking and public decorum influenced policy, but by the twentieth century, most Americans did not place abstinence from alcohol high in their personal value hierarchies. The erosion of a particular value can be a criterion for making a new judgment.

The final way in which value changes occur is through a *change in the oper- ating environment* of the society, the "whole range of social, cultural, demo- graphic, economic, and technological factors that comprise the way of life in that society" (Rescher, 1969, p. 117). Some of the demographic changes that have influenced society in recent years include the entry of women into the workplace and the cultural dominance of the baby boom generation. These are the same people who will cause another change at the beginning of the next century as they reach retirement age. Among the technological changes that have brought about value changes are the widespread availability of television, personal computers, and robotics in the workplace.

Social, cultural, demographic, economic, and technological factors that influence values cause them to come into conflict with one another. Two impor- tant values may have to be placed in a hierarchical relationship to each other to resolve this conflict, as is the case in the controversy over whether a clean envi- ronment or a healthy economy should be our priority. Value conflict forces a reconfiguring of the value hierarchies. The advocate's use of definitions of key terms to create a primary inference should establish this reconfiguration.

Value judgments are frequently made on the basis of long-standing values. Core American value systems are of particular importance to your analysis of a value proposition. There are certain dominant patterns of valuing that can help you identify societal value hierarchies that may apply to the present controversy. Daniel Yankelovich (1994) describes ten core values for America in the 1990s: freedom, equality, opportunity, fairness, achievement, patriotism, American superiority, community, religion, and luck. There is no rank ordering to these values and many of them may exist in combination in a given situation.

Freedom is the core value that embodies our beliefs that we have the right to choose our leaders, to speak out for those things we believe in and against those we do not. Freedom is the right to read, watch, and listen to what we want. It is also the right to live anywhere we choose, visit anywhere we choose, and to do so without interference from the government. Freedom is also the right to choose our spiritual path and to live our personal lives as we see fit.

Equality is the core value that reflects the American sense of justice. Regard- less of race, income, physical or mental ability, or where we live, all Americans expect equal treatment under the laws of the United States. This value is embod- ied in the affirmative action laws and programs of the last several decades.

Opportunity is the core value behind the American dream that all of us have the right to pursue ideas, education, and employment. This value suggests that all Americans have the chance to use their abilities, to compete for the good life, to test their mettle.

Fairness is related to the core value of equality, but extends this value on the basis that people should get what they deserve for the efforts they put forth. The cards of sex, age, race, social status, and so on should not be stacked against them. Americans have a fundamental belief that every institution of our society should treat all Americans evenhandedly but not make special allowances for a lack of effort.

Achievement is a core value based on the Protestant work ethic. We believe that hard work pays off and that the accomplishments of the individual should be rewarded. A corollary to achievement is the belief that we should not be idle, that we should always be progressing toward some goal, even in our leisure activities.

Patriotism is the core value of loyalty to the United States and our concept of democracy. This loyalty extends to the symbols of the United States—the flag, those who serve in the military, our historical traditions and celebrations, and sometimes our leaders. Patriotism can also be regional, as in loyalty to one's section of the nation, state, hometown, or alma mater.

American superiority is a core value derived from the Pilgrims. Americans have a vision of their nation as a special place, forged from a wilderness with blood and dedication, ordained by heaven. This is an idealized view of America as a nation with God-given rights and responsibilities that make us superior to every other nation.

Community is the core value of the group, the belief that we should work together to accomplish things. This core value embraces the values of family, neighbors, members of our ethnic group, loyalty to an employer or labor union, or any other group a field or audience deems significant. Community values take the individual outside of self and into the society of others.

Religion is the core value of spiritualism that suggests we benefit from believing in a higher power. America often defines itself as a Christian nation, so religious values are often those of Christian doctrine. As a core value, religion is also a source of moral standards, of an appreciation of our insignificance when compared to the magnificence of an entity that created the cosmos, and of our awe at the orderliness of the universe.

Luck is the core value that good fortune exists and will come to all of us at some time. Americans believe that luck exists, and if they try hard enough, it will come to them. This may explain why there are so many thriving state lotteries.

These ten core values are typical of American culture in the 1990s. They may be combined or stand in logical opposition to one another. Luck and achievement, for example, are often at odds. Some people seem to have luck but achieve little and vice versa. Consider how these core values complement and compete with one another. Also consider how value changes and values in opposition are capable of creating social tension.

Advocating Propositions of Value

The analysis of value propositions will lead you to the definition of the value object, its placement in a particular value hierarchy, and a choice of criteria to use in judging the value object against the standards of the value hierarchy. Information you gain from locating immediate causes will be used in developing units of argument and may also be used to focus on what is being evaluated and why. Historical background is particularly important because it provides you with information about the core values that pertain to your proposition. Defining terms and making the primary inference is critical to determining how you will organize your case as an advocate.

Construction of a prima facie case for value advocacy is a four-step process that begins by defining key terms and proceeds through considering the competing values within a hierarchy to identifying criteria. It ends with applying the criteria to the value object.

Let us suppose that our advocate has been assigned the proposition: *Rock 'n' roll is the most aesthetically significant music genre.* She will be arguing this proposition in her "mass media and society" course. First, she must define the value object.

Defining the Value Object

In some instances, the value object may be instantly recognizable and may not require lengthy definition. If the advocate was arguing that rock music has had great impact on young people, she might not feel compelled to provide an extensive technical definition of rock in order to clarify the nature of the value object. Such is not always the case. Since she is charged with arguing that rock's aesthetic properties make it significant, it will be necessary for her to approach the value object in more depth. Rock has several genres, and she must first decide whether her definition will include all of them or whether she will limit her definition in some way. Her definition must clarify the value object's meaning for the audience.

Next, the advocate utilizes the stock issues for analyzing value propositions:

1. By what value hierarchy is the object of the proposition best evaluated?
2. By what criteria is the value object to be located within this hierarchy?
3. Do indicators of the effect, significance, and inherency of the value object show that it conforms to the criteria?

Identifying the Hierarchy

Value hierarchy identification is the second step for the advocate. A value hierarchy is a complex set of attitudes and core values that members of a field or audience share. These hierarchies can vary widely from audience to audience. For example, "the majority of audiences will probably regard both beauty and profitability as values, but if they have to be weighed against each other the preference . . . will probably be different" (van Eemeren et al., 1987, p. 224) if one audience consists of record company executives and the other of rock critics. It is not the core values that change drastically but the way different audiences and individuals combine those core values into hierarchies (van Eemeren et al., 1987).

In arguing that one core value, or a certain combination of them, should take preeminence in making this evaluation, the advocate wants to move the audience in the direction of a particular set of standards for making evaluations. She wants the audience to view the value object in terms of the "right" hierarchy so that they will understand and accept the criteria she uses to make her evaluation.

For example, if she placed the value object "rock 'n' roll" in the hierarchy of the core values, American superiority and patriotism, her evaluation might not make much sense to the audience if she is talking about the infusion of aesthetic properties that African and Latin American folk songs have given to rock 'n' roll.

The appropriateness of the advocate's positioning of the value object within the hierarchy can be verified by arguments that (1) prove the superiority of the advocate's interpretation of the value object relative to all other possible interpretations, (2) offer the testimony of "admirable people" who support valuing the object of the proposition in this way, and (3) identify signs demonstrating that this interpretation best fits the existing societal value hierarchy.

Conflicting values are framed by value propositions, and value argumentation is aimed at resolving this conflict. The advocate attempts to resolve the conflict in her favor by creating a decision rule: (1) proving the advocate's value maximizes another agreed-upon value, (2) proving the advocate's value subsumes opposing values, (3) proving the advocate's value has more desirable consequences, or (4) arguing from definition in which the advocate's value is the defining property of the opposing value, (Zarefsky, 1976). This initiates argumentation on the first stock issue, By what value hierarchy is the object of the proposition best evaluated? The advocate's next responsibility in building a prima facie case is to decide what criteria she will use to evaluate the value object.

Specifying the Criteria

Statement of the criteria for evaluation is the third step in value advocacy. Description of the criteria for evaluation occurs first as the advocate states what criteria will be used. Because the criteria defining values lie at the heart of argumentation over these propositions, the two approaches that can be taken in identifying and applying them need to be considered: criteria discovery and criteria development.

Criteria discovery uses an existing framework of values—one already understood and generally accepted—as a standard by which phenomena may be evaluated. These criteria may be set forth in a general statement, but because they are so commonly accepted, advocate and opponent focus all argumentation on the appropriateness of judging the value object as a member of the class of phenomena to which this evaluation is commonly applied. Consider the general outline of advocacy using criteria discovery:

VALUE PROPOSITION: Drug XYZ is an effective treatment for cancer.
CRITERIA AS DISCOVERED FROM THE MEDICAL FIELD: The effectiveness of a
    drug rests on its ability to cure, contain, or prevent a disease, without
    producing adverse side effects.
INFERENCE RELATIVE TO THE OBJECT OF THE PROPOSITION: If drug XYZ
    can safely cure and contain cancer without producing adverse side effects,
    it can be considered an effective treatment.

CONTENTIONS: Drug XYZ can cure cancer.
Drug XYZ can contain cancer.
Drug XYZ has no adverse side effects.

In this instance, the decision to adopt discovered criteria is reasonable. Most listeners and readers would consider a substance with purported medicinal properties to be effective if it had curative powers. Three criteria, the ability to cure cancer, the ability to contain cancer, and the absence of adverse side effects, are applied.

Criteria development is used in situations where the advocate finds the criteria by which value may be determined either do not exist or are not commonly understood and, therefore, require explanation. This approach may also be used in situations where the criteria may be understood but are not readily accepted and, therefore, require substantiation. If upon analyzing the proposition the advocate decides to combine value standards from different fields or to use a relatively unknown value standard, criteria development will be her best approach. In criteria development, the locus of controversy may include the stock issues of hierarchy and criteria as well as the issue of whether the value object is appropriately measured by them. A prima facie case is established only if proof and reasoning relevant to all three stock issues of value are presented.

In arguing value propositions, a reasonable question to ask is, "Should I use discovered criteria or should I develop them?" Sometimes, a controversy over values has its genesis in a misunderstanding of the value term. A "good" sandwich may be tasty to you, economical to me, and nutritious to someone else. For this reason, criteria development may be the best approach because it has the potential of better assuring clarity of focus in argumentation rather than assuming it will occur naturally. By identifying and defining specific criteria to measure values, the advocate is less likely to find her arguments dismissed out of hand because they were misunderstood.

However, the advocate must exercise good judgment. Remember that argumentation is an instrumental process, and you should consider the audience as well as your opponent. If the advocate and her audience share an understanding of the criteria that define a particular value at the outset, it is a waste of time and an insult to the audience's intelligence to use anything but a criteria discovery approach.

The advocate then establishes the necessary and sufficient characteristics of these criteria. For example, in the case arguing that drug XYZ is an effective treatment for cancer, the necessary characteristics were (1) that it could cure cancer, (2) that it could contain cancer, and (3) that it did not have seriously harmful side effects. Notice that these conditions individually are insufficient to warrant acceptance of the proposition. A drug that merely has no seriously harmful side effects is not acceptable. This single criterion is insufficient to warrant the drug's use. It must also possess some other properties. The criteria advanced by the advocate must include all necessary and sufficient properties for proving her primary inference about the value object.

The decision to employ single or multiple criteria, which are either necessary or sufficient, is one of the strategic choices the advocate makes in deciding how best to advance her value proposition. These choices reflect the advocate's consideration of the information the reader or listener may legitimately require in order to assent to the value proposition. Contentions and claims in support of value propositions must be worded so that argumentation over them focuses on the stock issues of value. In analyzing the value proposition's topic area, look for resources that will provide support for these claims.

You might be wondering at this point, what happened to the advocate's responsibility to define the other key terms in her proposition and complete the primary inference? One of the secrets of making a primary inference for a value proposition is that defining the predicate in terms of the specific criteria for evaluation meets that responsibility. Our advocate of rock music's aesthetic superiority has defined the value object to include all those subsets of rock music that *Rolling Stone* identifies as constituting its genre. She now defines "aesthetically significant" in terms of the following criteria, which she discovered from a published source by a scholar who studies the aesthetics of rock:

1. Aesthetically significant music has a wide variety of sonic symbols.
2. Aesthetically significant music has imposing visual imagery.
3. Aesthetically significant music has lyrics that offer social and personal narratives.

The advocate might have created her own criteria for aesthetic significance, but since her audience consists of her professor and mass media classmates, she decided to use criteria from a source her audience would acknowledge as credible. She chose the three aesthetic criteria of measuring the significance of music on the basis of sonic, visual, and lyric properties because those were what her credible source offered. Using her discovered criteria as contentions, she then builds her case by developing units of argument to apply each criterion to the value object.

In some instances, value advocates need to consider two other aspects of discovered or created criteria. If the connection between the criteria and the value object is not readily apparent, the advocate must establish the relevance. If our advocate had elected to use criteria she discovered from literary criticism to evaluate rock music, she might have had to explain the relevance of these standards to rock music. If she combined criteria from more than one field, but the proposition seemed to lie in only one, she would have had to explain their pertinence to the field of the proposition. In both instances, she would advance arguments from parallel case in order for her proposition to satisfy requirements of logical progression.

Consider a more transparent example. Although questions of abortion, euthanasia, and genetic engineering lie in a scientific-medical field, the criteria you use to evaluate them could come from legal, ethical, or moral hierarchies. As an advocate, you would have to explain how criteria from these fields are pertinent to the medical-scientific aspects of the quality of human life.

Measuring the Value Object

Measuring the value object with the criteria for value judgment is the fourth step in value advocacy. Three subissues must be addressed as the advocate confronts the third stock issue of value argumentation, Do indicators of the effect, significance, and inherency of the value object show that it conforms to the criteria? The amount of proof and the number of arguments used in establishing effect, significance, and inherency are matters of choice, but all three subissues must be discussed for each criterion, or the case will not be prima facie.

By *effect* we mean what the value object is purported to do. Arguments of effect in value argumentation often are found when you locate immediate causes. For example, critical praise and huge album sales for a rock band that incorporates Ethiopian instruments and folk song traditions into their music might focus attention on the effects of the aesthetic properties of sound and rhythm.

In discussing the kinds of arguments to use in factual propositions, we told you that a contention should always have at least one unit of argument that proves significance. In value argumentation, *significance* is related to the magnitude, severity or frequency, with which the effect occurs. Making value judgments is a form of measurement of the value object; we use the term significance because the criteria are a measuring instrument.

Does the object of the proposition do what it is purported to do with important or serious consequences, and does this happen with regularity? Arguments of significance also result from investigation of the immediate controversy; they show how consequential the value object's effect is. For example, if most rock songs do not have videos or other visual images, the criterion that aesthetically significant music has imposing visual images will be difficult to argue as having any effect in judging rock 'n' roll as aesthetically significant on the basis of its visual imagery. Although an effect may exist, if it does not have some significance, it may not be worth the audience's concern.

Effect and significance arguments are both necessary elements of value advocacy. If a value object is shown to exist extensively, but not have much effect on society, interest or concern may not be justified. Equally, if the effect of the value object is very serious or has consequence, but does not extend to a significant number of individuals, interest or concern may not be justified.

Inherency pertains to causation. Are the effect and its significance the result of something intrinsic to the value object? In value argumentation, inherency often results from societal attitudes toward the value object. For example, if other rock critics and musicologists do not consider visual imagery an important component of the aesthetic properties of music, this criterion would have little or no inherency, little or no cause for the audience to use it as a standard for measuring the aesthetic significance of a musical genre. Inherency arguments examine attitudes to determine what might produce these attitudes and their identified effects. Keep in mind that causality is often the consequence of complex, interrelated factors, so inherency arguments have to consider the possibility of multiple causes.

Effect, significance, and inherency arguments must be present for a case to be prima facie. This is only logical. If the significance of the effect is not inherent to the fundamental nature of the value object, then measurement of the value object by the criterion is invalid. Inherency arguments prove that the effect and significance attributed to a value object are central to the value system of society or some elements of it. The most carefully constructed arguments about the effect of visual imagery on the quality of rock music will not warrant the audience's acceptance of the advocate's evaluation if she cannot demonstrate that visual imagery is an inherent aesthetic property for evaluating music.

Argument in Action

Value argumentation attempts to resolve questions regarding an object's appropriate place in the value hierarchy. The political field has placed "don't restrict free speech" relatively high in its value hierarchy. This value ordering was translated into law and policy and created the circumstances that Susan Baker decries in her value judgment about the marketing of rock albums.

Susan Baker of the Parents Music Resource Center (PMRC) was the first witness to testify during the Hearing on Contents of Music and the Lyrics of Records conducted by the Senate Committee on Commerce, Science, and Transportation. Her statement, part of which is reproduced here, opened debate on a proposition of value that was never explicitly stated: "A system for rating the content of record albums, similar to that used to rate movies, poses less of a threat to society than the message contained in the lyrics of rock music." As you read her testimony, try to identify the claims Mrs. Baker makes and decide whether you think her grounds and warrants are sufficient, identify her use of patterns of argument, and look for the preemptive argument in her case.

The Parents Music Resource Center was organized in May of this year by mothers of young children who are very concerned by the growing trend in music toward lyrics that are sexually explicit, excessively violent, or glorify the use of drugs and alcohol.

Our primary purpose is to educate and inform parents about this alarming trend as well as to ask the industry to exercise self-restraint.

It is no secret that today's rock music is a very important part of adolescence and teenagers' lives. It always has been, and we don't question their right to have their own music. We think that is important. They use it to identify and give expression to their feelings, their problems, their joys, sorrows, loves, and values. It wakes them up in the morning and it is in the background as they get dressed for school. It is played on the bus. It is listened to in the cafeteria during lunch. It is played as they do their homework. They even watch it on MTV now. It is danced to at parties, and puts them to sleep at night.

Because anything that we are exposed to that much has some influence on us, we believe that the music industry has a special responsibility as the message of songs goes from the suggestive to the blatantly explicit.

As Ellen Goodman stated in a recent column, rock ratings:

The outrageous edge of rock and roll has shifted its focus from Elvis's pelvis to the saw protruding from Blackie Lawless's codpiece on a WASP album. Rock lyrics have turned from "I can't get no satisfaction" to "I am going to force you at gunpoint to eat me alive." The material we are concerned about cannot be compared with Louie Louie, Cole Porter, Billy Holliday, et cetera. Cole Porter's "the birds do it, the bees do it," can hardly be compared with WASP, "I f-u-c-k like a beast." There is a new element of vulgarity and violence toward women that is unprecedented.

While a few outrageous recordings have always existed in the past, the proliferation of songs glorifying rape, sadomasochism, incest, the occult and suicide by a growing number of bands illustrates this escalating trend that is alarming.

Some have suggested that the records in question are only a minute element in this music. However, these records are not few, and have sold millions of copies, like Prince's "Darling Nikki," about masturbation, sold over 10 million copies, Judas Priest, the one about forced oral sex at gunpoint, has sold over 2 million copies. Quiet Riot, "Metal Health," has songs about explicit sex, over 5 million copies. Motley Crue, "Shout at the Devil," which contains violence and brutality to women, over 2 million copies.

Some say there is no cause for concern. We believe there is. Teen pregnancies and teenage suicide rates are at epidemic proportions today. The Noedecker Report states that in the United States of America we have the highest teen pregnancy rate of any developed country; 96 out of 1,000 teenage girls become pregnant.

Rape is up 7 percent in the latest statistics, and the suicide rates of youth between 16 and 24 have gone up 300 percent in the last three decades while the adult level has remained the same.

There certainly are many causes for these ills in our society, but it is our contention that the pervasive messages aimed at children which promote and glorify suicide, rape, sadomasochism, and so on, have to be numbered among the contributing factors.

Some rock artists actually seem to encourage teen suicide. Ozzie Osbourne sings "Suicide Solution." Blue Oyster Cult sings "Don't Fear the Reaper." AC/DC sings "Shoot to Thrill." Just last week in Centerpoint, a small Texas town, a young man took his life while listening to the music of AC/DC. He was not the first. . . .

Today parents have no way of knowing the content of music products that their children are buying. While some album covers are sexually explicit or depict violence, many others give no clue as to the content. One of the top 10 today is Morris Day and the Time, "Jungle Love." If you go to buy the album "Ice Cream Castles" to get "Jungle Love," you also get, "If the Kid Can't Make You Come, Nobody Can," a sexually explicit song.

The pleasant cover picture of the members of the band gives no hint that it contains material that is not appropriate for young consumers.

Our children are faced with so many choices today. What is available to them through the media is historically unique. The Robert Johnson survey on teen environment states that young people themselves often feel that they have: One, too many choices to make; two, too few structured means for arriving at decisions; and three, too little help to get there. (Record Labeling, 1985, pp. 11–12)

Summary of Value Advocacy Strategies
1. Define the terms of the proposition's value object.
2. Place the value object in the appropriate field, and state the value hierarchy of the field in which the value object is now placed.
3. State the criteria for evaluation.
   A. Have the characteristics of the criteria been defined or described?
   B. Are the criteria identified as necessary and/or sufficient to warrant acceptance?
   C. Has the relevance of the criteria to the value object been established?
   D. Are the criteria consistent with placement of the value object in a given field?
4. Measure the value object against the value judgment criteria, demonstrating that the value object fits the criteria on the basis of the following:
   A. What element of the society is influenced by the value object? (arguments on effect)
   B. To what degree or in what amount does the effect occur? (arguments on significance)
   C. What is the cause that produces the effect and significance of the value object? (arguments on inherency)

Opposing Propositions of Value

As was the case with fact, the opponent of the proposition of value has his choices constrained by both his resources and the advocate's choices. The uncertainty that this creates for the opponent of value change, and for that matter opponents of fact and policy, is partially offset by the asset of presumption. The opponent can also anticipate what the advocate is most likely to argue based on his analysis of the proposition, his knowledge of the stock issues she must address, and his understanding of audience beliefs and attitudes that the advocate might emphasize to encourage a value change.

The analysis of the proposition and search for issues is just as important for the opponent as it is for the advocate. To gain any advantage from presumption, the opponent must be aware of how the value object is presently viewed. The opponent should investigate every possible aspect of the value object—how it is regarded in its field, what opinions have been formed about it, what value standards are used to judge it, and what controversies exist concerning it. On the basis of this analysis, the opponent chooses his strategies for refuting the advocate's case.

Establishing Strategy

The opponent normally begins with an overview of the value proposition reflecting the position he will take in presenting arguments refuting the advocate's case.

This is his philosophy, and it expresses the essence of the opponent's perspective on the controversy, including a preview of his strategy. It tells the listener or reader that he will defend present values, present alternative values, or demonstrate the weakness of proof and reasoning in specific areas of the advocate's arguments; in short, it elucidates whatever strategy he chooses to employ. The purpose is to clarify where he stands on the proposition's value object.

Examining Definitions and Hierarchy

Since the first step in advocacy was to define the value object, that may be the opponent's next area of concern. Has the value object been properly defined? Does the opponent agree with the method of definition used by the advocate? If he feels that the value object should include elements the advocate has failed to consider or exclude elements she has included, his first point of clash with the advocate will be over how to define the value object. Our opponent may choose to accept the advocate's definition of rock 'n' roll based on *Rolling Stone*'s classification of the music, or he may choose to argue that this definition is too broad, and therefore it is impossible to judge using the criteria the advocate has discovered.

The opponent's next step is to make use of the stock issues of value argumentation. Recall that the first stock issue asks by what value hierarchy the value object is best understood. There are two questions the opponent should ask himself in preparing arguments about this issue. First, is the hierarchy the advocate has chosen really as important in the field and to the audience as the advocate suggests? He may attempt to demonstrate that society or those in the topic's field do not accept the validity of the value hierarchy the advocate has identified.

Second, has the advocate identified a value hierarchy appropriate to better understanding the value object? Does he see other more appropriate value hierarchies that the advocate has failed to recognize? Does the advocate provide an adequate justification for her choice of a value hierarchy? Would a different value hierarchy be more appropriate for this proposition?

The advocate's choice of hierarchy and criteria restrict her opponent's options. That does not mean that he has no choices. He may choose to dispute the core value she places at the top of her value hierarchy. If our advocate has identified the core value of achievement as the most important value in making her judgment, and she has justified this choice by arguing that aesthetic superiority is best understood as a form of achievement that is particularly appropriate to judging music, should the opponent dispute the core value? He may choose to argue that freedom is a much more important core value, in the world of rock 'n' roll as well as in every other area of American life. He could argue that it is unreasonable to place any other core value at the pinnacle of a hierarchy for this value object.

This illustrates one of the fundamental differences between fact and value argumentation. It is inappropriate and results in fallacious factual argumentation for the opponent to do too much shifting of the relationship between the subject and predicate of the proposition. An opponent for Richard Fraser's argumentation that Lincoln's doctors caused his death would be misleading the audience if he responsed that, "Yes the doctors were inept, but it wouldn't have mattered if Booth had not shot Lincoln." This response bypasses Fraser's argument and does nothing to refute his points about medical care of the 1860s.

In value argumentation, opponents do have the option of attempting to shift the hierarchy—asking the audience to view the value object from a different value system—without necessarily engaging in fallacious reasoning. This is not an instance of avoiding the issue, as long as the opponent develops arguments that will allow the audience to understand that shifting hierarchies is appropriate to understanding the proposition. The opponent may deny that there is any utility or probable truth in the advocate's evaluation of the value object. Or, he may choose to accept the general idea that making such a value judgment is a good thing to do, but the advocate does not go about it in quite the right way. The opponent then offers a new interpretation of the value hierarchy and suggests other criteria are more appropriate.

Suppose that our opponent had asked the audience to view the aesthetic significance of rock, not from the achievement value hierarchy of aesthetics as interpreted by music critics but from the aesthetic view of a mathematician. On the surface, you may not see values from the field of mathematics and music as all that compatible. The opponent must develop arguments from his investigation of the historical background demonstrating that there has long been a connection between the two fields and that mathematics is the most appropriate source of criteria for making aesthetic judgments about any musical genre.

Challenging the Criteria

Whether the opponent chooses to refute every aspect of the advocate's case, or asks the audience to shift to a different field for viewing the value object, his next concern is with the appropriateness of the criteria used in measuring the value object in terms of its effect, significance, and inherency. Has the advocate established unique criteria for a value object for which other, more commonly understood or accepted criteria exist? He may choose to argue that the value criteria are inappropriate for the value object because these criteria are too unusual or more appropriate to measuring some other value object. He would then provide arguments establishing that better criteria exist that are more appropriate to the value object or more widely recognized by experts in the field or society, or that the advocate has misinterpreted the value in question.

Refuting the Measurement

Finally, the opponent will turn to the third stock issue to determine if the value object is appropriately measured by the value criteria. With the concepts of effect, significance, and inherency clearly in mind, the opponent considers his strategies for opposition. First, remembering that the advocate must establish a prima facie case, he asks himself, "Have effect, significance, and inherency been argued by the advocate?" If one or more have not, a prima facie case has not been established. He should begin refutation by pointing this out. Second, since arguments of effect, significance, and inherency are advanced as claims, they require supporting proof and reasoning. He should examine the advocate's support for claims, asking, "Does the proof and reasoning offered by the advocate meet the tests established to determine their validity?" If it does not, the existence of a prima facie case would be in serious doubt.

If after analyzing the advocate's strategy, the opponent decides that the value criteria are fairly drawn, he must concentrate refutation on the goodness of fit between the criteria and the value object in the proposition. In employing denial and extenuation to oppose the value advocate, the opponent searches for proof and reasoning to ground arguments (1) stating that the effect suggested by the advocate occurs only in an exceptional case or that extenuating circumstances produce the effect, (2) denying that the value object's influence is as significant as the advocate suggests, (3) showing that only a small segment of those who place value on this object are influenced, (4) showing that prominent sources in the field do not consider the effect or the significance to be of great importance, (5) showing that either the effect or the significance is a temporary phenomenon brought about by the unusual circumstances, a passing fad, and (6) challenging inherency by demonstrating that the value in question is either not central to the society or is subject to change over time.

Argument in Action

The following is part of the statement made by Stanley M. Gortikov, president of the Recording Industry Association of America, Inc. (RIAA), in response to earlier testimony before the Senate Committee on Commerce, Science, and Transportation. Gortikov's testimony did not immediately follow Susan Baker's, coming instead several hours later. Thus, we have created something of an artificial debate between the two of them, although the PMRC's concerns were well known to the RIAA. As you read what Gortikov had to say, identify the points of clash between his position and Baker's, examine how he handles her preemptive arguments, and decide whether his opposition to what she had to say restored presumption to the music business.

> In this hearing today you have heard some understandable protests by the PMRC. We plan to act upon these concerns seriously. However, I also must spotlight five equally important truths that are essentially ignored by the PMRC in its media pronouncements, but hopefully which will be recognized by this committee.
>
> The first relates to unfairness. The sheer number of offensive recordings is minute compared with the total mass of recordings released by the industry. Yet the narrow targeting of the PMRC unfairly characterizes all artists and all companies as universal practitioners of evil.
>
> Second, positives. Whereas some lyrics may be objectionable, the mass of lyrics reflects pure entertainment or socially positive attitudes and practices.

If recordings do in fact affect young minds, as maintained by the PMRC, then the heavy thrust of our industry's input is positive, not negative.

Other forces. The PMRC, and therefore this committee, is focusing solely on rock music. But why is only rock music unfairly singled out for the scrutiny of the PMRC and the U.S. Senate while all other explicit negative influences on younger children go untargeted? What about movies and magazine ads, prime time television, soap operas, books, cable programs? If there is to be a negative review of negative forces in the environment of younger children, let it be a review of all such forces, not one which focuses on rock music alone. If the PMRC somehow were to be able to purify all music according to its own standards, who is going to purify the remainder of their children's world?

Fourth, behavior. The PMRC concentrates on modes of human behavior that it finds objectionable, but those realities are not invented by record companies, songwriters or performers. Adults in the society, some of them parents, are the real initiators of those extremes. Recorded music reflects rather than introduces society's values and the realities of human conduct, both good and bad.

And last, in respect to rights, although in this forum we address the rights of parents and younger children, we cannot submerge the rights of others. We are on delicate ground here in respect to censorship and the first amendment. We must not trample the rights of parents and other adults whose standards do not coincide with those of the PMRC or any other group. Further, recording artists and songwriters have their own rights and freedoms of expression and even have contractual protections that legally must be respected. We must assure that the noble intentions of the PMRC do not somehow get translated into a dilution of the rights and freedoms of others.

Those five realities which I have just articulated merit the consideration of this committee, too. And as to the PMRC, I am getting a little apprehensive about its motives and fervor. . . .

The PMRC now seems committed to impose its will on an entire creative community and on broadcasters, on record retailers, and thus on all who buy and hear recorded music. . . .

The members of the PMRC are parents. I and many of my colleagues are parents too. The PMRC has no monopoly on love and concern for kids. Child supervision is my personal parental responsibility, and degrees of control versus freedom are mine alone to set. I certainly would not be content to assign any part of my responsibility to some outside surrogate, like a record company, a radio station, a censorship panel, a government body, or a parent organization.

"Censorship" can take subtle forms and need not be confined to a deliberate surgical excising of dirty words. Censorship, in one of its manifestations, can be the stifling of the creative act—an insidious filtering out of creative energy—a homogenizing of creative output.

Some musical content may be considered offensive. We offend some people some of the time. Down through the ages, there always has been shocks in popular music—even from prime shockers like Cole Porter, Elvis Presley, and the Beatles. I cannot recall, however, definitive damage to children from any one of them. We here today, in fact, are ourselves some of those "victimized" children.

Some of our music, then, may cause one to wince. That wincing, the fleeting moments of discomfort, are the occasional prices one pays to get access to basic creative energy, to the talent pool, to the resources of excitement from which music and all art forms flow. One risks strangling those precious energies by rules and criteria and panels and coalitions and inquiries and even inscriptions. (Record Labeling, 1985, pp. 96–98)

Summary of Value Opposition Strategies

1. Give a statement of the opponent's philosophy that overviews the stand to be taken against the advocate's case.
2. Challenge or accept the advocate's definition of the value object.
3. Consider what criteria should be used to measure the value object.
   A. Is the asserted value as good as the advocate claims?
      1. Does society recognize it as good?
      2. Do experts in the field recognize it as good?
   B. Have the value criteria been correctly identified?
      1. Are there other values involved in the standard used?
      2. Does the advocate provide adequate justification for the value criteria selected?
      3. Is there a better standard by which to evaluate the value object?
4. Evaluate how appropriately the value object has been measured by the value criteria.
   A. Does the value object fit the stated criteria?
   B. Is the effect of the value object created by an exceptional case or extenuating circumstances?
   C. Is the significance temporary, inconsequential, or improperly measured?
   D. Is the value inherent in the value hierarchy of society or the field of the value proposition? Is there some alternate causality?

Propositions of value attempt to establish how something or someone ought to be judged. They are argued by determining the criteria or standards by which the evaluation ought to be made and then determining the fit between the object being evaluated and these criteria. Advocates of value propositions must be sure their argumentation considers effect, significance, and inherency, regardless of whether they proceed by means of criteria discovery or criteria development. The opponent, besides employing techniques applicable to arguing propositions of fact may also use the strategies of proposing different criteria and charging improper classification. Understanding how propositions of both fact and value are argued provides important insight into the next chapter's subject—how policy propositions are argued.

Learning Activities

1. Review Susan Baker's statement that a system for rating the content of record albums would be valuable. Analyze her advocacy position in terms of the following:

A. Into what value hierarchy does she place the value object, rock music albums?
B. What criteria does she use for making her evaluation? Are the criteria discovered or created?
C. Identify her use of arguments of effect, significance, and inherency in developing her evaluation.

2. Review Stanley M. Gortikov's opposition to the value of a rating system for rock music albums. Analyze his opposition in terms of the following:
A. What was his overall strategy of opposition? How does he express his philosophy of opposition?
B. Identify his use of denial and extenuation arguments; were they effective? Why or why not?

3. Choose an article that reviews a film from a magazine such as *Premier* or *Entertainment Weekly*. What hierarchy does the reviewer use as a source for evaluative criteria? What specific criteria are used in evaluating this film? What arguments of effect, significance, and inherency are used?

4. In the field of speech communication, one area of scholarship, rhetorical criticism, is devoted to making value judgments about the relative merits of human communication. Read one of the following articles and prepare an oral or written report using the questions listed below.

Trujillo, N., & Ekdom, L. R. (1985, September). Sportswriting and American Cultural Values: The 1984 Chicago Cubs. *Critical Studies in Mass Communication, 2*, 262–281.

Rushing, J. H. (1989, February). Evolution of "the New Frontier" in *Alien and Aliens:* Patriarchical Co-Optation of the Feminine Archetype. *Quarterly Journal of Speech, 75*, 1–24.

A. How does the rhetorical critic identify the value hierarchy used in doing criticism?
B. Is a theory of rhetoric used to discover criteria, or does the critic create criteria by combining ideas from rhetorical theory and other fields?
C. How are criteria applied to the communication examples of the value object?
D. How does this value argumentation differ from other types you have read or heard?

5. Discuss each of the following value propositions in terms of the value(s) to be supported by the advocate, the field(s) from which value criteria could be taken, and the specific judgmental criteria that might be used in measuring the value object.
A. Students will benefit from classical literature studies in grades 6 through 12.
B. For most people, buying a home computer is a waste of money.
C. The rights of endangered species ought to take precedence over the rights of indigenous human populations.
D. Humanitarian rather than geopolitical objectives ought to govern foreign policy decisions.

Suggested Supplementary Readings

Aaron, H. J., Mann, T. E., & Taylor, T. (1994). *Values and Public Policy.* Washington, D.C.: Brookings Institute.

This is an anthology of articles on making value judgments about existing and proposed policies. How changes in the economy bring about value change, the influence of culture on public policy, the changing nature of the family, multiculturalism, and the problems of gang violence and law enforcement are all described in terms of how we apply core values in our decision making.

Berg, J. L., Jr. (1992). *The Great American Priorities.* Lanham, MD: University Press of America.

This anthology excerpts speeches on major business, social, and political trends that are expected to take place by the end of this century. Berg chooses speeches about education, health care, and regulation of business and speeches that reflect the interests of groups such as veterans, women, African Americans, and youth to illustrate the values Americans apply to their personal and public lives.

Church, R. T., & Buckley, D. C. (1983). Argumentation and Debating Propositions of Value: A Bibliography. *Journal of the American Forensic Association,* 19, 239–250.

A comprehensive bibliography on value argumentation covering the work published prior to 1983 in the field of speech and related disciplines.

Warnick, B. (1981). Arguing Value Propositions. *Journal of the American Forensic Association,* 18, 109–119.

The author examines the basic issues found in value propositions. She suggests that to be prima facie, the advocate's case must establish a set of values that, when applied to the value object, are shown to be more fundamental than those presently associated with the value object. As a result, analysis of value propositions must be centered on how the audience/society views what is evaluated. An outline of the steps to follow in analyzing a value proposition is provided.

Young, M. J. (1980). The Use of Evidence in Value Argument. In J. Rhodes & S. Newell (Eds.), *Proceedings of the Summer Conference on Argumentation.* ERIC Document ED 181 503.

A very good discussion of what is necessary to ground value arguments. In particular, the concepts of *harm* and *significance* are discussed as value judgments intrinsic to policy argumentation.

Chapter Eleven

How Are Propositions of Policy Argued?

Policy argumentation contemplates a potential course of action. Where do we find examples of policy argumentation? In the field of law, we see examples of policy making as criminal codes are devised and revised, judges set penalties for those who are found guilty, and both professionals and ordinary citizens debate the merits of capital punishment and other issues involving the law and its implementation.

One of the more obvious places to see policy making and policy argumentation in action is in legislative bodies—national, state, and local. The establishment of new programs and the evaluation of existing ones takes place in city councils and commissions, in state legislative houses, and in the U.S. House of Representatives and the Senate. Your school may have a decision-making body that sets university policy. Since many policy proposals create both strong support and strong opposition, deliberations can become lengthy and fraught with emotion.

In business, management concerns itself with the creation and implementation of policy and subsequent reviews of its effectiveness. Issues related to productivity, labor relations, purchasing, sales, and public relations lead to policy development in business, where the deliberative process normally includes a definition and limitation of the problem, analysis of the problem, establishment of criteria to evaluate possible solutions to the problem, and subsequent review of the efficacy of the chosen solution after it has been implemented (Koehler, Anatol, & Applbaum, 1981).

Those who successfully advocate and oppose propositions of policy employ their understanding of how fact and value are argued. They also may benefit from the fact that the field of speech communication has historically devoted a great deal of critical attention to the unique requirements of policy argumentation. High school and intercollegiate debate have served as both an academic context for testing ideas and a crucible for examining the means by which those ideas may best be tested. As a result, a considerable body of knowledge has emerged relative to how propositions of policy, and more recently value, are argued. While the Appendix discusses intercollegiate debate in more detail, the ideas discussed in this chapter apply many of the concepts developed in contest debating to policy argumentation in general.

Advocating Policy Propositions

Creation of a prima facie case for a policy proposition begins with the advocate's research to find immediate causes, historical background on the topic, and information to develop three stock issues:

1. Is there a reason for change in a manner generally suggested by the policy proposition?
2. Does the policy proposed resolve the reason for change?
3. What are the consequences of the proposed change?

    The first step in creating a prima facie case is to discover whether a disparity between what exists and what would be desirable represents a problem to be solved. For example, suppose a group of people were endangering public safety, and the societal response was inadequate to prevent them from continuing to do so. Many people believe this is what is actually happening in the case of drunk drivers and that a disparity exists between the way things are and the way things ought to be. The analysis of stock issues in a policy proposition leads to discovering the existence of this disparity. The first stock issue asks what unresolved problems exist or will exist in the future: *Is there a reason for change in the manner generally suggested by the policy proposition?*

Advocacy of the First Stock Issue

Answering this question is important because if no reason for change exists, change is unwarranted. If someone walks up to you and asks to borrow ten dollars, they are advocating the policy proposition, "You should give me ten dollars." Your probable response will either be no, because they've given you no reason to warrant action on your part or why? because you would like to know their reason. Inquiry into the reason for change involves consideration of what the advocate perceives the disparity between actual and ideal to be.

    The advocate's response normally takes the form of a value contention, and four subissues must be advanced to win assent. These subissues provide the answers to questions customarily asked to determine whether a reason for change exists.

1. What is the nature of the disparity?
2. How extensive is the disparity?

3. Does the disparity cause harm to something or someone?
4. Is the disparity inherent in the present nature of things?

Advocacy of the first stock issue, reason for change, makes the listener or reader aware of an unresolved problem now, or in the future, that is a consequence of the way things are at present.

Identify the Disparity

The first subissue, the nature of the disparity, requires the advocate to substantiate at least one definitional claim; something that presently exists can be defined or classified as representing a disparity of a certain type. Because there is a natural resistance to change, people will usually be unresponsive unless the disparity is a serious one. "Accidents caused by drunk drivers kill innocent victims." The seriousness of the disparity is suggested in the definitional claim and further supported by arguments on the next two subissues, significance and effect. This should sound familiar since it is basic value argumentation. The advocate may discover that more than one disparity must be identified to produce a case that is compelling or prima facie. "Accidents caused by drunk drivers kill and injure innocent victims and increase the cost of auto insurance for us all."

Quantify the Disparity

The second subissue explains or quantifies the significance of the disparity, alleging the magnitude of this present or future problem. If the significance of the problem is demonstrable in quantitative terms, the advocate will advance and substantiate a factual claim. If the question is addressable only qualitatively, the claim will be definitional; the disparity is to be classified as being of a certain qualitative type, widespread or all-encompassing for example.

Characterize the Consequences

The third subissue concerns the effects, or consequences, of the disparity. A value claim is presented, suggesting that the consequences are in some way harmful to those experiencing the disparity. Why is this important? We could probably prove that every person reading this book is not presently a student at the University of Tokyo, a disparity that is extensive; but unless we could demonstrate that as a result you are being hurt, our advocacy of the policy proposition "you should transfer to the University of Tokyo" would be unwarranted. Thus, the advocate uses the third subissue to examine the consequences of the present or future disparity. She evaluates them in negative terms by first establishing the criteria for harm and then demonstrating the goodness of fit between those criteria and the present disparity.

Establish Inherency

The final subissue used in developing argumentation on the first stock, reason for change, concerns itself with inherency. You might review the discussion of inherency in Chapter 2. In policy propositions, inherency is argued to determine the cause of the serious and harmful disparity. Blame for the existence of the disparity is placed at the doorstep of things as they are now—existing laws, institutions, or beliefs. A factual claim is used to establish the causal relationship between what exists and the disparity. The demonstration of inherency is critical. Subscribing to the philosophy of "if it ain't broke don't fix it," the advocate's readers or listeners will be unwilling to change something that is apparently innocent of having caused the problem for which a remedy is sought.

If the reason for change rests on the hypothesis that some more desirable future state will not be achieved because of things as they are now, the advocate must demonstrate that this desired state will probably not be reached because of the way things are now. People tend to give existing laws, institutions, or beliefs the benefit of the doubt, assuming they are likely to change naturally in ways that result in a future that is better than our past or present. The advocate must preclude this kind of thinking by demonstrating that existing barriers render the more desirable future state she supports unavailable by any means other than those she will propose.

Having successfully upheld the burden of proof with regard to the first stock issue, reason for change, the advocate must now propose a way to remedy the disparity. The remedy is a new policy by which a preferred state, one in which the disparity would cease to exist, is reached. *Does the proposed policy resolve the reason for change?*

Advocacy of the Second Stock Issue

Assuming change is warranted because the advocate has proven the existence of a problem, she must then provide the solution if she hopes to win assent. This solution, or proposed policy, should explain exactly what is to be done, and it should include the following elements:

1. *Change*—What behaviors are to be enacted that are not presently being enacted? What will be done differently?
2. *Mechanism*—On whose authority will these behaviors be undertaken? Will a new law be passed, a new agency or institution created, or will individuals do this on their own?
3. *Financing*—If the change or mechanism incurs any costs, how much will they be, and how will they be paid?
4. *Enforcement*—Unless everyone is willing to go along with the change, how will violations be detected? Who will be responsible for this detection, and how will violators be dealt with? What means are used to assure compliance?

Unless a separate definition of the key terms in the proposition is provided, the advocate's proposal serves as an operational definition of the meaning of the proposition.

Suppose the advocate has suggested that present laws regarding drunk drivers should be changed because of the number of deaths and injuries attributable to them. The proposal for change might include the following:

The federal government will remove the requirement of probable cause and mandate that law enforcement officers randomly stop one vehicle per shift and administer a test of sobriety to the driver. Drivers with blood alcohol levels above the legal limit shall be subject to license revocation for one year. Persons caught driving during the period of revocation will receive a one-year jail sentence. Since this proposal involves the addition of no new manpower or facilities, it is essentially a free solution to the problem.

All four elements a policy proposal should have are contained in this example. After its details are spelled out, the advocate will be obliged to demonstrate how the reason for change has been satisfied. This involves considering the third stock issue: *What are the consequences of the proposed policy?*

Advocacy of the Third Stock Issue

At the very least, we expect solutions to work, to solve the problems that called them into being. If, in addition to this workability, other good things happen coincidentally, we are very pleased. The advocate guides the listener or reader through the consequences of the proposed policy by considering four questions:

1. How does the proposed policy address the disparity?
2. How does the proposed policy overcome its inherency?
3. How workable is the proposed policy?
4. What are the subsidiary effects of the proposed policy?

These four questions represent the subissues the advocate must develop in support of the third stock issue of policy argumentation, the consequence of change.

Demonstrate Solvency

The first question pertains to the concept sometimes referred to as solvency. Does the proposed policy address the disparity in such a way that it eliminates or substantially minimizes it? Does the proposed policy get us to, or at least nearer to, the more ideal state the advocate seeks? The proposed solution to the problem created by drunk drivers rests on the laws of probability. If 10 percent of the people who are driving could not pass a sobriety test, then 10 percent of the random stops should result in arrests and convictions. The penalties are hoped to be severe enough to deter people from driving while intoxicated or to incapacitate them if they were not deterred but were caught. The advocate of this policy would have to offer proof and reasoning in support of these claims alleging the solvency of the proposal.

Overcome Inherency

The second subissue is important. If existing institutions cannot address the reason for change because of inherent barriers, the advocate must demonstrate how her proposal is not hamstrung by these same barriers. Normally, the mechanism section of the policy proposal will fiat the necessary change. If the barrier was structural, for example, the present requirement of having probable cause before stopping a driver and administering a sobriety test, the advocate would argue that her proposal removed or altered it in such a way that it no longer constitutes an impediment. If inherency was a consequence of something's absence at present, for example, the lack of a federal mandate and determinant sentencing for drunk drivers, the advocate must show how her proposal fills these gaps. If inherency resulted from attitudes, the advocate must be able to prove these same attitudes will not undermine the solvency of the proposal, or she must provide some means to change them. For example, if inherency was due to the attitudes of police, who feel that catching murderers, rapists, and thieves is more important than stopping someone who may have had too much to drink, the advocate would be in serious trouble because those charged with enforcing her proposal would not attach much importance to the task.

Establish Workability

The third subissue turns attention to the fundamental nature of the proposal itself and analyzes its workability. A proposal may solve problems and overcome inherent barriers but be totally unrealistic and unworkable. To suggest that the most effective solution to the problem of drunk driving would be to prohibit the manufacture and sale of alcoholic beverages may be true but unworkable. The nation tried that particular policy for moral reasons in the past and discovered that most Americans not only did not favor it but also willfully violated it. The advocate must develop and use criteria of effectiveness to argue that the proposed policy is more workable than what it replaces.

Identify Subsidiary Effects

The fourth subissue, identifying the subsidiary effects of the proposed policy, allows the advocate to conclude discussion of the consequences of change by pointing to whatever desirable side effects occur as a result of assent to her proposal. Do the members of her audience get something for nothing? The advocate of tougher action against drunk drivers could claim they might. While her reason for change concerns deaths and injuries attributable to those who drive while intoxicated, a problem the proposed policy is thought to remedy, a subsidiary effect of the policy might be lower insurance premiums for everyone.

To be considered a subsidiary effect, something must be an inherent consequence of the success of the proposed policy, over and above remedying the disparity that motivated its being proposed. Subsidiary effects are like fringe benefits; they are nice to have, but they are not always available. Therefore, the absence of subsidiary effects does *not* render an advocate's case nonprima facie. Nor do subsidiary effects constitute a warrant for change in and of themselves. If a reason for change does not exist, or if the proposal for change fails to remedy the problem it is intended to resolve, the advocate's cause is lost even if her proposal produces some pleasant side effects.

Patterns of Organization

Before we turn to an example of policy advocacy, some comments about patterns of organization are in order. While we have labeled the stock issues first, second, and third, the logic of the advocate's approach should dictate the order in which they are presented. The overall pattern presented here reflects traditional organization, known as need-plan-advantage. It is used when the reason for change involves righting past wrongs and showing the subsidiary benefits of the proposed policy. For this type of advocacy, the order in which the stock issues have been discussed in this chapter is most appropriate.

However, if the reason for change relates to the attainment of a more desirable future state, then the means to attain that state, the second stock issue, should be discussed first. This is called comparative advantage structure. It compares the advocate's proposed policy to existing policy and argues that the advocate's proposal is more advantageous. It is used when serious present problems under the stock issue of reason for change cannot be discovered or are not widely accepted. It is also used when there is almost universal agreement that a reason for change exists, but controversy surrounds the question of what is the best future course of action. This is often the case in legislative debate. Argumentation compares the proposed solution to existing policy. The second and third stock issues, the proposed change and the consequences of change, provide the focus for argumentation.

Although there is no rule regarding how many advantages are necessary to warrant a change, the advantages must be demonstrated to result from the new policy, and their value must by qualitatively or quantitatively measurable. The same is true of advantages claimed in the traditional need-plan-advantage case. The organization of comparative advantage advocacy begins with the presentation of the policy proposal that specifies change, mechanism, financing, and enforcement. The advocate then indicates one or more advantages to be achieved by adopting this proposal. Each advantage should be unique. Only the proposed policy, when compared to existing policy, is capable of achieving it. In addition to demonstrating uniqueness, the advocate establishes a quantitative and/or qualitative measure of each advantage's value to society.

A third type of organization exists for policy advocacy that uses many of the features of value argumentation. Goals-criteria advocacy begins by examining what society values and what goals it has set to achieve these values. If full employment is a goal of society stemming from our valuation of the work ethic, a proposal to achieve full employment might be advocated on the basis that it better achieves the goal and, therefore, more fully realizes the relevant value. Criteria are used in the same manner as in value argumentation. The proposed policy is then examined in terms of value criteria that measure its ability to obtain the desired goal.

The advocate's presentation may be organized in accordance with different philosophies—traditional, comparative advantage, or goals-criteria—but arguments will still address the same stock issues. As you read through the following example of policy advocacy, decide which pattern of organization the advocate is using.

Argument in Action

On October 29, 1991, popular songwriter and recording artist Debbie Gibson offered the following policy argumentation in support of proposed legislation to enact a royalty payment charge on digital audio recording equipment and media. She does not provide an extensive discussion of the proposal since it was already spelled out in the legislation. Notice, though, how she does address the issue of solvency as she offers arguments in support of the legislation.

My name is Deborah Gibson. I'm a songwriter and performer. I'm a member of ASCAP, and today I am proud to represent songwriters and music performers from around the world.

I'd like to thank you all for the opportunity to speak to you about the Audio Home Recording Act, and I'd like to thank Senator DeConcini for introducing S.1623.

Let me tell you how I became interested in a career in music. I guess you could say that from the time I could talk I had the dream of being on the stage. When I was eight, I bought my first pop album, which was Billy Joel's "52nd Street." One year later, I saw him in concert and ever since that day, I knew that I wanted to be a writer/artist like him.

My parents set up a recording studio for me in our basement at home in Long Island, and I practiced and wrote songs and auditioned and shopped my tapes around.

I was fortunate to be signed to a recording contract, when I was 16, with Atlantic Records. The song that became my first hit really summed up my feelings about my success. It was called "Only in My Dreams," and it was a single off my first album, "Out of the Blue" which also launched three other top five singles, including a song that went to No. 1: "Foolish Beat." By the way, the RIAA certified this album triple platinum, and to those RIAA representatives who are here today, I still say thank you.

My second album, "Electric Youth," was a No. 1 album with two "gold" singles: "Electric Youth" and "Lost in Your Eyes." It was also certified multi-platinum and I certainly was very encouraged.

But it's the title of my third and most recent album that I'd like to focus on because it's called "Anything Is Possible." That's certainly the story of the popularity of my records to date, the great people I've worked with and the fact that I've been part of a system that gives young people an incentive to follow their dreams.

And that's why I'm here today. To make certain that others like me will have the same opportunity to follow their dreams.

By supporting S.1623, you are protecting the future of all songwriters and artists and that of the entire music industry.

Let me explain how the DAT bill can accomplish this. I was born into a musical era that is both the best of times and the worst of times. Because of the wonders of modern technology, there are more outlets than ever before for playing music and because of that fact, my hits were truly worldwide hits in every sense for which I'm grateful.

On the other hand, the music trades and consumer press carried stories about countless financial losses due to unauthorized copying of our records both at home and abroad. And, unfortunately, those losses were not just press items, they were real.

I, along with other songwriters and performers worried would we ever have the same chances at success as those who came before us? More important, would there be an industry left for us to be part of?

S.1623 removes these sizeable [*sic*] fears because it compensates us for the losses we will suffer from copying by digital audio equipment.

There's certainly no doubt that the DAT machines will generate more copying of our records than ever before. We all know how much copying went on with analog machines, which made *imperfect* copies of the original. Can you imagine how much more will go on with machines that make *perfect* copies of the original? I can and that's why I'm scared. And I'm not alone.

Digital Audio technology is a great advance, our music sounds better than we ever imagined possible. All of us who write and perform applaud it. But we don't want to see the hard-won protections for creators and performers of music that have come about over the past century stripped away.

As I understand it, the present law does not deal adequately with the problem of how we would be paid for the perfect copies that would be made of our copyrighted musical works.

As a result, all factions of the entertainment business including the hardware and software industries worked hard and long to achieve the compromises which address the interests of all of us and, most important, of the public. The public benefits when creators are encouraged to create and when the fruits of technology are there for the public to enjoy.

We believe that your bill, S.1623, embodies the protections we so desperately need. It provides an updated legislative framework that will assure fair compensation for creators and a stable business climate for everyone.

There's also another concern. Several other countries have already responded to the problem of unauthorized copying of music through the use of a royalty like the one proposed in S.1623. Some of these countries do not protect foreign authors unless their governments also have this kind of legislation. In fact, in a recent report to this subcommittee, our own Register of Copyrights, Ralph Oman, has stated that 17 nations have a royalty provision similar to the one in your bill. I'd hate to think that American creators won't be receiving any home taping royalties from those countries because the United States doesn't provide the same kind of protection.

S.1623 is a wonderful solution. It represents a compromise resulting from years of controversy and negotiations; it enables a new recording technology to enter the United States; it provides for a modest royalty on digital tapes and recording equipment; it also contains a computer chip that prevents "copies" of copies to be made, thereby reducing our losses.

I may be young, but I've worked very hard for the success I've had to date. My entire family has worked just as hard, as my sister, Karen, who is here with me today will verify. I've staked my future on music, I'm giving it everything

I've got. I want to keep working at what I love; to concentrate on my writing and performing without worrying about whether I will be paid for the copying of my music, or whether the industry I'm so happy to be in will survive.

Let me sum up the impact of S.1623 by quoting, if I may, from a lyric I wrote: "There is a world of endless resources. There is a mind full of outrageous dreams. There is a place where the two meet. Anything is possible." S.1623 proves that anything is possible by bringing all the different parts of our industry together to arrive at legislation that will nurture the incentive to create. (The Audio Home Recording Act of 1991, 1991, pp. 63–66)

Ms. Gibson's argumentation is developed on the first stock issue that a disparity exists in the recording industry and the third stock issue, that this disparity will be resolved by the proposed legislation. Since this example was taken from legislative debate, she was not responsible for developing the second stock issue. The details of the proposal had already been specified by the those who submitted the legislation. Her role was to advocate the reason for change and the solvency of the bill in protecting the rights of musicians to be compensated for their work. In order to be prima facie, the advocate's case must include arguments that address the following questions:

Summary of Policy Advocacy
1. Is there a reason to change in the manner generally suggested by the policy proposition?
   A. What is the nature of the disparity?
   B. How extensive is the disparity?
   C. Does the disparity cause harm to something or someone?
   D Is the disparity inherent in the present nature of things?
2. Does the policy proposed resolve the reason for change?
   A. What will be done differently?
   B. Who will be responsible for doing it?
   C. What will it cost, and how will costs be paid?
   D. What means are used to assure compliance?
3. What are the consequences of the proposed change?
   A. How does the proposed policy address the disparity?
   B. How does the proposed policy overcome its inherency?
   C. How workable is the proposed policy?
   D. What are the subsidiary effects of the proposed policy?

Opposing Policy Propositions

The opponent of the policy advocate attempts to demonstrate that good and sufficient reasons exist to consider the proposed policy unacceptable. Remember that the advocate must develop arguments in support of three stock issues. Although the second one may become essentially noncontestable as soon as a proposal for change is advanced, the advocate must win the two remaining stock issues. There must be a reason for change and the consequences of the proposed policy must be such that, at a minimum, the reason for change is remedied. Must the opponent also win both these issues in order to defeat the advocate? No, in fact, he doesn't even have to contest both. Thus, the first strategic choice the opponent makes concerns whether to argue one or both of the remaining stock issues. If he feels one is clearly winnable and the other is not, he may choose to attack only where he has the advantage, focusing audience attention on that portion of the contested ground where his arguments are strongest.

Why is this strategic choice possible? A prima facie case is one that can be taken at face value, meaning that the reason for change, the proposed change, and the proposed change's ability to resolve the reason for change must be present in the advocate's case before it can be termed prima facie. If the opponent can successfully attack the advocate's position on the first or last of these stock issues, the case is no longer prima facie. It no longer offers good and sufficient reasons for a listener's or reader's assent. As a rule, the advocate's position will not be so clearly deficient in its development of the three stock issues to make this decision an easy one. Therefore, the opponent usually attacks on both fronts and determines the real strengths and weaknesses of the advocate's case based on the arguments used to defend it.

Establish Strategy

The opponent's case usually begins with an overview of his rationale for rejection. What will he defend? What does he oppose? How does he wish the listener or reader to view the proposed policy? The opponent examines the advocate's case, identifies the central idea behind the proposed change, and asks himself the following questions. Does the reason for change contain assumptions that are unwarranted because they have not been fully proven? Are there implied values the reader or listener is asked to accept without explanation? What is the advocate's burden of proof and has it been met? In addition to determining whether the advocate has fulfilled the responsibility of the burden of proof, the opponent assesses the evidence and reasoning contained in individual arguments, applies tests of evidence to the proof grounding and backing claims, and examines the reasoning for fallacies.

Examine Definitions

The opponent also determines whether he wishes to contest the advocate's definition of terms. If the proposition has been defined operationally, his refutation of the ability of the proposal to do what the advocate claims it will do is equivalent to contesting the definition of terms. But if the advocate chose to define the subject of the proposition independently, the opponent applies the same tests he employed in opposing fact and value propositions—has the advocate excluded something important or included too much?

Refute the Reason for Change

Opposing argumentation on the first stock issue uses the strategies discussed in Chapters 9 and 10 since the stock issue of reason for change is advanced by fact and value arguments. The opponent may use arguments to deny that the disparity exists or to show that it is not as great as the advocate suggests. The opponent may use arguments that deny the harmfulness of the disparity, or he may attempt to prove the harm is insignificant. He may also argue that extenuating circumstances, which are only temporary, explain the existence of the disparity.

Challenge Inherency

In regard to reason for change, the opponent may offer arguments showing that the disparity is not inherent to the field or society, its institutions, or its policies. In arguing inherency, the advocate wants the reader or listener to believe that what presently exists causes the problem and, by implication, that the only remedy lies beyond the reach of existing laws, institutions, or patterns of belief. If this were absolutely true, we would be locked in place, totally incapable of change. In reality, what exists at present is, to a certain degree, in a state of flux and in the process of becoming something else. The opponent may capitalize on this, denying the inherency of the reason for change on the basis of a field's or society's self-correcting abilities. This is normally referred to as a *minor repairs* argument.

The philosophy of minor repairs does not give the opponent license to claim whatever he wishes. Whatever minor repairs are suggested to what exists must meet certain tests. First, minor repairs must be attainable within the foreseeable future. To assert that someday the state of the art in automotive safety technology will be such that people will no longer be killed or injured in an accident, thus rendering unnecessary an advocate's proposal to crack down on drunk drivers, stretches both an audience's credulity and the limits of the foreseeable future beyond their breaking points.

Second, a minor repair must be attainable without benefit of a structural or attitudinal change—it must be a natural consequence of what presently exists. To argue that states could decide to suspend probable cause without the federal mandate provided by the advocate would violate this second standard. However, arguing that there is a current trend toward tougher sentences for those convicted of drunk driving, which causes many to think twice before driving while intoxicated, and that this trend will continue into the future, conforms to the second standard.

Third, minor repairs are subject to the same standards of proof, insofar as their solvency, inherency, and workability are concerned, as the policy proposed by the advocate. Fourth, and finally, minor repairs should not themselves be interpretable as a legitimate part of the policy proposition. If the proposition calls for the prevention of drunk driving, the opponent could not propose the installation of ignition interlock devices, which prevent intoxicated drivers from starting their cars, as a minor repair. While the suggestion differs from the specific interpretation of the proposition presented by the advocate, it still constitutes "advocacy" of the proposition's intent. Because it also constitutes a structural change in the way society attempts to control drunk driving, it is neither a defense of present policy nor a reasonable interpretation of what present policy is in the process of becoming.

Refute the Consequences of Change

Question Solvency

Opposing argumentation on the third stock issue requires creativity, along with a firm belief in the principle whatever can go wrong, will go wrong. What might preclude solvency? Almost anything or anyone whose actions are necessary to remedy a problem has the potential to interfere. In the drunk-driving example, suppose the accuracy of some devices used to determine blood alcohol content could be shown to be questionable. The advocate's proposal provides no funding to purchase the right kind of equipment. As a result, a police department with the wrong kind of equipment could find all the cases it brings to court dismissed. In addition, if most police cars are not sent into the field with testing equipment because of the expense, how are the officers to make their daily determinations of sobriety?

Identify Barriers

What might preclude inherency being overcome? While the proposal will normally fiat a means to overcome present barriers, two things must be remembered. First, attitudes cannot be legislated. Second, people resist change, especially when they are not sure that a change is in their best interests. This leads the opponent to an analysis of what are commonly called *circumvention arguments*. How might circumvention occur in the present example? Police are only human. Some of them may even have a drink from time to time. One of the current impediments to convicting drunk drivers is the there but for the grace of God go I syndrome. Enforcement relies on the police, and if they suffer from the aforementioned syndrome, they may choose to let marginal cases go or only stop those whose driving indicates they are obviously intoxicated, those for whom they would have had probable cause under the old system anyway.

Dispute Workability

What renders a proposal unworkable? If the means by which it operates are so slow, so inconvenient, or so time consuming that the cost of making a proposal work outweighs the benefits gained when it does, we deem it unworkable. Simple proposals are rarely all that simple. The efforts expended by those who make the system work should not be excessive. In the drunk-driving case, for example, requiring the police to spend time either waiting by the roadside for the test equipment to arrive or driving around late at night on deserted streets looking for a car to stop suggests a relatively high proportion of wasted effort.

Present Disadvantages

Up to this point we have said nothing about the fourth subissue, subsidiary effects. Proposals are like pebbles tossed into ponds, they make waves. Sometimes these waves are small, but usually one or more may be of epic proportions. The opponent should look for these, since they constitute the *disadvantages* to the advocate's proposal. Development of arguments of this kind rests on performing a "worst case" analysis of a situation in which the consequences of the proposal are portrayed to be as bad as or worse than the problem the proposal was intended to remedy.

What would be a worst case situation in the proposal we have been discussing? A man who would not fail the sobriety test, but who has had a drink, is driving home. A police car pulls up behind him and turns on the red light. The driver panics and flees, resulting in a high speed chase in a congested area. Or consider a woman who has lost her license but has continued to drive as the driver in our worst case. Although she has not had a drink, she knows she will be arrested for driving without a license. The result is the same and the consequence is at least as potentially serious as the problem the policy was designed to remedy.

How are disadvantage arguments developed? The opponent begins by assuming the policy will do exactly what the advocate says it will. This means that solvency, inherency, and workability are, partially or wholly, granted to the advocate. The argument is then developed in the same manner that an argument advocating a value proposal would be. The opponent establishes criteria for evaluating the advocate's proposal as if it were in existence, and then demonstrates the goodness of fit between these criteria and the proposal. This also means that he assumes a burden of proof similar to that of the advocate of a value proposition.

A final note concerning disadvantage arguments. Opponents must resist arguing disadvantages indiscriminantly. To be effective, disadvantages must possess *uniqueness;* they must occur only in the presence of, and as a consequence of, the advocate's proposal. If the same disadvantage would occur as a result of a minor repair the opponent has suggested, or would occur even without the repair as a consequence of what presently exists, its impact in dissuading the reader or listener is diminished.

If the opponent has to concede so much and be so careful in arguing a disadvantage, why bother? Because disadvantages are the potential "service aces" of argumentation. The opponent can concede everything, the stock issues of reason for change and the ability of the proposed change to remedy the problem; but if he can convince the audience that a single disadvantage, or series of disadvantages, to the advocate's proposal represents a greater harm to society than the one the proposal remedies, he can win their assent.

Consider the relationship between the pharmaceutical industry and the Food and Drug Administration (FDA) as an example of the power of disadvantages in determining the outcome of argumentation. A drug company makes a product intended to produce certain health-improving effects. Assume the drug produces these effects, along with some dangerous side effects. If the FDA determines that these side effects are so harmful and extensive that they outweigh the benefits the drug produces, it would not allow the company to market the product or would force it to take the product off the market if they were discovered later.

The burdens placed on the advocate seem great, and the opponent may defeat a policy proposal with one telling disadvantage, so why bother to argue? Why risk advocacy? The advocate actually has a number of natural advantages, not the least of which is the ability to define the nature of the ground over which argumentation is joined. The policy advocate makes the best possible case for a proposal's adoption. However, if the good to be achieved would be outweighed by the greater evils that would occur, rational decision making suggests that the reader or listener ought to reject it.

Offer a Counterproposal

One final strategy the opponent may elect to employ is to accept as valid the advocate's reason for change and offer a *counterproposal*, an equally acceptable alternative to it. This strategy is used in many fields and has become common in academic argumentation. In law making, business, and family decision-making situations, all parties may agree a problem exists that must be solved, but they may disagree over which policy would represent the best solution. In the legislative context, this often results in an amendment to a proposal being suggested.

In many fields, opponents would sometimes happily acquiesce to the advocate's proposal if she would withdraw one part of it or make some revision to it. The opponent in academic argumentation normally does not follow this strategy. Opponents usually seek rejection of the advocate's case as a whole. In academic argumentation, the requirement that the proposal must be *nontopical* applies to counterproposals and minor repairs alike. In addition, the counterproposal in academic argumentation must be *competitive*, which means that its adoption must preclude the ability to also adopt the advocate's proposal. The audience is asked to choose between two mutually exclusive proposals. If the opponent chooses to use a counterproposal, he assumes the same burden of proof as an advocate and uses the subissues of the second and third stock issues in his argumentation to demonstrate the superiority of his proposal.

Patterns of Organization

Opponents typically follow the pattern of organization provided by the advocate, arguing first things first and proceeding to subsequent arguments in an order that juxtaposes each with the advocate's argument. This helps listeners and readers clearly understand the points of clash and disagreement. While the opponent has a number of strategic options available, all of these options can never be used simultaneously.

Argument in Action

Philip Greenspun, a research assistant at the Massachusetts Institute of Technology, was one of the opponents who spoke against S.1623, the Audio Home Recording Act of 1991. His opposition is highlighted by two important strategic choices: denial that any change will occur as a result of this policy and arguments that prove how technology will outstrip the mechanism of the legislation and render its workability and solvency questionable. We have edited out some of Mr. Greenspun's transitional observations on problems with vendors, the potential for lawsuits, and using trademarks.

I'm from the MIT Department of Electrical Engineering. Everybody else has said something about their organization. I guess all I can say is that MIT is known worldwide as probably the finest engineering school in East Cambridge. . . .

I guess I'd like to read a quote here. "The most sensitive ear could not detect the slightest difference between the tone of the singer and the tone of the mechanical device." Metropolitan Opera soprano Anna Case found that "everybody, including myself, was astonished to find that it was impossible to distinguish between my own voice and Mr. Edison's recreation of it." Now, they weren't speaking of Kiyoaki Edison, designer of DAT machines, but of Thomas Edison, inventor of the Diamond Disk phonograph. This was in 1915, and it was purely acoustic technology that didn't even depend on electricity.

I maintain that digital audio technology will not change the amount of copyright infringement in America, and Mr. Oman pointed this out. He said that teenagers will continue using these $49 boomboxes, and he said that the audiophiles will buy these things and copy. Well, even the current DAT machines are actually inferior in quality in many ways to the best cassette decks, Nakamichi cassette decks, which audiophiles already own, and the new technologies that are being proposed now are inferior to Nakamichi cassette decks. So I don't see who's going to buy this except for computer users, because the new media is ideal for storing computer data.

Americans would rather buy than copy. Despite ample tools distributed throughout this country for copyright infringement, Americans bought $6.5 billion worth of recordings last year. I think it's premature to say that America is full of people who are intent on not paying for their music.

I'd like to say that copyright exists to promote the progress of the arts so that society benefits. Copyright was created not to enrich authors, but because it was thought that society as a whole would benefit if authors could earn more money from their creations. Let's see if S.1623 will benefit society.

Consider first the case of the small American firm manufacturing digital audio equipment. To implement the SCMS as required by the bill, a small American company would most likely have to buy chips from foreigners. I understand that Mr. Roach's $4 billion dollar company [Tandy Corporation] hasn't had much trouble getting the chips, but in a decade of designing consumer electronics and industrial electronics, I can tell you that it can be very difficult to get things that the Japanese don't want to sell you. Federal Express will come every day with engineering data books, samples, and prices. But when I tried to buy TV tuners, it was a different story. I had to pay $100 apiece for 2,000 TV tuners that are incorporated in products that cost $200. A recent GAO study confirms my personal experience.

S.1623 will enable foreigners to decide who in America may enter the digital audio business and what prices they charge for their products.

Let's consider that you are in fact making digital audio recorders. You manage to get the chips, and the digital audio recorders are rolling out of your factory in Peoria. Let's also assume you manage to hire an army of lawyers and accountants to romance the new bureaucracy created by S.1623. You'll file your quarterly reports, annual reports, and pay royalty tax. Where does the tax go? A lot of it goes into the pockets of your biggest competitors, Sony and Matsushita, since they own CBS and MCA Records. S.1623 changes you from a small-time manufacturer into a financier of the Japanese electronics and software oligopoly. . . .

Now here's where I guess I don't agree with the other witnesses. You in fact do need to copy music back and forth between two machines many times in order to make a master tape. You even need to do this if you make a video recording. If you do a video of your daughter's wedding, for example, if you don't want all that raw footage, then you're going to have to copy that onto another recorder, and if you later decide that you don't in fact like the way you edited that, if you want to make another copy with certain scenes removed, you have to copy it again. You have to copy, copy, copy, copy, copy.

For someone who can't afford one of these new, fancy digital microphones that was mentioned, they won't be able to buy low cost consumer digital audio recorders. They'll have to buy expensive professional ones, which would increase the barrier to entry in the already concentrated record industry, making it harder for individuals and small American companies to compete with large, foreign-owned companies. Slightly increased revenues for established companies and artists would not make up for the loss of variety and opportunities for newcomers. . . .

The multimedia revolution in computers will make S.1623 appear laughably shortsighted. In the 16 months since I last testified before Congress on this issue, more than five new technologies capable of storing both digital audio and computer data have been introduced.

Digital audio stores music as ones and zeroes. Digital video is stored the same way. So are spreadsheets and documents. This started out as a bunch of ones and zeroes on my Macintosh. Computers today store digital data on consumer video tape and consumer digital audiotape. Every indication is that within the next 5 years, computers and home stereos will use identical recording media, as indeed they already do in some cases. Blank media will be subject to royalty tax by S.1623, so every time an American uses his computer, he's going to pay a tax to Japanese conglomerates that own record companies but also happen to manufacture computer equipment. So American audio consumers and American computer users will be subsidizing Japanese companies that compete with our computer industry.

Computers subvert the intent of this bill in more ways than one. Last year George Wilson and I, the two electrical engineers testifying, proved that anyone could defeat SCMS with a handful of common electronic parts. By the time there are enough digital audio recorders in America to contribute to a copyright infringement, even the cheapest personal computers will be able to read and write digital audio. A 10-line computer program would then suffice to defeat SCMS. . . .

The most egregious effect of S.1623 will be on blind Americans who purchase a disproportionate amount of audio recorders and blank tape. Digital audio offers tremendous promise to the blind not because of sound quality, but because of convenience, indexing, and the ability to store dozens of hours of a talking book on one tape. Blind people mostly record audio letters and talking books, so it is unfair that S.1623 forces them to pay a tax to foreign-owned record companies or even fellow Americans like Michael Jackson.

SCMS is a particularly nasty thorn in the side of blind consumers. When SCMS prevents a digital copy from being made, the sighted consumer notes the flashing "Congress says you can't do this" on the front panel and switches to the analog input. He then sets the recording level by watching two meters while adjusting a knob. The sighted consumer ends up with a nearly perfect copy as opposed to a perfect bit-for-bit copy. A blind consumer cannot see the flashing SCMS indicator. Even if he did understand why the machine wasn't recording, he wouldn't be able to see the level meters. S.1623 prevents blind people from using consumer digital audio recorders for noninfringing purposes. . . .

Does S.1623 benefit society? Will Michael Jackson produce better music if S.1623 increases his income by 1 percent? Or will we be deprived of a future Michael Jackson because an unknown artist could not afford a professional digital recorder? If S.1623 makes a composer slightly wealthier, will that make up for an increased trade deficit, lost American jobs, and inconve-nienced, poorer consumers? Is it worth shipping millions of extra dollars to reduce copyright infringement by a few percent or to shift it from digital machines to my boombox? Should computer users in America be subsidizing computer vendors in Japan by paying royalty tax to Sony and Matsushita? Should blind Americans suffer inconvenience and pay taxes to Matsushita, Phillips, and Sony for the privilege of recording their own voice? (The Audio Home Recording Act of 1991, 1991, pp. 127–130)

The examples of policy advocacy and opposition from the debate over the Audio Home Recording Act of 1991 were specifically chosen to demonstrate how an advocate and opponent clash on the stock issues of a need for change and the workability of a proposal. Ms. Gibson's argument demonstrates how an advocate can be both passionate and logical in making a case for policy change. Her argu-mentation has the possibility of being very compelling because she herself has a certain authoritative status as someone who is affected by the disparity. Also com-pelling is her use of song lyrics to ground some of her claims. Mr. Greenspun's argument is particularly strong in his use of the historical background of audio recording and his projections about what technology will mean to this topic. Both arguers represent effectiveness in their creation of sound reasons.

Summary of Policy Opposition
1. Is the advocate's case prima facie, and does it fulfill the burden of proof?
   A. Has the advocate failed to provide a rationale for change?
   B. Has the advocate failed to provide a specific proposal for change?
   C. Has the advocate failed to consider the consequences of change?
2. Will the opponent choose to argue both the first and third stock issues or only one of them?

3. What is the philosophy on which opposition rests?
   A. What will the opponent defend?
   B. How does the opponent wish the audience to view the proposed change?
4. Will the opponent accept the advocate's definition of terms?
   A. Has the advocate broken faith with the audience by distorting the meaning of the proposition?
   B. Has the advocate improperly included or excluded things in defining terms?
5. How will the reason for change be opposed?
   A. Is the disparity as great as the advocate has alleged? (challenges to significance arguments)
   B. Is the disparity as severe as the advocate has alleged? (challenges to effect arguments)
   C. Are there extenuating circumstances that produce the disparity? (challenges to inherency arguments)
   D. Are there other possible causes for the alleged disparity? (challenges to inherency arguments)
6. Will existing institutions ameliorate the disparity?
   A. Will the normal pattern of societal change resolve the disparity given time?
   B. Short of the change called for by the advocate, what minor repairs are available to remedy the disparity?
7. What are the deficiencies in the proposed solution?
   A. Is the solution capable of solving the problem?
   B. Are conditions necessary for the solution to work present or will something preclude the proposal's ability to solve the problem? Can the proposal be circumvented?
   C. Is the solution workable?
8. What are the consequences of the proposed solution?
   A. Will the proposal bring about the advantages claimed by the advocate?
   B. Will the proposal cause disadvantages, or greater evils?
   C. Are these disadvantages unique to the advocate's proposal?
9. Will a counterproposal be offered?
   A. Is it an equally acceptable alternative to the advocate's proposal?
   B. Is it nontopical and competitive with the advocate's proposal?

As you have probably concluded, the range of potential issues may vary greatly with propositions from different fields of argument. The number of potential reasons for change might not be as extensive for some topics as for others. The range of potential new policies may be vast or narrow depending upon the topic area. Some proposed policies may cause more problems than they solve, or they may accrue benefits in a number of different areas. Regardless of the field of the proposition, the stock issues common to all policy propositions can be used to identify the general areas of concern that you should analyze and argue.

Learning Activities

1. In class, present a brief description of a topic you believe suitable for policy argumentation. Lead your classmates in a discussion of which approach to case construction for policy advocacy (traditional, comparative advantage, or goals-criteria) would be most feasible for the topic you described.

2. From the *Congressional Record,* choose a recent example of a legislative debate that addressed some disparity. In a written or oral report, discuss the argumentation. How were the issues of reason for change, proposal for change, and consequences of change handled by both advocates and opponents?

3. Identify the disparity implied in each of the following policy propositions. In small groups, brainstorm possible fact and value arguments that could be used in developing the advocate's case and proposals to achieve the change. Now discuss the arguments you would use in opposing the cases just brainstormed.

   A. Puerto Rico should be granted statehood.
   B. The federal government should institute a national sales tax.
   C. The ability to pass a nationally standardized proficiency test of basic skills should be a requirement for high school graduation.
   D. Private ownership of firearms should be more rigorously controlled.
   E. The United States should significantly decrease its foreign military commitments.

4. Identify one or more problems at your school that seem to create a disparity. Analyze this disparity in terms of its nature, extent, harm, and inherency. Suggest proposals to solve the disparity. How would each proposal solve the disparity? What advantages does each proposal have?

5. Take on the role of opponent for the policy proposals constructed in #4. What would be a strategy of opposition? What minor repairs might be made to remedy the disparity? What would be the consequences of adopting the changes suggested?

Suggested Supplementary Readings

Chesebro, J. W. (1971). Beyond the Orthodox: The Criteria Case. *Journal of the American Forensic Association, 7,* 208–215.

> Chesebro discusses the requirements and strategies of the goals-criteria case. He provides a rationale for using this approach in policy argumentation, suggesting it embodies value principles that are necessary conditions for policy formation. The article contains an excellent discussion of the standards of proof such a case must meet in order to be prima facie, along with a description of the pattern of case construction.

Hobbs, L., & Hamilton, H. (1993). Counterplan Permutations in Contemporary Practice. In R. E. McKerrow (Ed.), *Argument and the Postmodern Challenge: Proceedings of the Eighth SCA/AFA Conference on Argumentation* (pp. 50–54). Annandale, VA: Speech Communication Association.

The authors explore the uses of counterplans in contemporary academic debate. This is a useful review of current thinking on the competitiveness of the counterplan as a winning strategy for opponents and has some interesting examples of counterplans.

Hollihan, T. A., & Baske, K. T. (1994). *Arguments and Arguing.* New York: St. Martin's Press.

This is a basic argumentation text with a fresh perspective on how people argue. Hollihan and Baske introduce the idea that we make extensive use of narratives—stories about our experiences—when we argue. Their discussion of academic debate in Chapters 10 and 11 explains how narrative theory can be used for developing the stock issues of value and policy debate.

Chapter Twelve

How Do I Present My Arguments to an Audience?

U p to this point, you have been primarily concerned with preparing the ideas that communicate your views to an audience, constructing rational units of thought. Presenting your arguments and having them accepted by an audience depends not only on the quality of your reasoning but also on the clarity and expressiveness of your technique as a communicator. In Chapter 1 we told you that argumentation is part of persuasion. In addition to argumentation or logos, the logical subset of persuasion, there are two other subsets: ethos and pathos. Today, we refer to these as the communicator's credibility and the communicator's ability to create a particular psychological climate in the minds of audience members.

Logical arguments, the arguer's credibility, and the creation of a favorable mind-set combine to make up the persuasive presentations of advocates and opponents. In this concluding chapter, we will make some suggestions about the persuasive presentation of arguments that derive from skills of audience analysis, style and language use, brief writing, delivery technique, and credibility building.

Argumentation is audience-centered communication. To be of any use, to have any impact, your preparation and presentation of arguments must center on the receiver. Unless you consider who your audience is, argumentation becomes nothing more than an exercise in your ability to construct units of argument. Successful argumentation involves much more, adapting those units of argument in such a way that they constitute a message that is both appropriate and compelling to your receivers.

Adapting arguments to an audience in public communication is generally known as using rhetorical strategies. A *rhetorical strategy* is a choice that you believe will increase the probability that an audience will see your message as both appropriate and compelling. Your choice of a rhetorical strategy begins with the units of argument you construct—the claims you make, the evidence you use, the reasoning process that allows you to ask the audience to accept these claims based on the evidence you provide. Rhetorical strategies also include the choices you make in framing individual units of argument through style and language choices, organizing your arguments into a complete message, selecting appropriate delivery techniques, and building your credibility.

Audience Analysis

Perfecting your technique in presenting arguments begins with a consideration of your audience. We can consider the audience on two levels: the general audience suggested by the field in which argumentation takes place and the specific individuals who make up the audience you actually address your message to.

The General Audience

A field of argument is the context in which argumentation takes place, such as medicine, law, film, or politics. The field of argument sets up expectations about how arguments will be presented. The field also determines the *rules of engagement* under which arguments are created and presentations are made (Toulmin, 1958, and Toulmin et al., 1984). Some fields, such as law, have very rigid rules of engagement. In legal argumentation, if the rules are not closely followed, a jury's decision may be overturned on a "technicality." The rules of engagement for academic debate, which specify what advocates and opponents must do to win the debate, are presented in the Appendix that follows this chapter.

The rules of engagement for a particular field also specify the *degree of precision* the general audience will demand in the arguments they hear and read. Audiences have predispositions, based on their knowledge of the field, about how much accuracy in the use of evidence and reasoning they expect from arguers. In scientific fields, standards of accuracy may be rigidly predetermined; in artistic fields, accuracy may be more open to interpretation by the arguers (Toulmin et al., 1984).

The way in which argumentation is concluded, its *mode of resolution*, is also a part of the rules of engagement. People argue to achieve specific outcomes—to determine a winner, to reach consensus, or to justify or clarify a position they have taken. The rules of engagement in a field specify the kind of outcome arguers seek. In intercollegiate debate, the losing side does not concede the accuracy or justness of the winner's case, even though the debate judge names a winner and a loser. In other fields, such as the deliberations of legislative groups, the goal of argumentation is usually to reach a consensus that produces a majority coalition voting for or against a piece of proposed legislation. A third goal, justifying or clarifying a position, is represented in the argumentation a corporation might use in stating its case for a change in the laws concerning environmental protection.

To be a successful arguer, you must understand the unique demands of the field in which you argue. How much formality is expected? What demands for accuracy in the use of evidence and reasoning exist? What goal or outcome does an arguer in this field pursue? Your ability to meet the expectations of the field is an important factor in how successful you will be in presenting arguments.

The Actual Audience

In discussing the concept of presumption, we said that it has important implications for audience analysis. By virtue of being associated with a field of argument, you can make some guesses about your audience and what they will expect of you. Within a field, however, there can be a lot of variety among the individuals who make up the audience that actually hears your message. The rhetorical strategies you should choose in adapting your message to these receivers can be discovered by asking certain questions about them:

> What do they think is important?
> What issues concern them?
> What kinds of things do they value?
> How knowledgeable are they on this topic?
> Do they share my views?
> What opposing views might they hold?
> What sources of evidence are they likely to respect?
> What reasons are they likely to find most persuasive?

Sometimes you will have the opportunity to specifically answer these questions by surveying members of the audience and asking them these questions before preparing your argumentative message. Lawyers prepare for trials by surveying sample jurors, selected at random from jury lists, just as real jurors will be drawn. They ask questions about prejudices, understanding of evidence, or beliefs about issues to determine how the real jurors are likely to respond to a line of argument. Political candidates survey voters to determine how well they understand the issues, what they strongly believe, and what qualities they think a candidate must have to obtain their votes. In your classroom exercises in argumentation, you can find the answers to many of your questions about your classmates as an audience by asking directly or by listening to what they have to say in class discussions.

When a survey or direct questioning is not feasible, it is still possible to learn much about those who will make up your audience by turning to other sources. The same sleuthing techniques used to discover evidence to present to an audience can be used to discover information about the audience itself. Professional polling and survey research is constantly being done and reported by the mass media. If you want to know what audiences composed of individuals from the business field value and perceive to be important, you might find information from the Bureau of Labor Statistics, the Commerce Department, the Federal

Trade Commission, the President's Council of Economic Advisers, the *Wall Street Journal, Business Week,* or Cable News Network's financial programming. Finding out as much as you can about an audience's expectations and the extent of their knowledge is a key factor in making a successful presentation before them. In addition to knowing the rules of engagement under which you must argue and the demands of the field of argument for precision in creating your arguments, analyzing your audience will also help you discover what type of style and language use will be most acceptable, which delivery techniques are likely to be preferred, and what you must do to be perceived as a credible arguer.

Language Choice and Style

Language and style are the vehicle for communicating your ideas to the audience. Both language and style choices influence the ability of the audience to understand your arguments as you wish them to be understood.

Words As Symbols

The smallest unit of language is the word. In communication we typically refer to words as *symbols* because a word represents something else. The symbol is not the thing but is used to represent someone's direct experience with people, places, objects, and concepts. This makes choosing words a tricky business since the meaning you assign to a symbol is not necessarily the same meaning your audience will assign.

You can improve your chances of having an audience correctly assign meaning by considering your symbol choices in terms of what you know about your audience. Choose the most concrete term. For example, when arguing about something "the government" (an abstract term) does, refer to the specific government office or agency, such as "the Federal Trade Commission" (a concrete term). In adapting your language, choose the symbols your audience is most likely to assign meaning to in the same way that you do. Define key terms, particularly if they may be unfamiliar to your audience. When you are uncertain about what meaning they will assign a term, provide the appropriate interpretation.

There is another aspect of language that is important to consider in making sure your choices of word-symbols do not impair an audience's ability to properly understand your arguments. The language you choose reveals your attitudes, prejudices, and values and acts as a filter for your view of the world. In communication, language is said to act as a *terministic screen;* the choice of a particular term sets limits, directs attention in a certain way, or creates a certain feeling based on the symbol chosen.

Being insensitive to how you choose your language can lead to problems in how your audience perceives your arguments. For example, if every reference to people in general used the terms *mankind, men, he,* or *manpower,* these choices all function as a male terministic screen. Your audience may perceive that you view the world as male dominated and feel that only men are important. You would be guilty, at a minimum, of using sexist language.

Terministic screens are a product of the connotative and evaluative dimensions of language. Your own terministic screens are not necessarily bad, but you should become aware of them and of how your use of language works to convey meaning. Defining terms creates the specific terministic screen through which you want your audience to interpret meaning. Devoting equal care to choosing the language in the remainder of your message prevents your audience from becoming caught up in the screen your choice of language dictates. Be sensitive to connotative meanings and the evaluative properties a word might have for an audience. Avoid language that conveys sexism, racism, or other types of discrimination. Of equal importance, be conscious of the language choices you make in terms of how your audience assigns meaning to those terms. Understanding the fallacies of language use, discussed in Chapter 8, can help you avoid some of these problems.

The Elements of Style

The arrangement of words into complete thoughts and of those thoughts into units of argument reflects style in argumentation. Style includes the rules of correct English usage, the necessity to be clear, and the quality in using language termed *eloquence*. Style in communicating arguments is the element that makes them interesting to the audience. While good style will not compensate for poorly reasoned arguments, good reasoning alone does not guarantee your audience will be receptive to your message. Audiences expect good argumentation to possess eloquence as well as substance.

The first characteristic of effective style is that the arguer must follow the rules of English usage. This means using grammar, spelling, and punctuation correctly in written argument and using correct grammar and pronunciation in oral argument. The sentence is the basic unit of thought in English, and constructing sentences to provide variety and interest improves style. Sentence structure can be varied by using clauses, compound sentences, and active rather than passive verbs. Knowing the rules of English usage and following them in creating arguments will improve your credibility since we tend to estimate the intelligence and competence of someone based on how closely he or she follows the rules of grammar, spelling, punctuation, and pronunciation.

The second characteristic of effective style in argumentation is that the arguer must strive for clarity. You can improve your ability to be clear by paying attention to how you use language and how you organize both individual units of argument and the several units of argument that comprise your case. Clarity is a product of the economical use of language. Do not use more words than you need to express an idea, and use repetition only when it helps your audience follow your main lines of argument. Specifically choose language that quantifies, names, or describes things in concrete terms. Always choose the simplest term, avoiding jargon or ambiguous and vague terms. Remember that there are differences in how you achieve clarity in oral and written style.

The principal difference between oral and written style is that written style tends to be more formal and to more closely observe the rules of English usage. Oral style uses the less formal modes of expression that are not appropriate for formal written style, including colloquialisms, contractions, interjections, and sentence fragments. Oral arguments need to be expressed with a more restricted vocabulary than written ones. Personal pronouns and rhetorical questions are more frequently used in oral style and it tends to use more direct quotations of evidence, connotative words, elaborate figures of speech, and restatement of key ideas. Oral style must be punctuated nonverbally by the speaker's use of pauses, gesture, facial expression, voice, or movement.

The final characteristic of effective style in argumentation is the eloquent expression of ideas. Eloquence refers to the beauty of using language. While you want to exercise care in making language choices, avoiding choices that interfere with your audience's assigning the meaning you intended, you do not want your listeners or readers to become bored and tune out your message. If you are advocating a proposal to solve the problem of homelessness in America, you should present clear statistical evidence and reason that these statistics point to a need for your proposal. However, that argument may not be very compelling because it does not capture the interest of your audience. To be persuasive, you must do more. Make the audience visualize what it is like to be a part of those statistics. You want the audience to sense the experience of homelessness so they will support your proposal.

The hallmark of an eloquent style is that it uses imagery and creates interest for the listener or reader. To create imagery in arguments, use descriptive language that calls up a sensory experience in the receiver's mind. An illustration or example vividly describing what it is like to live on the street will shape that sensory image. Combined with your reasoning and use of a statistic enumerating the extent of homelessness, the illustration or example will make your argument much more persuasive.

Although oral style typically uses more figures of speech than written style, both depend upon these devices to create imagery and stimulate interest. The following list represents figures of speech commonly used (Rybacki & Rybacki, 1990).

> *Alliteration* is the repetition of opening sounds of two or more words in sequence: The slippery slope of symbol selection. A related figure of speech, *assonance* is the repetition of vowel sounds: Take now our counsel.
>
> *Allusion* refers to shared cultural heritage, usually referencing a legend or myth: We are like Johnny Appleseed, planting the seeds of a federal deficit from which future generations will harvest bitter fruit.
>
> *Antithesis* contrasts two opposing ideas: From our darkest hour can come our finest moment. When the contrast is stated in inverted parallel phrases, it is called a *chiasmus:* Let us never negotiate out of fear, but let us never fear to negotiate.

Climax builds to a high point: At the local level the homeless are a nuisance; at the state level a budget item; but at the national level, they are a reflection of our inhumanity.

Hyperbole uses great exaggeration: Listening to this argument is about as compelling as watching paint dry.

Metaphor compares things that are different: The drug problem is a cancer, eating away at our society. *Analogies* are more fully developed metaphors. Metaphors and analogies are the most commonly used devices of style in argumentation.

Metonymy substitutes a given name or title for something the name or title is associated with: The White House held a press conference today. *Synecdoche* substitutes the whole for a part or a part for the whole but does not necessarily use a formal name or title: Science does not recognize the efficacy of homeopathic medicines (using the whole "science" for the part "physicians").

Oxymorons are seeming contradictions in language use which may or may not represent actual contradictions: The silence following the advocate's speech was deafening.

Personification gives human characteristics to non-human things: The defense budget is fat with waste. Congress needs to put it on a diet.

Repetition repeats words or phrases: We shall arrest them where they live; we shall arrest them where they work; and we shall arrest them where they play.

Rhetorical questions do not ask the audience for an overt response, but instead focuses their thoughts in a particular direction: We must ask, are we really our neighbor's keeper?

These devices of style help create the psychological climate within which you want the audience to interpret your arguments. Figures of speech help provide the terministic screen through which you want the audience to view the world. One of the most important functions of style is that it helps the audience remember what you had to say. We may no longer recall all of Abraham Lincoln's analysis of how to establish peace between halves of a warring nation, but we remember the psychological climate he created in the conclusion of his second inaugural address of 1865.

> With malice toward none, with charity for all, with firmness in the right as God gives us to see the right [repetition and assonance], let us strive to bind up the nation's wounds [personification], to care for him who shall have borne the battle and for his widow and his orphan [synecdoche], to do all which may achieve and cherish a just and lasting peace among ourselves with all nations. (Andrews & Zarefsky, 1989, p. 296)

Achieving eloquence in argument is a matter of choosing figures of speech wisely to create imagery and add interest. A cautionary note on style, while it can be a stimulating mental exercise to see how many figures of speech you can include in an argument, be careful to not overdo eloquence. A speech or essay that uses too many figures of speech may be perceived as empty eloquence rather than substantive argumentation. You do not want to become so caught up in creating images that you lose sight of what you were trying to achieve through reasoning.

Brief Writing

The actual oral or written presentation of an argument should be preceded by the preparation of an argumentative brief. *The brief outlines the essential elements of the advocate's or opponent's development of arguments on the proposition.* At a minimum, the advocate's brief contains the following elements:

1. A full statement of the proposition.
2. A definition of key terms.
3. An interpretation of the proposition of fact, value, or policy that establishes how the advocate will argue the proposition.
4. The development of each stock issue through units of argument, which include the claims and evidence that make up the body of the case. Warrants and their backing should be included only as necessary.

The minimum requirements for the opponent's brief include the following:

1. A full statement of the proposition from the opponent's perspective.
2. Any counter arguments on the definition of key terms. (Note: Since the opponent is free to accept the advocate's definition of terms, this step may be omitted.)
3. A statement of philosophy that forecasts the opponent's choice of strategies to be used in responding to the advocate's case.
4. The claims and evidence that make up the opponent's arguments, including warrants and backing when necessary.

The idea of using a brief in developing arguments into final message form is adapted from the field of law and legal brief writing. In preparing for trial, or in appealing a decision to a higher court, a lawyer develops a written brief that includes all of the arguments and evidence. The brief provides a system for organizing the lawyer's arguments into a whole that will make sense to the intended audience. Like a lawyer's legal brief, an argumentative brief is an outline of claims to be made and the evidence to be used in advancing them.

Argumentative briefs are organized as an outline, "a visual representation of the relationships among ideas" (Campbell, 1982, p. 222). Earlier, in discussing how propositions of fact, value, and policy are argued, we provided suggestions for patterns of organization that are appropriate to each. All of these patterns can be described as *logical structure* because each arranges units of argument in a logical relationship. As an advocate, you would obviously arrange your units of argument in terms of the case structure—interpreting fact; applying value criteria to a value object; comparing two value systems; describing a problem and its solution, a goal and the proposed policy that better meets it, or the consequences of two policies, one existing and the other proposed—that your approach to the proposition will take. As an opponent, your brief would contain what you intend your response to be if an advocate argues a particular claim, and your actual presentation would include that response only if the advocate's presentation warranted it.

Organizing your arguments in a logical outline increases your ability to clearly present the reasons for or against the change you want the audience to consider. The key to organizing logically starts with the proposition and the issues you discovered while analyzing it. Each issue is a main point on the outline. In argumentation, a main point is called a contention. Under each contention, you will arrange the individual units of argument that develop that contention. The claim statements from these units of argument form the outline's substructure. A third level of substructure under the claim statements would be the individual pieces of evidence, warrants, and backing supporting your claims. While you do not always need to supply warrants and backing, when you prepare your first argumentative brief, it is a good idea to include all of the third-level subpoints in your outline. Writing out the warrant is a good way to test the soundness of your reasoning, and providing the backing ensures that you have it in case audience analysis suggests you need to back a particular warrant.

Since the purpose of the brief is to promote clarity, paying attention to the rules of outlining is important. In talking about claims, we emphasized the importance of phrasing a claim as a complete, declarative statement. If you have followed that advice, you already have the basis for a logical outline. As you construct your outline, follow these rules:

1. State each contention as a complete, declarative sentence.
2. Each contention is a main point and must have appropriate subpoints under it. A claim must be subordinate to the contention it develops and stated as a complete declarative sentence.
3. At the third level of subordination, the evidence that grounds a claim must be stated. Warrants and backing may also be included.
4. Use a consistent set of alpha-numeric symbols to show subordination. Contentions are typically given Roman numerals, with capital letters used for claim statements under each contention, and Arabic numbers used for evidence, warrant, and backing under claim statements.

In preparing a brief, remember that it is not the finished product in argumentation. The finished product is a speech or essay. The brief provides a logical framework that organizes your arguments. It is refined for oral or written presentation. For oral argument, you can usually think of the brief at this stage of development as a speaking outline. For written argument, it would serve as a very rough first draft that you would revise, rewrite, and polish into a completed essay.

Formats for Brief Writing

Formatting your brief is easy to accomplish—you simply follow the guidelines for case development of fact, value, or policy. The number of contentions you advance and the number of claims you use as subpoints under each contention will be determined by your analysis of the issues and research on the proposition. The formats in Figures 12-1, 12-2, 12-3, and 12-4 show how advocates and

---

FIGURE 12-1   Advocate's Fact Brief

Proposition: State the factual proposition.
Definitions of Key Terms (repeat for as many terms as you choose to define):
   1. First Key Term is defined as:
   2. Second Key Term is defined as:
Primary Inference: Restate the proposition as now interpreted by the primary inference.
Overview: State introductory material.
Contention I: State your first contention.
   A. Claim: State the claim for a unit of argument for this contention. (The claim may be one of effect, significance, or inherency).
      1. Grounds: Quote or paraphrase the evidence you will use to ground the claim. At the end of the quotation or paraphrase, list the full source citation (author, date, title, periodical or publisher, page number).
      2. Warrant: Identify the link between grounds and claim you want the audience to make. (Review Chapter 5 for how to phrase the warrant.)
      3. Backing: Quote or paraphrase the evidence used as backing, or state the general principle that serves to support the warrant. (If quoting or paraphrasing evidence, be sure to include full source citation).
   B. Claim: State the second claim for this contention.
      1. Grounds
      2. Warrant
      3. Backing
   C. Claim: State the third claim for this contention.
      1. Grounds
      2. Warrant
      3. Backing
Contention II: State your second contention and develop with units of argument as described for the first contention.
Contention III: State your third contention and develop with units of argument as described for the first contention. (Continue the process if there are additional contentions.)
Conclusion: State the material you will use to conclude.

---

opponents might structure their fact and value briefs. Following the one appropriate to the kind of argument your are constructing will help you in organizing the results of your research and analysis. We have not included similar models of policy briefs because organizational strategies for policy argumentation are discussed in the preceding chapter.

To format the advocate's brief, Figure 12-1, for a factual proposition, state the proposition, define key terms, make the primary inference, and proceed to develop the contentions. The advocate is required to develop a minimum of three units of argument for each contention, proving effect, significance, and inherency. The opponent is not so limited, Figure 12-2, and may choose as many or as few units of argument for each contention as his strategies of opposition

---

FIGURE 12-2   Opponent's Fact Brief

Proposition: State the factual proposition.

Definitions of Key Terms: If your strategy is to contest one or more of the advocate's definitions, provide your own definitions of terms.

1. First Key Term is defined as:
2. Second Key Term is defined as:

Primary Inference: Restate the proposition as you want the audience to perceive the primary inference.

Overview: State introductory material and the philosophy of opposition strategies for refutation of the advocate's case.

Contention I: State your first contention.

   A. Claim: State the claim for a unit of argument for this contention. (The claim may phrased as denial or extenuation of one of the advocate's claims. The claim may also be phrased as the opponent's defense of existing beliefs.)

      1. Grounds: Quote or paraphrase the evidence you will use to ground the claim. At the end of the quotation or paraphrase, list the full source citation (author, date, title, periodical or publisher, page number).
      2. Warrant: Identify the link between grounds and claim you want the audience to make. (Review Chapter 5 for how to phrase the warrant.)
      3. Backing: Quote or paraphrase the evidence used as backing, or state the general principle that serves to support the warrant. (If quoting or paraphrasing evidence, be sure to include full source citation).

   B. Claim: State an additional unit of argument that logically develops this contention. (Claim C and Claim D would be added and supported as necessary.)

      1. Grounds
      2. Warrant
      3. Backing

Contention II: State your second contention and develop with units of argument as described for the first contention.

Contention III: State your third contention and develop with units of argument as described for the first contention. (Continue the process if there are additional contentions.)

Conclusion: State the material you will use to conclude.

---

require. Our models for briefing formats provide complete details for the first contention's first unit of argument and then abbreviates the description of what each remaining unit of argument contains.

To format the advocate's brief for a value proposition, Figure 12-3, state the proposition, identify the value hierarchy to be used to judge the value object, define key terms, make the primary inference, and proceed to develop the contentions. The advocate of a value proposition is once again required to develop a minimum of three units of argument for each contention, proving effect, significance, and inherency. The opponent in value argumentation is not restricted in this way and may choose as many or as few units of argument for each contention

---

FIGURE 12-3 Advocate's Value Brief

Proposition: State the value proposition.
Statement of the Value Hierarchy:
1. Identify the field in which the value hierarchy is found.
2. Identify (defining if necessary) the core value or value combination that forms your value hierarchy.
Definitions of Key Terms:
1. Definition of the Value Object:
2. Statement of the Value Criteria:
Primary Inference: Restate the proposition as the application of your list of value criteria to the value object.
Overview: State introductory material.
Contention I: State your first criterion for measuring the value object.
   A. Claim: State the claim for a unit of argument applying this criterion to the value object. (The claim may be one of effect, significance, or inherency).
      1. Grounds: Quote or paraphrase the evidence you will use to ground the claim. At the end of the quotation or paraphrase, list the full source citation (author, date, title, periodical or publisher, page number).
      2. Warrant: Identify the link between grounds and claim you want the audience to make. (Review Chapter 5 for how to phrase the warrant.)
      3. Backing: Quote or paraphrase the evidence used as backing, or state the general principle that serves to support the warrant. (If quoting or paraphrasing evidence, be sure to include full source citation).
   B. Claim: State the second claim for this contention.
      1. Grounds
      2. Warrant
      3. Backing
   C. Claim: State the third claim for this contention.
      1. Grounds
      2. Warrant
      3. Backing
Contention II: State your second criterion for measuring the value object. Develop with appropriate units of argument, proving effect, significance, and inherency.
Contention III: State your third criterion for measuring the value object. Develop with appropriate units of argument, proving effect, significance, and inherency. (Continue the process if there are additional criteria.)
Conclusion: State the material you will use to conclude.

---

as his strategies of opposition require, Figure 12-4. Our models for briefing formats for value once again provide complete details for the first contention's first unit of argument and then abbreviates the description of what each remaining unit of argument contains.

Remember, a brief is not the final form your presentation will take; it just provides the essentials of case content. The conventions of effective speaking and writing also mandate that arguers have introductions, make transitional

---

FIGURE 12-4   Opponent's Value Brief

Proposition: State the value proposition.
Statement of the Value Hierarchy:
1. Accept the advocate's interpretation of the value hierarchy, or identify the field from which you want the value hierarchy to be taken.
2. Accept the advocate's choice of core values, or identify (defining if necessary) the core value or value combination that forms your value hierarchy.

Definitions of Key Terms:
1. Accept or reject the definition of the value object; if rejecting, supply your definition.
2. Accept or reject the advocate's statement of the value criteria; if rejecting, supply your interpretation of value criteria.

Primary Inference: Restate the proposition as your interpretation of this value judgment.

Overview: State introductory material and the philosophy of opposition strategies for refutation of the advocate's case.

Contention I: State your first contention in response to the advocate's first criterion or your application of alternative criterion to the value object.
  A. Claim: State the claim for a unit of argument for this contention. (The claim may phrased as denial or extenuation of one of the advocate's claims. The claim may also be phrased as the opponent's defense of existing value judgments.)
    1. Grounds: Quote or paraphrase the evidence you will use to ground the claim. At the end of the quotation or paraphrase, list the full source citation (author, date, title, periodical or publisher, page number).
    2. Warrant: Identify the link between grounds and claim you want the audience to make. (Review Chapter 5 for how to phrase the warrant.)
    3. Backing: Quote or paraphrase the evidence used as backing, or state the general principle that serves to support the warrant. (If quoting or paraphrasing evidence, be sure to include full source citation).
  B. Claim: State an additional unit of arguments that logically develops this contention. (Claim C and Claim D would be added and supported as necessary.)
    1. Grounds
    2. Warrant
    3. Backing

Contention II: State your second contention and develop with units of argument as described for the first contention.

Contention III: State your third contention and develop with units of argument as described for the first contention. (Continue the process if there are additional contentions.)

Conclusion: State the material you will use to conclude.

---

statements between main ideas, and offer conclusions. The differences between oral and written style further influence the final form your message will take. However, whether you are speaking or writing, there are some basic principles of introductions, transitions, and conclusions that will help you make your presentation a polished whole.

Introductions, Transitions, and Conclusions

In argumentation, an effective introduction accomplishes four things. First, it gains the audience's attention. Second, it states the proposition from your perspective on the controversy. Third, it gives the audience a reason to listen or read further, establishing what they stand to gain from accepting your point of view on the dispute. Fourth, the introduction should connect you personally to the dispute. This last step helps to establish your credibility by revealing your motives for engaging in argumentation.

There are several rhetorical strategies that help create an effective introduction. In oral argument it is sometimes customary to greet the audience and acknowledge the occasion for your speaking to them. You may want to begin with an appropriate quotation from a respected authority who sees the issues as you do or who expresses a perspective that supports your development of the proposition. Alternative beginnings include using statistics that show significance, rhetorical questions to focus the audience's attention, or a statement of the values you will support through your arguments. A reference to the field of argument and the place of your arguments in that field can also be effective. As part of your introduction, you may also provide a presummary to overview the main points you will develop. In complex situations, where it is necessary to develop several contentions, a presummary is a useful strategy.

Transitions are used to move from one contention to the next and to link units of argument to the contentions they support. Transitions can enumerate the point or subpoint you are arguing, restate claims, or forecast the subpoints you are about to argue. Transitions tell the audience that one unit of argument is finished and another is about to begin. Oral style tends to make greater use of transitions that summarize because they help the audience retain what has been said.

Since the conclusion is the last thing the audience hears or reads, it is particularly important to have a memorable one. The passage from Lincoln's second inaugural address used to illustrate figures of speech contains one of Lincoln's most often quoted thoughts: "with malice toward none, with charity for all." The conclusion is your final opportunity to create credibility for yourself as an arguer.

An effective conclusion must accomplish three things. First, it must underview or summarize the main ideas in your message. Second, it must reference the role of the audience in the process of argumentation, acknowledging their part in the rules of engagement as decision makers, judges, or those asked to concur with one side or the other in a controversy. Third, the conclusion must provide closure for your advocacy or opposition to it by telling the audience what you want them to do on the basis of having heard your arguments.

A final summary of main ideas, a synopsis of one or two key pieces of evidence or reasoning, or a restatement of your strongest argument are effective techniques for concluding. Your final words might be an appeal for the audience to respond favorably to your stand on the proposition, or you might choose an appropriate quotation or a reference to the field of argument that has given you the opportunity to present your message to the specific audience.

Many of the traditions of argumentation in our society have emerged from oral debate and discussion. In certain fields, such as law, oral argument seems to dominate although written argumentation is important. In the classroom, even when written assignments are used, it is common practice to present them orally as well. To assist you in the practice of oral argument, the next section covers specific delivery techniques that can be strategically employed in turning your brief into a speech.

Delivery Techniques

Delivery refers to the physical presentation of arguments before an audience. Delivery includes appropriate use of your voice and body and the effective use of visual aids in communicating ideas.

Use of Voice

The properties of voice include articulation, pronunciation, pitch, volume, rate, and pauses. By knowing what each appropriately involves, you can improve your oral presentation of arguments.

Articulation is the intelligible production of various vowel and consonant sounds of a language. The tongue, teeth, lips, hard and soft palate, and the vocal cords all work together to produce sounds by manipulating the air you exhale. Good articulation neither adds anything to nor omits anything from each sound. While some people have articulation problems caused by a physical impairment in the vocal mechanism, most speakers can clearly articulate the sounds of a language. The most common problems in articulation are caused by laziness, inattention to how sounds are made, and haste, trying to say too much too rapidly.

Pronunciation is often confused with articulation. While both are a matter of agreement, articulation represents the sounds of language, while pronunciation concerns agreement on the sounds and the order in which they must be articulated in uttering a particular word. Agreement on pronunciation is not as universal as agreement on articulation. The correct pronunciation of a word may vary from region to region. In some parts of the nation "apricot" is pronounced with the long "a" sound, in other parts it is pronounced with the short "a."

Standards of correct English pronunciation were first codified in the eighteenth century and reflected the pronunciation of the British upper class. The first American standards of pronunciation were the work of language scholars. In today's dictionaries the first pronunciation given is usually the preferred one, with regional alternatives listed second. One factor influencing American standards of pronunciation is the mass media. Radio and television have promoted a standard of American speech that is primarily middle-western. The regional accents of the upper east coast, New York and New Jersey, the deep south, and the southwest are obliterated. Aside from the potential for confusion, the biggest problem with mispronouncing words, or failing to follow standards in pronunciation, is that it can undermine an arguer's credibility.

Pitch is the tonal range, the highness or lowness, of the voice produced by the vibration of the vocal cords. Women's voices are generally higher pitched and men's voices are generally lower. Whether you are female or male, you can still vary your pitch by practicing. One of the uses of a pitch change is to punctuate thoughts, slightly raising pitch toward the end of a sentence asking a question, slightly lowering it when making a statement. A problem occurs when the same pattern of raising and lowering pitch is used habitually, producing a sing-song vocal pattern.

Volume is the loudness or intensity of the voice. Speaking too softly can cause your audience to tune you out because they must work too hard to hear, let alone understand, you. Good speakers vary their volume as a way of focusing audience attention on a key idea or word. Increasing volume can also be used to drown out extraneous noise, to compensate for speaking in a large room with poor acoustics, or to overcome a normally soft speaking voice. However, speaking too loudly can cause your audience to perceive you as harsh and strident.

Rate of speaking is the speed with which words are uttered. Audience-preferred rates of speaking range from 160 to about 200 words a minute. Anything less gives an audience too much time to drift away mentally. Anything more than 200 words a minute is a rate of speaking that is too taxing for all but the most skilled or practiced audience members to listen to. Like volume, the rate of speaking can be varied to keep the audience's attention focused on what you are saying, as in slowing down to emphasize key words and ideas.

Pauses punctuate speaking and also give the speaker time to draw a breath. A pause of a few seconds draws the audience's attention back, if for no other reason than to see if the speaker has finished. Pauses are used most effectively to signal the end of a complete thought or point, to allow the audience time to reflect on a rhetorical question, or to emphasize a key point. Vocalizing the pause, "uh," "um," "er," "ok," or "you know," is a distraction rather than an effective delivery technique. It is probably impossible to completely rid your speaking of vocalized pauses. Discover which vocalized pauses you are most prone to use and work to eliminate as many as possible from your speaking.

Taken together, these characteristics add up to *voice quality*. Whether a voice is described as rich, smooth, polished, and pleasing or harsh, nasal, scratchy, and irritating depends upon how the speaker manages use of voice. It is important to learn your own voice quality. Working with an audio or video tape will allow you to determine the characteristics of your speaking voice. If you discover you have a serious problem with some aspect of using your voice, it may be worthwhile to take a course in voice and diction, work with a therapist, or get advice from a speech coach. Most problems, however, are minor and can be effectively managed by carefully listening to yourself, determining your vocal strengths and weaknesses, and practicing to eliminate weaknesses while maintaining strengths.

A final consideration of voice quality concerns the attitude your voice communicates. Pitch, volume, rate, and pauses all send a nonverbal message to your listeners about your attitude. How you feel about the arguments you are advancing will come across in your voice. If you do not sound enthusiastic, like you believe in your message, the audience may not accept you as competent, sincere, or credible. You should try to project a sense of belief in, and commitment to, your arguments through your voice.

Use of Body

The properties of your body that communicate include eye contact, facial expression, gesture, posture, and movement. The verbal elements of your arguments can be undermined if conflicting nonverbal messages are sent. Just as an unenthusiastic voice that is hard to hear can influence how an audience interprets your message; casual, sloppy, informal, random body language can also undermine your arguments.

Eye contact is the person-to-person impression of communication you create by looking directly at the people in your audience. Eye contact is one of the most important aspects of effective delivery. In our culture, failure to make eye contact may be associated with a lack of honesty or self-confidence on the part of the speaker. Your eye contact with an audience should be frequent and take in the whole audience. With very large groups, this can be difficult but can be managed by consciously looking at people in all areas of the room. Be sure that you do not favor one side of the room over the other and that you actually look out at the people to whom you are speaking, rather than gazing over their heads.

Facial expression communicates feelings. The human face is very expressive in showing anger, fear, concern, joy, sadness, and the whole range of human emotions. In addition to your voice, your facial expression also indicates your belief in what you have to say. Speakers who believe what they say tend to have animated faces.

Gesture refers to the movement of hands and arms. Probably the most common gesture in oral argument occurs when speakers enumerate points on their fingers. Gestures also include reaching out to the audience, pointing or extending the arm and hand. For this to be effective, gestures have to be natural. The two greatest weaknesses of inexperienced speakers are that their gestures are either wooden and unnatural or they are so numerous that their hands and arms seem to be constantly in motion, like the wings of a bird ready for flight. To observe gesture as a natural communication device, watch people in conversation. Almost no one talks as though they were sitting on their hands. Instead, the arms are raised, move in circles or from side to side, and the hands are in motion. Take these basic techniques, enlarge the movement to compensate for the increased distances imposed by the speaker-audience setting, and beware of overusing a gesture to the extent that it loses its potential to communicate.

Posture is how a speaker stands before the audience. Ideally, posture should communicate the sense that the speaker is in control of the situation and has confidence in what is being said. A speaker should stand up straight, avoid leaning on the podium or slouching, and keep both feet flat on the floor. Good posture conveys a sense of formality that tells the audience the speaker is a competent person who can be trusted.

Movement is the speaker's use of space. How you occupy and use space is a means of establishing control over the speaking situation and projecting confidence in yourself and your arguments. You want to avoid standing rigidly in one place, as though you had been planted on that spot. Coming out from behind the podium, taking a step forward, or moving to one side can be used to signal a transition between points or to emphasize a point. The most important caution to keep in mind, to ensure that your use of movement is effective, is that it should occur for a reason. Avoid wandering around or setting a pattern of pacing back and forth.

Use of Visual Aids

In discussing kinds of evidence, we talked about the use of artifacts—objects, photographs, audio and video tapes, and diagrams. Such visual aids offer a visible demonstration or representation of information in an oral presentation. Because too much evidence, particularly statistics, can bewilder or bore an audience, visual aids are fairly common in speaking. Charts, tables, graphs, and diagrams can be used to present statistical information visually, making it easier to understand. Visual aids can be used effectively to show changes, compare data, point out significance, or establish trends. It is also possible to use a flip chart with a brief list of key ideas to help the audience keep key points in mind and follow the progression of arguments.

In choosing visual aids, there are two principles to keep in mind. First, a visual aid must be pleasing in its presentation of information. If the audience cannot see it, if it is messy, or if it crowds too much information into too little space, as frequently occurs when a speaker uses a single visual aid when several would be more appropriate, the visual aid is useless. Using the graphic capabilities of a computer to generate charts, graphs, and the like, using the printed output to produce transparencies are good ways to create visual aids. You can also create visual aids without a computer if you remember to keep your lines straight, your lettering neat, and the contrast between foreground and background high.

The second principle to keep in mind when you plan on using visual aids is that you must practice with them before actually giving your speech. Practice ensures your visual aid will fit smoothly into your presentation and you will feel comfortable using it. Observing the following requirements in your practice sessions will help you effectively incorporate visual support for arguments into your delivery:

1. Use the visual aid as a form of support for your argument; explain the visual aid as you are using it.
2. Talk about the visual aid while you are using it; do not assume that the audience will figure out what it is supposed to mean.
3. Remove the visual aid from sight after you are finished with it.

Visuals aids are much like figures of speech in terms of their ability to enhance recall, add interest, and focus an audience's attention. As with figures of speech, overusing visual aids can hinder rather than help your cause. Use them sparingly and make sure you relate them to the unit of argument they support. If you are using electronic equipment, it is extremely important to practice using it. Few things will undermine your credibility as a speaker more than spending several minutes fumbling with an overhead or slide projector, searching a video tape to find the right spot, or discovering that your electronic equipment has malfunctioned.

The effectiveness of your delivery can make or break your credibility with the audience. While your analysis of the audience, choice of language and use of style, and organization of your case are all important factors to your being perceived as a competent, credible advocate or opponent of change, poor delivery of an oral presentation will surely diminish your effectiveness.

Building Credibility with an Audience

Credibility refers to an audience's perception of a speaker's reliability. It is not something that you automatically have although what you do to prepare and present your arguments has a strong impact on whether your audience will perceive you as credible. There are two kinds of credibility: external credibility, which is the product of your prior reputation, and internal credibility, which is the product of an audience's direct experience with you and your arguments.

External Credibility

Initially, external credibility is a more important factor in determining how an audience perceives an arguer. A person's prior reputation determines the degree to which an audience is willing to trust his or her words. External credibility is a product of what the audience already knows about the arguer's socioeconomic status, profession, education, race, sex, and established position on the issues or the proposition being argued.

The field of argument is important in assessing prior reputation. Someone who is either respected or notorious in a particular field has an established prior reputation with potential audiences. For locally or nationally known individuals, mass media coverage may have helped establish prior reputation. The field of politics and candidacy for public office provides one of the best demonstrations of the effect of prior reputation. Long before elections are held, in some cases before campaigning has gone on very long, voters are made aware of the most intimate details of the candidates' lives along with their stands on issues. In other fields, external credibility occurs in the same way. For example, Oliver Stone's success as a maker of award-winning films gives him external credibility that a less successful filmmaker might not have, something that he himself has acknowledged, that gives him the ability to get skeptical studios to listen to his proposals for projects they would not otherwise consider. The more information about an arguer that an audience has prior to directly experiencing his or her arguments, the more likely they are to have formed strong opinions about the arguer's credibility.

Internal Credibility

A speaker may not have the kind of public reputation that produces strong positive or negative feelings in an audience prior to their direct experience with his or her ideas. Internal credibility, which is assigned by the audience as a result of their direct experience, is ultimately more important in determining whether the audience perceives an arguer as credible. While you cannot always manage your prior reputation with an audience, you can manage the part of your credibility that is a product of your audience's exposure to your message.

In Chapter 1, we said that in argumentation, you have ethical responsibilities to thoroughly research the proposition, to promote the common good of society, to use good reasoning, and to observe the rules of free speech in our society. Managing your internal credibility with an audience is a matter of demonstrating how effectively you have met these responsibilities. Internal credibility is also influenced by your skill in organizing your case, your clarity and specificity in language use, and your performance as a public speaker while presenting your case.

Managing Your Credibility

First, arguers with high credibility are perceived as competent and trustworthy. You want to be perceived as an expert, thoroughly prepared to argue your side of the proposition. If you follow the rules for selecting and using evidence presented in Chapter 6, you will build your credibility as an arguer. This means using qualified sources of evidence that will be recognized by your audience as authoritative, accurate sources of information. Acknowledging and explaining any biases or inconsistencies in your evidence will further enhance your credibility. Competence and trustworthiness are also demonstrated through sound reasoning.

Second, arguers with high credibility are well organized. It is not enough to simply create sound units of argument. You must organize them in a way that makes sense to your audience. Following the recommendations for brief writing in developing messages on propositions of fact, value, or policy will help you present arguments that are clear and easy to follow. Being organized in presenting arguments will increase the probability that your audience will perceive you as competent. Moreover, you will be free of any suspicion of attempting to conceal things from them by clouding the issues with disorganization, thus increasing your trustworthiness.

Third, arguers with high credibility demonstrate that they are fair and have their audience's best interests in mind. Managing your image as fair and concerned for the common good of your audience is a matter of associating your arguments, or your perspective on the proposition, with what your audience values. In business, an audience may value success, progress, scientific research, or beating the competition. Relating your position to something your audience values and explaining how your position reflects their own interests in terms of achieving or maintaining that which they value will build your credibility in your listener's or reader's minds.

Fourth, arguers with high credibility are sincere. This final element in managing internal credibility combines elements of language use, style, and delivery. Sincere arguers project social responsibility by avoiding prejudicial uses of language and examples. They also avoid ambiguity by being clear and direct in expressing both their intentions for arguing and their arguments. Sincerity is also a product of delivery techniques that cause a speaker to be labeled a vital, interesting person, whose message is worth the audience's attention. This means projecting confidence in speaking and avoiding apologetic phrases or nonverbal mannerisms that contradict this confidence.

Ultimately, your audience decides whether you are credible. Deciding which rhetorical strategies will help you manage your credibility begins with your audience analysis. Knowing what expectations your receivers have, what sources of information and reasoning techniques they find credible, what language and delivery techniques they find appealing, and what they believe to be in their own best interests can be used in choosing rhetorical strategies that enhance your credibility.

Remember, if the field of argument has rules of engagement stating a winner and loser must be determined, losing does not necessarily mean you had no credibility with your audience. Whatever credibility you built in the course of presenting arguments becomes part of your prior reputation with the audience and may influence them to give credence to your arguments in the future.

Presenting your arguments to an audience involves more than constructing sound arguments through effective issue analysis and the use of evidence and reasoning. Your arguments and the manner of their presentation must be adapted to your listeners or readers. This means taking an audience-centered perspective on argumentation. You must consider the field in which you are arguing and the audience expectations it creates. You must also consider who will make up your actual audience and what role they play as decision makers or participants hearing or reading your message. Adapting your arguments into an effective message involves making appropriate language choices, using appropriate techniques of style and organization, and, in oral argumentation, practicing appropriate delivery skills. Together with the content of the arguments in your message, these presentational aspects of oral argument will influence your credibility and the probability that your audience will perceive you as a competent, trustworthy advocate or opponent of change.

Learning Activities

1. Analyze the people in your class as an audience for your argumentative messages. What do members of the class think is important about the subject

you are going to argue? Which issues might concern them most? What values do they hold in regard to this subject? Are they likely to share your views or oppose them? How knowledgeable are they on this subject? What sources of evidence are they most likely to find compelling? What reasons will they find most persuasive?

2. Find an essay or opinion piece in *Time* or *Newsweek* and a speech from *Vital Speeches* on the same subject. Discuss the differences between oral and written style demonstrated by the two examples.

3. Make an audio tape of yourself delivering an oral argument. Analyze your voice in terms of your articulation, pronunciation, pitch, volume, rate, and use of pauses. How would you characterize your voice quality? Assess your strengths and weaknesses in managing your voice.

4. Conduct a discussion of the external credibility of members of your class. After you have determined how each class member's external credibility has been established, analyze ways of managing internal credibility with the class audience.

Suggested Supplementary Readings

Campbell, K. K. (1982). *The Rhetorical Act.* Belmont, CA: Wadsworth.
This is an advanced public speaking text that provides information on all aspects of speech construction and public speaking technique. We recommend Chapter 11, The Resources of Language, for a complete discussion of language use as a rhetorical strategy, use of figures of speech, and the concept of what constitutes oral style. A new edition of this book is in press.

Lakoff, R. T. (1990). *Talking Power.* New York: HarperCollins, Basic Books.
Robin Lakoff examines the logic and magic of how we use language. She delves into a variety of fields to explore why unintelligibility seems to be valued in academics, what power our everyday uses of words have, how language use varies across regions of the U.S. and cultures, and how men and women use language differently. This is a very readable discussion of language and style with some excellent examples of how a field influences language use.

Appendix

One specialized format for argumentation is competitive debate. The setting in which argumentation takes place is formalized, and specific time limits and responsibilities are imposed on those who participate. Debates may take place in argumentation classes as a learning experience or in an intercollegiate contest between teams representing different schools. There are even national debate championship tournaments.

Since the orientation of this book has precluded a focus on the specialized form of competitive debate, this Appendix provides an introduction to debate forms and techniques. Entire books are devoted to the tactics and strategies of competitive debate, as well as numerous articles in the *Journal of the American Forensic Association*. Once you have learned the basic skills of arguing, you may choose to delve further into debate technique. Winning debates is a matter of skill and preparation. Had we cast this Appendix in the interrogative paradigm of our chapter titles, we would have called it What Are the Rules of the Game?

Debate Formats

While there are many different debate formats and there are different kinds of propositions argued, academic debate in general has the following characteristics:

1. Teams of debaters, usually two to a side, will be prepared to argue both sides of a proposition. In debate parlance, they are called affirmative and negative rather than advocate and opponent.
2. All teams will argue the same proposition, often a policy proposition, for the entire year although value topics that change at midyear are used by the

Cross Examination Debate Association (CEDA). Propositions address broad issues of national concern.

3. The debate is judged by a single individual or a panel of three, five, or seven individuals who determine the winner of the debate based on which team demonstrated the greater skill or had the better arguments.

Like all communication, debate is rule-governed behavior. One set of rules pertains to the order in which members of both teams make their presentations and the length of time they have for each presentation. This is commonly referred to as the *format* for the debate. While slight variations may be found, most debates use one of two formats. The first is called the *traditional format*, in which each team member presents a constructive and a rebuttal speech. While the time limits for the speeches may vary, the format looks like this:

Traditional Format

First Affirmative Constructive Speech	10 minutes
First Negative Constructive Speech	10 minutes
Second Affirmative Constructive Speech	10 minutes
Second Negative Constructive Speech	10 minutes
First Negative Rebuttal Speech	5 minutes
First Affirmative Rebuttal Speech	5 minutes
Second Negative Rebuttal Speech	5 minutes
Second Affirmative Rebuttal Speech	5 minutes

Notice that the affirmative team has the first and last speeches, and that the negative team has two speeches in a row (we will have more to say about this when we discuss the responsibilities of the speakers). We should also point out that the debate may take longer than an hour to complete, since it has become customary to allow both teams a total of five or ten minutes preparation time during the course of the debate. This is time that may be used as the team members see fit.

The second commonly used format is the *cross-examination format*. The order and length of constructive and rebuttal speeches stays roughly the same, but both teams are given the opportunity to interrogate each other. The format looks like this:

Cross-Examination Format

First Affirmative Constructive Speech	10 minutes
Cross-Examination of First Affirmative Speaker	3 minutes
First Negative Constructive Speech	10 minutes
Cross-Examination of First Negative Speaker	3 minutes
Second Affirmative Constructive Speech	10 minutes
Cross-Examination of Second Affirmative Speaker	3 minutes
Second Negative Constructive Speech	10 minutes
Cross-Examination of Second Negative Speaker	3 minutes
First Negative Rebuttal Speech	5 minutes
First Affirmative Rebuttal Speech	5 minutes
Second Negative Rebuttal Speech	5 minutes
Second Affirmative Rebuttal Speech	5 minutes

The length of constructive and rebuttal speeches are sometimes shortened to eight and four minutes respectively to reduce the amount of time that it takes to complete the debate, since preparation time is generally provided. The Cross Examination Debate Association does this in its debates on value propositions. Regardless of the subtle variations, debate formats establish fixed amounts of speaking and preparation time and give equal time to both parties to the dispute.

Less common than either of these formats for debates between teams of individuals is the *Lincoln-Douglas Format*, named after the historical one-on-one debates between these two candidates for the Senate. This format is often favored for in-class debating. The variations in this format are numerous. The basic rules for Lincoln-Douglas debating are that "each speaker presents a constructive position, questions the opponent, replies to questions, refutes the opponent's position, and defends his or her own position" (Patterson & Zarefsky, 1983, p. 13).

Speaker Responsibilities

In both the traditional and cross-examination styles of debating, each speaker has certain duties he or she must perform. The order of presentation, with affirmative speakers beginning and ending the debate, is based on presumption, which lies with the negative, and the requirements of the burden of proof, which fall on the affirmative. The debate begins with the *first affirmative constructive speech*. This presentation establishes the basis of the affirmative case and normally includes all the claims, evidence, and reasoning that would, if unanswered, allow the judge to vote in favor of adopting the proposition.

In value debate, this would involve presenting a case as discussed in Chapter 10: identifying the value object, establishing the criteria by which it is to be evaluated, and providing arguments supporting the appropriateness of judging the value object in this manner. In policy debate, the first affirmative speaker might only discuss the first stock issue, reason for change, if the affirmative is employing the traditional need-plan pattern of organization. However, if one of the other patterns of organization is used, the first affirmative is responsible for presenting both a proposal and a reason for change. Regardless of whether the proposition is one of value or policy and irrespective of the pattern of organization followed, the first affirmative speaker establishes her team's interpretation of the proposition. The second affirmative may add new arguments that further develop, or in the case of the traditional organization pattern complete, that interpretation, but if the first affirmative speech fails to establish a prima facie position the affirmative has lost before the debate has even begun.

Assuming a prima facie case has been presented, what are the duties of the *first negative constructive speech*? The first negative speaker establishes the philosophy of the negative team—their stand on the proposition. If the negative team plans to question the definitions of key terms offered by the affirmative, those questions are raised in this speech and alternative definitions are offered. If the affirmative definitions are so outrageous that their case appears to be nontopical, the first negative speaker normally argues this as well. If the negative team intends to defend the present system of values or policies, the first negative presents these arguments. This speech responds directly to the first affirmative presentation and establishes the points of clash between the two teams. In policy debating, this speech usually focuses on the first stock issue, leaving the second and third stock issues to the second negative speaker. This is called *division of labor*, and you will see the wisdom of it when we discuss the rebuttal speeches.

The *second affirmative constructive speech* attempts to repair the damage done to the affirmative case by the first negative speaker. Since the initial points of clash between the two teams were defined by the first negative, the second affirmative must respond point by point—for three reasons. First, if there are arguments relating to definitions or topicality, the affirmative will be unable to carry argumentation forward successfully unless an attempt is made to resolve these disputes in the affirmative's favor. Second, the negative team is about to get two turns, back-to-back. If the second affirmative does not respond to the first negative arguments, the first affirmative rebuttalist will be swamped. Third, it is a rule in debate that *while new evidence may be introduced in rebuttal speeches, new arguments may not be*. The constructive speeches are the appropriate place for presenting original arguments.

In addition to repairing any damage, the second affirmative should point out arguments that still stand, arguments with which the first negative chose not to clash. This is best accomplished if the second affirmative responds to the negative arguments in terms of the basic case structure used in the first affirmative constructive speech. Finally, in policy debating, the second affirmative must present the proposal for change if it was not included in the first affirmative's speech. In general, the second affirmative has the responsibility of rebuilding and extending the affirmative case.

The *second negative constructive speech* is the final speech in the constructive phase of the debate. The second negative generally deals with the stock issues that his partner left unargued. In value debate, this frequently takes the form of examining society's willingness to accept the new value hierarchy proposed by the affirmative. In policy debate this means examining the affirmative proposal in terms of solvency, circumvention, workability, and disadvantages.

The second negative speaker must be careful to listen to his partner so that their arguments are not contradictory. The easiest way for the affirmative team to get off the hook on a disadvantage or solvency argument is to point out that one of the first negative's inherency or minor repair arguments reduces the disadvantage's impact or eliminates the solvency problem. Affirmative speakers have to listen to each other as well, but they usually do not have as much of a problem with contradictions, since they know where they do and don't want to go with their case. They have argued it many times before. The negative may be hearing it for the first time, grasping for anything to defeat it.

The *first negative rebuttal speech* begins the final phase of the debate. These back-to-back speeches are sometimes called the negative block. If the negative speakers do not maintain a clear division of labor, the first negative will waste time repeating what the second negative has just said; thus, any advantage that might have been gained from consecutive speeches will have been squandered. The first negative rebuttalist's responsibilities are similar to the second affirmative constructive speaker's—rebuild and extend on the points of clash established in the constructive speeches. It is important for the first negative rebuttalist to respond to the second affirmative's arguments, not merely repeat his own. This rebuttal should identify arguments the negative has "won" outright because they were not contested by the second affirmative. It should crystalize the important arguments to which the affirmative, during their rebuttals, must respond with new evidence and further reasoning, but add no new arguments. If it suddenly dawns on the first negative that all the affirmative's evidence is more than twenty years old, too bad. These are rebuttal speeches and no new arguments can be advanced.

The *first affirmative rebuttal speech* is, strategically speaking, the most important and most difficult speech in the entire debate. Attacks that took the second negative ten minutes to present must be answered in half the time, and the first affirmative rebuttalist cannot totally ignore what the first negative has had to say, especially if definitions and/or topicality are still in dispute. In policy debate, the drill goes like this: First, answer challenges on definitions and/or topicality. Second, respond to second negative constructive arguments. Third, respond to key issues extended in the first negative rebuttal. In value debate, the order of priority is the same although the nature of the issues discussed is different.

The *second negative rebuttal speech* is the negative team's last speech. While he should respond to what the first affirmative rebuttalist had to say about arguments presented in the second negative constructive speech, the second negative rebuttalist must remember that his primary mission is to give the judge a reason to vote for the negative team. This speech should cover the main arguments favoring rejection of the affirmative team's arguments, regardless of whether they were initiated by the first or second negative speaker. This is the only point in the debate where observing the division of labor between the negative speakers hurts the team.

The *second affirmative rebuttal speech* is the final speech in the debate. Like the second negative rebuttal, it summarizes the debate but from the affirmative team's perspective. The second negative rebuttalist probably established reasons why the decision should favor the negative. The second affirmative rebuttalist should respond to these, as well as point out things the negative team has not contested, which suggest an affirmative decision. In essence, both final rebuttal speakers attempt to provide the judge with a set of rules or criteria that favors their side's interpretation of the proposition.

Burden of Clash

As already indicated, the order of speeches reflects the exigencies of presumption and burden of proof. The order of speaking also puts certain obligations on both teams in terms of going forward with the debate. Recall that the first affirmative speech must be prima facie, otherwise the debate is over before it really begins, even though the rest of the speeches will be given. The negative team must move the debate forward by *establishing clash*. The negative is obligated to respond to what the affirmative has presented in some way, even if their only argument is that the affirmative case is so far off the topic that topicality is the only thing they have to argue.

Successive speakers have the responsibility of *maintaining clash*. Each speech moves the judge closer to making a decision by responding to what the other side has just said. The only exception might be the second negative constructive speech, which, because of division of labor, usually leaves second affirmative constructive arguments to the first negative rebuttalist. It is not sufficient merely to repeat your arguments. You must respond to your opponent's arguments to move the controversy toward resolution. Not only must arguments be presented, but the points of clash between the two teams must be identified. In so doing, both sides have the obligation to make an honest effort to develop arguments that do not distort, deceive, or misrepresent what they know to be true.

Cross-Examination

The responsibilities of the speakers and the obligations to establish and maintain clash are relevant to both traditional and cross-examination debating. You may have figured out the speaker's responsibilities from having read this book. However, cross-examination gives debaters some unique opportunities. You should approach the opportunity to ask and answer questions as a chance to advance the debate in a way that favors your side.

Cross-examination usually covers the speech immediately preceding it although it might cover lines of argument extending through several preceding speeches. Use cross-examination for various purposes:

Cross-examination allows you to gain information about your opponent's reasoning. What kinds of inferences link evidence to claims, and what kinds of inferences link one argument to another? If they are illogical, you can point this out in a later speech.

Cross-examination allows you to prevent possible misunderstandings. If you are not sure whether the speaker said "million" or "billion," ask. In this way you ensure that the argument you advance in a later speech cannot be dismissed because it is based on a misinterpretation.

Cross-examination allows you to probe for and point out inconsistencies either within a single speech or between two speakers. If you are a first affirmative rebuttalist, remember that negative teams are especially vulnerable to contradictions if they do not listen to each other. Finding the contradictions makes your task much easier.

Cross-examination allows you to advance your own position. You can ask questions whose answers point toward the conclusion you wish the judge to draw.

Notice that all these purposes represent means to an end, rather than ends in and of themselves. Cross-examination is used to set up arguments in subsequent speeches. No one ever won a debate with an imitation of Perry Mason during cross-examination. Debates are won in the constructive and rebuttal speeches. Whatever gains you think you may have made will be realized only if you capitalize on them in your speeches.

Preparation is as important to success in cross-examination debate as it is in traditional debate. Preparation begins with a thorough understanding of your topic. Cross-examination quickly exposes limited knowledge. Be prepared to take the role of both questioner and respondent. In terms of the first three purposes discussed here, you obviously have to listen to what your opponent says and decide on the spot what you need to ask. However, in regard to the fourth, you can plan a series of questions in advance. A series of questions is needed because even the dullest respondent will not readily admit to something favoring your position. If your position is that the poor are denied access to cable television because of its cost, asking "Don't you agree that the poor are denied access to cable because of cost?" will probably elicit a no. Assuming you had the supporting evidence, you would be better served by asking the following series of questions:

> The poor own just as many television sets, proportionally speaking, as the rest of the population, don't they?
> They watch television just about as much as everyone else, don't they?
> The majority of them live in urban areas served by cable systems, don't they?
> Yet few poor people are cable subscribers. Doesn't this suggest that the cost of cable service is a barrier to access for the poor?

Even though this last question might still elicit the same answer, your position would be advanced for two reasons. First, you would have planted a seed in the judge's mind that a series of signs point to your conclusion. Second, you could always ask one more question: "OK, can you tell me why the poor don't subscribe to cable?"

You may want to think twice before you ask that question. When attempting to advance your position through cross-examination, always ask questions to which you already know the answer. Your motive is to educate the judge, not yourself. Thus, if you do not know the answer to a question, it is sometimes safer not to ask it, lest you discover, too late, that you have presented your opponents with an opportunity to advance their position. While you will be fairly sure of the answers your questions will elicit, you still need to listen to the answers and adapt subsequent questions or even abandon a line of questioning if it is going nowhere.

Like the role of questioner, which allows for some prior planning, the role of respondent allows you to prepare your position. While you cannot anticipate every question that might be asked, you can anticipate the kinds of questions that will probably be asked about your affirmative case and the negative arguments you typically use. Prepare for answering by having your partner interrogate you.

Just as the various speaker positions in the debate have different responsibilities, the roles of questioner and respondent carry with them specific requirements as well. Neither questioner nor respondent may confer with colleagues during the cross-examination period. The questioner is in charge during cross-examination. She asks the questions, being careful that the respondent does not try to turn the tables. Questions should be as brief and clear as possible to encourage brief and clear responses. While the questioner cannot require yes or no responses, she need not tolerate filibustering by the respondent. The respondent should attempt to be as direct as possible but may qualify answers if necessary and refuse to answer questions that are patently unfair. If it becomes necessary to qualify an answer or refuse to provide one, it is important that the respondent explain why.

Both the questioner and respondent should remember that the debate is a public-speaking situation. Both parties should refrain from making speeches during the cross-examination period, and questions and answers should be articulated clearly and distinctly so that the judge may understand both. The most important thing to remember is to remain composed. Do not become hostile or defensive, and do not do things that would produce these behaviors in the other person.

Knowing what to ask in cross-examination, or what to argue in your next speech, requires not only argumentative skills but also a sense of what is going on in the debate as a whole. What is your team's position? What has the other team disputed? What has the other team conceded? What has your partner said? What are you going to say? No matter how good your memory is, learning how to keep a flow sheet of the debate as it unfolds is your best memory aid. A flow sheet tracks the progress of arguments during a debate and is nothing more than a specialized outline.

Flow Sheeting

In class, you fill page after page with notes on what your professor has to say. Now suppose that you have two professors who constantly disagree with each other. The only way you can keep things straight when you study is to have two sets of notes side by side. Suddenly you realize things would be much easier if you drew a line down the middle of a page of notebook paper, and put what one professor has to say on one side and what the other says on the other. If you rewrote the notes for one professor in black ink, and the other in red, you could tell at a glance who said what, and exactly what the points of disagreement between the two of them were. You have just discovered the flow sheet.

Instead of two columns, most people divide their paper into as many as eight columns, one for each speech. Unless you are able to write very small and have very good eyesight, something bigger than the standard eight and one-half by eleven inch notebook paper is helpful; contest debaters often use large artist's sketch pads. Outline each successive speech in the next column to the right, placing opposite each other arguments that clash and connecting them with arrows. If nothing is to the right of an argument, it probably means it has gone uncontested. To cram lots of information into a narrow column, use special symbols and abbreviations. You will have to develop your own because there is no standard set. For instance, one of your authors uses the acronym NAIR for "new argument in rebuttals." With a little practice you will quickly develop your own shorthand.

Debate Judges

Debates are judged and winners and losers are determined, but unlike the audiences for argumentation, which may vary considerably, the audience that counts in debate is somewhat more predictable. For the most part, debate judges are trained professionals who engaged in the activity themselves as undergraduates, presently coach or have coached debate teams, and teach courses in argumentation and debate. For debaters this means that concepts like presumption and burden of proof will not be alien to the judge as they might be to a lay audience for oral or written argumentation. Debaters are well advised to avoid "teaching" the debate judge in the same way they would the lay audience. If you intend to make a topicality argument, make it and go on. Debate judges dislike being lectured on theory, so they need not be informed of the gravity of a successful challenge to topicality. Unlike the lay audience, debate judges make a sincere effort to leave their biases at the door and judge the debate round on the basis of which team debated better rather than which team they agreed with most. For debaters this means that an idea that could have passed unproven or undeveloped before a lay audience, because it approached the status of a premise, must be proven to the debate judge. If, for example, the topic relates to unemployment, a trained debate judge will expect proof for the notion that full employment is a national goal and listen to counter arguments that it is not a goal.

That is not to say that debate judges are bias-free. In regard to style, some judges dislike what is sometimes referred to as NDT (National Debate Tournament) style, which is characterized by rapid rates of delivery, the reading of large quantities of evidence at the expense of explanation, and the excessive use of debate jargon ("On PMA 1 . . ."); other judges may not object to this style. The formation of the Cross Examination Debate Association (CEDA) was, in part, a reaction to some of the perceived excesses of NDT debate. While it is unlikely that many teams have ever lost rounds for talking too fast, rate can undermine your understandability and credibility with a particular judge.

In regard to the judging philosophy that shapes their decisions, some judges of policy debate see their role as that of a hypothesis tester while others see themselves as policy makers. Some judges will not consider successfully advanced topicality arguments as sufficient, in and of themselves, to warrant voting for the negative team. Other judges have a very narrow view of the range of possible meanings for the debate topic and seem to go out of their way to accept topicality arguments as a means of registering their displeasure with narrow interpretations of the topic. For debaters, the only saving grace is that they have to adapt only to one person, the judge, instead of to a group of people with undisclosed biases. The key is to learn the tendencies of those who judge and be flexible enough to adapt.

References

Andrews, J., & Zarefsky, D. (1989). *American Voices: Significant Speeches in American History, 1640–1945*. White Plains, NY: Longman.

Aristotle (n.d.). *The Rhetoric*. (1954). (R. Roberts, Trans.). New York: Modern Library. (Original work published in n.d.).

Begley, S. (1993, May 3). Hands off, Mr. Chips. *Newsweek*, 58.

Begley, S. (1993, November 29). Doin' What Doesn't Come Naturally. *Newsweek*, 84.

Boller, P. F., Jr. (1981). *Presidential Anecdotes*. New York: Penguin.

Brockriede, W. E. (1990). Where Is Argument? In R. Trapp & J. Schuetz (Eds.), *Perspectives on Argumentation: Essays in Honor of Wayne Brockriede* (pp. 4–8). Prospect Heights, IL: Waveland Press.

Brockriede, W. E., & Ehninger, D. E. (1960). Toulmin on argument: An Interpretation and Application. *Quarterly Journal of Speech, 46*, 44–53.

Bruce, D. R. (1993). Argumentation and the Reconstitution of Desire: A Lacanian Mediation of Presumption and Ideology. In R. E. McKerrow (Ed.), *Argument and the Postmodern Challenge: Proceedings of the Eighth SCA/AFA Conference on Argumentation* (pp. 113–118). Annandale, VA: Speech Communication Association.

Campbell, K. K. (1982). *The Rhetorical Act*. Belmont, CA: Wadsworth.

Children and Gun Violence. (1993, June 9 and September 13). Washington, D.C.: Committee on the Judiciary, Senate.

Children Carrying Weapons: Why the Recent Increase? (1992, October 1). Washington, D.C.: Committee on the Judiciary, Senate.

Cramer, J. (1991, July 1). The $40 Billion Controversy. *Time*, 43–44.

Drugs in the 1990's: New Perils, New Promise. (1989, August 31). Washington D.C.: Committee on the Judiciary, Senate.

Ehninger, D. E. (1974). *Influence, Belief, and Argument*. Glenview, IL: Scott, Foresman.

Eisenberg, A. M., & Illardo, J. A. (1980). *Argument: A Guide to Formal and Informal Debate*. (2nd ed.). Englewood Cliffs, NJ: Prentice Hall.

Elmer-Dewitt, P. (1993, December 6). First Nation in Cyberspace. *Time*, 62–64.

Fisher, W. R., & Sayles, E. M. (1966). The Nature and Functions of Argument. In G. R. Miller & R. Nilsen (Eds.), *Perspectives on Argumentation* (pp. 2–22). Chicago: Scott, Foresman.

Fraser, R. A. R. (1995, February/March). How Did Lincoln Die? *American Heritage, 46,* 63–64, 66–70.

Golden, J. L., Berquist, G. F., & Coleman, W. P. (1992). *The Rhetoric of Western Thought* (5th ed.). Dubuque, IA: Kendall/Hunt.

Hancock, L., (1994, October 24). In Defiance of Darwin. *Newsweek,* 61.

Hickey, N. (1994, August 13). New Violence Survey Released. *TV Guide,* 37–39.

Human Subjects Research: Radiation Experimentation. (1994, January 13). Washington, D.C.: Committee on Labor and Human Resources, Senate.

Innocence and the Death Penalty. (1993, April 1). Washington, D.C.: Committee on the Judiciary, Senate.

Japanese-American and Aleutin Wartime Relocation. (1984, June 20, 21, 27 & September 12). Washington, D.C.: Committee on the Judiciary, House of Representatives.

Johnstone, H. W., Jr. (1965). In M. Natson & H. W. Johnstone, Jr. (Eds.), *Philosophy, Rhetoric, and Argumentation* (Introduction). University Park, PA: Pennsyivania State University Press.

Juvenile Courts: Access to Justice. (1992, March 4). Washington, D.C.: Committee on the Judiciary, Senate.

Karp, W. (1984, March/April). Where the Do-Gooders Went Wrong. *Channels,* 41–47.

Koehler, J. W., Anatol, K. W. E., & Applbaum, R. L. (1981). *Organizational Communication.* New York: Holt, Rinehart & Winston.

Levy, S. (1995, February 27). Technomania. *Newsweek,* 25–29.

Lynne, J. R. (1990). Argument in the Human Sciences. In R. Trapp & J. Schuetz (Eds.), *Perspectives on Argumentation: Essays in Honor of Wayne Brockreide* (pp. 178–189). Prospect Heights, IL: Waveland Press.

Meiland, J. W. (1989). Argument As Inquiry and Argument As Persuasion. *Argumentation, 3,* 185–196.

Mills, G. E. (1968). *Reason in Controversy.* Boston: Allyn & Bacon.

Morganthau, T. (1994, October 24). IQ Battle. *Newsweek,* 52–54.

Morganthau, T. (1995, February 13). What Color Is Black? *Newsweek,* 63–65.

Mullen, J. (1995, February 3). Jim Mullen's Hot Sheet. *Entertainment Weekly,* 10.

Nilsen, T. R. (1974). *Ethics of Speech Communication* (2nd ed.). Indianapolis: Bobbs-Merrill.

Patterson, J. W., & Zarefsky, D. (1983). *Contemporary Debate.* Boston, Houghton-Mifflin.

Peterson, J. L. (1994). *The Road to 2015: Profiles of the Future.* Corte Madera, CA: Waite Group Press.

Record Labeling. (1985, September 19). Washington, D.C.: Committee on Commerce, Science, and Transportation, U.S. Senate.

Republicans. (1994, December 26/1995, January 2). *Newsweek,* 60.

Rescher, N. (1969). *Introduction to Value Theory.* Englewood Cliffs, NJ: Prentice-Hall.

Rieke, R. D., & Sillars, M. O. (1984). *Argumentation and the Decision Making Process.* Glenview, IL: Scott, Foresman.

Rives, S. G. (1964). Ethical Argumentation. *Journal of the American Forensic Association, 1,* 79–85.

Rokeach, M. (1973). *The Nature of Human Values.* New York: Macmillan, Free Press.

Rowland, R. C. (1987). On Defining Argument. *Philosophy and Rhetoric, 20,* 140–159.

Rybacki, K. C., & Rybacki, D. J. (1990). *Communication Criticism: Approaches and Genres*. Belmont, CA: Wadsworth.

Sandman, W. (1993). Gorgias and His Postmodern Cousins: Toward a Skeptical View of Argument. In R. E. McKerrow (Ed.), *Argument and the Postmodern Challenge: Proceedings of the Eighth SCA/AFA Conference on Argumentation* (pp. 97–104). Annandale, VA: Speech Communication Association.

Scott, R. L. (1987). Argument As a Critical Art: Re-Forming Understanding. *Argumentation*, *1*, 57–72.

Sproule, J. M. (1976). The Psychological Burden of Proof: On the Evolutionary Development of Richard Whately's Theory of Presumption. *Communication Monographs*, *43*, 115–29.

Sproule, J. M. (1980). *Argument: Language and Its Influence*. New York: McGraw-Hill.

Term Limits for Members of the U.S. Senate and House of Representatives. (1993, November 18, and 1994, June 29). Washington, D.C.: Committee on the Judiciary, House of Representatives.

The Audio Home Recording Act of 1991. (1991, October 29). Washington, D.C.: Committee on the Judiciary, Senate.

Toulmin, S. (1958). *The Uses of Argument*. London: Cambridge University Press.

Toulmin, S., Rieke, R., & Janik, A. (1984). *An Introduction to Reasoning* (2nd ed.). New York: Macmillan.

Urban Grocery Gap. (1992, September 30). Washington, D.C.: Select Committee on Hunger, House of Representatives.

van Eemeren, F. H., Grootendorst, R., Jackson, S., & Jacobs, S. (1993). *Reconstructing Argumentative Discourse*. Tuscaloosa, AL: The University of Alabama Press.

van Eemeren, F. H., Grootendorst, R., & Kruiger, T. (1987). *Handbook of Argumentation Theory: A Critical Survey of Classical Backgrounds and Modern Studies*. Providence, RI: Foris Publications.

Violence on Television. (1992, December 15). Washington, D.C.: Committee on the Judiciary, House of Representatives.

Walter, O. M., & Scott, R. L. (1984). *Thinking and Speaking* (5th ed.). New York: Macmillan.

Walton, D. N. (1988). Burden of Proof. *Argumentation*, *2*, 233–254.

Walton, D. N. (1992). *Plausible Argument in Everyday Conversation*. Albany: State University of New York Press.

Warnick, B. (1981). Arguing Value Propositions. *Journal of the American Forensic Association*, *18*, 109–19.

Wenzel, J. W. (1990). Three Perspectives on Argument: Rhetoric, Dialectic, Logic. In R. Trapp & J. Schuetz (Eds.), *Perspectives on Argumentation: Essays in Honor of Wayne Brockreide* (pp. 9–26). Prospect Heights, IL: Waveland Press.

Whately, R. (1828/1963). *Elements of Rhetoric* (Douglas Ehninger, Ed.). Carbondale: Southern Illinois University Press.

Wilcox, J. R. (1973). The Argument from Analogy: A New Look. Central States Speech Association, Minneapolis. Unpublished Paper.

Wilson, B. A. (1980). *The Anatomy of Argument*. Lanham, MD: University Press of America.

Witness Intimidation: Showdown in the Streets—Breakdown in the Courts. (1994, August 4). Washington, D.C.: Committee on the Judiciary, House of Representatives.

Yankelovich, D. (1994). How Changes in the Economy are Reshaping American Values. In H. J. Aaron, T. E. Mann, & T. Taylor (Eds.), *Values and Public Policy* (pp. 16–53). Washington, D.C.: The Brookings Institute.

Zarefsky, D. (1976, November 24). Criteria for Evaluating Non-Policy Argument. Western Speech Communication Association, San Francisco. Unpublished Paper.

Zeman, N. (1989, October 2). Buzzwords. *Newsweek*, 8.

Ziegelmueller, G. W., Kay, J., & Dause, C. A. (1990). *Argumentation: Inquiry and Advocacy* (2nd ed.). Englewood Cliffs, NJ: Prentice-Hall.

Index